Transnational crime and security are key modalities of governance in a globalizing world. World-wide, there is a tendency to treat every imaginable source of harm as a potential source of insecurity, and therefore as a crime. The catastrophic imagination is fueled by the precautionary logics of a world system troubled by systemic risk. As these logics become pervasive, security measures are invoked in an effort to control the imagined sources of harm, and the consequences are not always clear-cut. Further, the terminology of transnational crime, threat, risk and (in)security (and the phenomena to which they refer) is substantively deterritorialized, raising further theoretical and practical difficulties. Research and scholarship concerning these issues touches upon crucial features of the world system. This series offers wide inter-disciplinary scope for scholarship exploring these central aspects of global governance and governance globally.

More information about this series at
http://www.palgrave.com/gp/series/14398

Transnational Crime, Crime Control and Security

Francesco Vecchio • Alison Gerard
Editors

Entrapping Asylum Seekers

Social, Legal and Economic Precariousness

palgrave
macmillan

Editors

Francesco Vecchio
Anthropology
Chinese University of Hong Kong
Hong Kong, Hong Kong

Alison Gerard
Centre for Law and Justice
Charles Sturt University
Bathurst, Australia

Transnational Crime, Crime Control and Security
ISBN 978-1-137-58738-1 ISBN 978-1-137-58739-8 (eBook)
DOI 10.1057/978-1-137-58739-8

Library of Congress Control Number: 2017955067

Cover illustration: Derek Croucher / Alamy Stock Photo

Printed on acid-free paper

This Palgrave Macmillan imprint is published by Springer Nature
The registered company is Macmillan Publishers Ltd.
The registered company address is: The Campus, 4 Crinan Street, London, N1 9XW, United Kingdom

Alison – 'For Sebastien and Zadie'
Francesco – 'For my parents'

Acknowledgements

This book was conceived a number of years ago, out of the conviction that no matter what asylum seekers might endeavour to do in order to obtain safety, security and well-being, their agency is often (mis)understood as evidence that their behaviour is incompatible with that of those who were privileged enough to be born on the 'right' side of the globe.

Such a conviction is the product of years of working with and researching asylum seeker populations in several countries now struggling with self-made crisis, the management of which is an indication of hegemonic discourses of control and power, both over borders and underprivileged foreigners, which reveal how citizens are controlled through the threat 'we' are supposedly under when approached by deviant and resource-draining foreigners.

It is in this light that we are most grateful to the hundreds of asylum seekers we encountered over the years who generously shared their stories with us. It is impossible to name them all, but we certainly extend our thanks and hope this book may to some extent do justice to their lived experiences, on the one hand, and that it can be of practical use to improve their lives. Accounting for our responsibilities in shaping the contextual and relational space wherein asylum seeker behaviour can be understood is indeed the objective of this book, and in such an endeavour, we must extend our gratitude also to the wonderful contributors who participated in this project. They readily accepted the challenge and produced significant pieces of research that are collected in the pages that follow.

We finally thank the editors of the Transnational Crime, Crime Control and Security series and Stephanie Carey and the people at Palgrave that worked on the preparation of this book; Julia Farrell for her capable editing work; Charles Sturt University's School of Humanities and Social Sciences and the Centre for Law and Justice; and the Department of Anthropology at The Chinese University of Hong Kong. We would also like to thank our respective families for their understanding.

Contents

List of Contributors

Alison Gerard is Associate Professor of Law and Director of the Centre for Law and Justice at Charles Sturt University. Alison's articles have appeared widely and is the author of *The Securitization of Migration and Refugee Women* (Routledge 2014). Her research focuses on pressing social justice issues, with extensive focus placed on refugee mobility, deaths in custody, sex work and 'crimmigration' practices.

Stuart Hodkinson is Associate Professor of Critical Urban Geography at the University of Leeds, UK. His research focuses on neoliberal urban governance, austerity and contestation in relation to public housing, welfare reform, gentrification and the right to the city.

Olga Jubany is Serra Hunter Fellow in the Social Anthropology Department of the Universitat de Barcelona, Spain, and Director of the European Social Research Unit. Committed to the anthropological tradition of ethnography, she explores the social world of identity, diversity and social control, with a focus on migration, gender and multiple intersectional constructions. Dr Jubany is a nominated Expert at the Research Executive Agency of the European Commission and currently a coordinator of an international research project on discrimination, gender and diversity in Europe.

Hannah Lewis is Vice Chancellor's Fellow in Sociological Studies, University of Sheffield UK. Her research interests include forced migration, immigration and asylum policy, forced/unfree labour, integration, multiculturalism and community.

Michele Manocchi earned his PhD in Comparative Social Research in May 2010 at the University of Turin (Italy). Since the summer of 2013, he lives in Canada, where collaborates with Western University (London-ON) and Ryerson University (Toronto-ON). His work focuses on refugee reception systems and policies, as well as on border control policies and undocumented migrants.

Pierluigi Musarò is Associate Professor of Sociology at the Department of Sociology and Business Law and at the School of Political Science, University of Bologna. He is also Visiting Fellow at the London School of Economics and Political Science and at the Institute for Public Knowledge, New York University. His primary research interest focuses on the relationship between social justice and humanitarianism in contemporary mediated communication. His most recent publication is *Performative citizenship: Public Art, Urban Design, and Political Participation* (Udine 2016).

Elisa Pascucci is an Academy of Finland postdoctoral researcher at the University of Tampere, Finland. Her research interests involve the materialities and spatialities of humanitarian aid and theorizations of migrant and refugee political agency, including practices of transnational citizenship and collective mobilization and protests. She has started a project on the impact of ICTs and private sector involvement on refugee aid. Elisa has a Ph.D. in Human Geography (University of Sussex, UK, 2014) and a degree in Middle Eastern Studies (Ca' Foscari University of Venice, Italy, 2005). Her work focuses on North Africa and the Middle East.

Gabriella Sanchez is an assistant professor at the University of Texas at El Paso. Her work ethnographically documents the social organization of smuggling groups. She is the author of *Human Smuggling and Border Crossings* (Routledge, 2015). One of her projects documents the experiences of youth and children in drug and migrant smuggling markets.

Francesco Vecchio collaborates with a number of independent organizations such as Vision First in Hong Kong and Fondazione ISMU in Italy. He is an adjunct assistant professor at the Chinese University of Hong Kong and an adjunct research fellow at Charles Sturt University's Centre for Law and Justice, where previously he was a postdoctoral research fellow. He is the author of *Asylum Seeking and the Global City* (Routledge 2015).

Louise Waite is Associate Professor of Human Geography at the University of Leeds, UK. Her research interests span migration, citizenship and belonging, with a particular focus on discourses of 'modern slavery', unfree labour and exploitative work among asylum seekers and refugees in the UK. Web www.geog.leeds.ac.uk/people/l.waite.

Frances Webber is a retired barrister who specialized in asylum, immigration and human rights. She taught part-time for some years at Warwick and at Birkbeck. She is the author of *Borderline Justice: The Fight for Refugee and Migrant Rights* (Pluto, 2012) and writes regularly on the law and politics of asylum.

List of Figures

List of Tables

1

Entrapping Asylum Seekers: Introduction

Alison Gerard and Francesco Vecchio

Globally, the number of people forcibly displaced from their homes has reached record highs, at over 60 million (UNHCR 2016). Although exact numbers are difficult to obtain, the United Nations High Commissioner for Refugees (UNHCR) estimates that about a third of those displaced are refugees or asylum seekers. We use the term 'asylum seeker' to denote people who cross international borders seeking some form of humanitarian protection. Asylum seekers—although different from refugees in a strictly legal sense, as we explore below—resemble the broader sociological descriptor of 'refugees'. They symbolize displaced people seeking safety in times of unrest in countries neighbouring their own or further afield. In our usage, an asylum seeker embodies this label of 'refugee' for two reasons: for the hope that he or she might harbour to be granted refugee status, due to a well-founded fear of persecution for

A. Gerard
Centre for Law and Justice, Charles Sturt University, Bathurst, NSW, Australia

F. Vecchio (✉)
Anthropology, Chinese University of Hong Kong, Hong Kong, Hong Kong

F. Vecchio, A. Gerard (eds.), *Entrapping Asylum Seekers*, Transnational Crime, Crime Control and Security, DOI 10.1057/978-1-137-58739-8_1

reasons of race, religion, social group or political opinion; and for the often unbearably long process in which refugees become entangled when seeking asylum.

Traditionally, many countries within the Global North have demonstrated a clear preference for humanitarian programmes aimed at resettling limited numbers of refugees from the Global South. This was the practice during the Cold War, when asylum seekers were limited to sporadic cases and their acceptance helped western governments advance their political strategy of embarrassing the Soviet bloc countries—from where most asylum seekers originated at the time (Keely 2001). These programmes enabled western governments to screen and effectively manage the inflow of people whose circumstances called for the humanitarian intervention of wealthier states—thereby exercising moral authority and economic superiority over countries considered to be political opponents (Loescher 1993; Cohen 2006).

Since the late 1980s, however, the number of asylum seekers spontaneously travelling towards the Global North has increased (Black 1993), with their geographical areas of origin also diversifying (Van Hear and Crisp 1998). This has combined with an increase in restrictions on certain forms of migration targeted at preventing the arrival of asylum seekers (see Huysmans 2006). In the span of a few years, an unexpected inflow of asylum seekers began, whose arrival overwhelmed the reception systems of the countries receiving the highest numbers, causing a generally positive public and official attitude towards asylum seekers to change drastically towards one of closure and rejection (Muus 1997). Asylum seekers have consequently become a class of underprivileged people whose legal, social and economic precariousness—inherited from their home countries' inability or unwillingness to provide for their overall safety—is exacerbated by widespread hostility in countries that feel vulnerable in the face of, if not outright threatened by, the risk they are perceived to pose. As many contributors to this collection reveal, asylum seekers today face an ostensibly more intimidating and securitized environment in both the Global North and the ever-changing borderlands in or around destination countries. This book conceptualizes this precarity as entrapment, and seeks to identify the agents and processes that contribute to this cycle and produce the lived experience of immiseration that has been brought to bear on asylum seekers.

From a legal standpoint, asylum seekers who cross international borders seeking refugee protection are supported by international legal frameworks, such as, but not limited to, the 1951 *Convention Relating to the Status of Refugees* (Refugee Convention); the 1948 *Universal Declaration of Human Rights*; the 1948 *Convention against Torture and Other Cruel, Inhuman or Degrading Treatment or Punishment*; and the *International Covenant on Civil and Political Rights* and *International Covenant on Economic, Social and Cultural Rights*, both of 1966. In international law, and to some extent within the domestic legislation of signatory states, asylum seekers have access to certain rights and entitlements. This includes non-punishment for their method of entry and the prohibition on governments returning to their country of origin any person who is deemed to be a victim of persecution or whose claim in that respect has not yet been determined (the principle of 'non-refoulement') (Goodwin-Gill and McAdam 2007). Technically, these international refugee law mechanisms work to provide an 'exception to the general rule that sovereign states are free to decide who crosses their borders' (Dauvergne 2008, p. 62). Scholars highlight how this technical-legal position receives support by the influence of international agreements and conventions on border controls (Sassen 1996), and the 'legal process' of liberal courts (Joppke 1998). It is also supported by the machinations of 'client politics', bilateral relationships that serve particular interest groups and tend to increase rather than curtail migratory intakes (Freeman 1994).

Despite these legal and procedural safeguards, in today's world, asylum seekers are largely perceived and managed as unwanted and undeserving people. They are viewed as a security threat, deviant and ultimately prone to abusing asylum mechanisms. Asylum seekers have become ensnared in a stringent mesh of administrative, criminal and immigration laws, policies and practices that impinge upon their mobility across borders, while ensuring that their stay within borders remains unpleasant when unavoidable. They are increasingly contained between the promise and the reality of asylum (Gerard 2014; Vecchio 2013), between the diffuse, deregulated and often blatant denial of rights (Dauvergne 2008; Aas and Bosworth

2013) and the limitation on welfare that denies their basic needs (Webber 2012; Zetter 2007). Asylum seekers live, or are corralled into living, a liminal existence between a subtle 'culture of rejection' and new conditions of violence enacted by border controls (Weber and Pickering 2011) and the delivery of humanitarian assistance that perpetuates ahistorical conceptualizations of 'refugees'—a label that is now infused with victimization, paternalism, subordination and passivity (Malkki 1995). When asylum seekers exert their agency, these expressions may ironically support the politics, policies and practices that, while promising asylum, foster asylum seekers' legal, social and economic precariousness.

In this book, we aim to analyse and account for the policies, politics and practices that contribute to asylum seekers' daily lived experiences of entrapment. We define entrapment as the novel yet most common condition that hinders asylum seekers' capacity to lay down roots and feel safe and respected in the host country. In the realm of migration studies, entrapment has been conceptualized by Núñez and Heyman (2007, p. 354), who, drawing on a widely accepted notion of structuration theory (Giddens 1981), noted that 'police and other state agencies impose significant risk on the movement of undocumented people, while these people exercise various forms of agency by both forgoing travel and covertly defying movement controls.' Yet, the chapters contained herein reveal a relation between structure and agency that goes beyond such an interpretation. Our contention advanced in this volume is that the agency of asylum seekers, and that of their supporters, may in some respects reproduce the policies, politics and practices shaping their immiseration and criminalization. In other words, in negating the impact of border controls, asylum seekers' coping strategies may fuel expressions of agency that ultimately define their illegality, thus justifying the stringent policies aimed at deterring and protecting society from such behaviour—instating a mutually reinforcing cycle of entrapment.

Weber and Pickering (2011) have long argued that, once deterrent policies or otherwise stringent systems targeting asylum seekers are in place, they may easily become self-perpetuating and institute what Squire (2009) called a self-fulfilling cycle. Those responsible for this cycle are the agents who enable and enforce asylum seeker precarity, as well as asylum seekers themselves, who seek to mitigate their immiseration as a survival strategy. Through this process, entrapment becomes self-reinforcing. In this book, we employ a multilevel analysis to draw a map that is far from exhaustive, and yet expounds the evidence upon which it should be possible to critically rehabilitate the figure of the asylum seeker: namely, a map of the policies, politics, practices and *actors* that, on several levels, are responsible and should be held accountable for the entrapment of asylum seekers in precarious lives, through processes that are either consciously designed to do so, or unintentionally cause vulnerability and a daily lived experience that is criminogenic.

In what follows, we root the analysis in a brief account of the asylum seeker contemporaneous condition. We then introduce the framework of entrapment that provided the genesis for this international edited collection, and conclude with an overview of this book and the contributions contained within.

The Social, Legal and Economic Precariousness of Asylum Seekers

The precariousness of asylum seekers' social, legal and economic condition is suffered on several levels and at different times. Most notably, government and local policies can affect both the movement and lived experienced of asylum seekers (Koser 1997). At the same time, the discourses embedded within or supporting those policies have the potential to dehumanize asylum seekers and delegitimize the recognized legal status that comes with this form of humanitarian protection. This affects asylum seekers' agency and that of the actors who are required, or willing, to manage their arrival and provide for their protection and well-being. Huot et al. (2016) recently examined the 'othering' process at play for asylum seekers, whose estrangement from the host country's cultural, social and legal settings is escalated in the eye of the public by an overwhelmingly negative asylum discourse. Asylum seekers are generally deemed to be a threat associated with images of floods and waves that resonate with natural disasters (Crisp 2007). This perception of a threat is strengthened by asylum seekers' uninvited mobility, in sharp contrast to resettlement programmes that operate on quotas and enable refugees to arrive in an 'orderly fashion' (Gibney and Hansen 2005). Asylum seekers are thus understood as imposing an economic and resource burden on host countries (Hammar 2001). They are perceived as abusing the charitable nature of protection; their travel across borders raising suspicion as to both the motivation compelling their journey and the associated risks posed in relation to terrorism, crime and unemployment (Khosravi 2010). Their mobility thus epitomizes the threat they allegedly pose to host societies.

The paradoxical approach to refugee protection that governs policy towards asylum seekers across the Global North makes seeking asylum a turbulent experience. Refugees in humanitarian discourse are regularly objectified as helpless and in need of our assistance. Yet, when they arrive at our borders asylum seekers are portrayed as non-genuine, bogus or economic migrants. Governments are further frustrated when asylum seekers assert the right to apply for refugee protection, to work or even to request assistance (Pickering 2005; Harrell-Bond 2002). The Refugee Convention claims that 'Every refugee has duties to the country in which [he/she] finds [him/herself], which require in particular that [she/he] conforms to its laws and regulations as well as to measures taken for the maintenance of public order' (UNHCR 2010, p. 16). Asylum seekers who cross international borders and exercise their agency in ways that fall foul of the laws and regulations of the host country are an affront to this image of passive victim. Desirable refugees and asylum seekers are those who behave in a way that resonates with perceptions of their suffering brought on by displacement (cf. Stein 1986). On this view, refugees are faceless people, victims of their circumstances. Their survival is contingent upon governments' management of the manufactured crises sparked by their arrival (Mountz 2010); the spectacularization of refugee crises preventing us from thinking about the broader structures that cause their occurrence in the first place (Kapoor 2013; Zizek 2016). Asylum seekers confound by instilling both an urgency to provide for the most unfortunate and compliant, and the suspicion that the numbers of people involved in these mass movements are unjustified and unreasonable. In reality, crossing borders is anything but passive, and undertaking this challenge demonstrates considerable resilience and the ability to negotiate complex economic and political structures that enforce precariousness (Van Hear 1998; Haddad 2008). It is this agency that is rarely considered or valued in official and public discourse; but when the asylum seeker agency is acknowledged, it is portrayed as evidence of bogusness by governments unsteadied by globalization and eager to appeal to discontented constituencies through populist messages (Moore 2013).

Faced with refusal and rejection, asylum seekers find themselves constrained within a spiral of risks. On the one hand, their mobility may lead to experiences of violence at the border, a reflection of government efforts to prevent and deter their arrival against the background of an international legal framework that provides for international passage (Gibney 2004). On the other, a condition akin to 'social death' may ensue within host countries, whereby asylum seekers are denied access to basic rights such as housing, healthcare and education (Weber and Pickering 2011). Often barred from working legally, asylum seekers are made dependent on limited services that corral them into poverty (Webber 2012), raising precariousness while engendering their vulnerability to exploitation. Johansen (2013) speaks of a 'funnel' through which asylum seekers are subtly pushed that locks individuals into a situation wherein their actions can only comply with the state's desired outcome. For Johansen, this outcome is the irregular migrant's self-expulsion. In some settings, asylum seekers can nonetheless negotiate and resist their 'deportability' by engaging with the informal or underground economy (De Genova 2002). It can also be resisted by asylum seekers who assume coping strategies that, considering the structural limitations imposed on them, strengthen the values, norms and habitus that contribute to establishing their 'illegal persona' (Coutin 2010). These circumstances are essentially criminogenic, despite agency being expressed in the asylum seekers' pursuit of survival and a 'normal' life (Agnew 1992).

The precarious socio-legal condition of asylum seekers is born of the state's need to allocate and deny rights to particular groups in an attempt to strategically discipline both the population and the economy that sovereign states claim to govern (Polanyi 2001; Guarnizo 2012). Citizenship has indeed become a means through which national borders are reasserted at a time when they have become increasingly porous for economic reasons (Aas 2011). Further, belonging has become circumscribed and dependent upon the reproduction of a 'waste population' within the state (Bauman 1998; Tyler 2013). Tyler is clear that this population, among whom asylum seekers are the least privileged, is not the by-product of state oversight of the market economy. Rather, in Tyler's view, it is the intended consequence of the realization of a precise class structure, at the bottom of which certain people are turned into 'abjects'—namely, individuals populating zones of social life that are made unliveable. The existence of these non-citizens reinforces the domain of the entitled and rightful citizen, and disciplines the 'identities of citizens as well as those of foreigners', writing the nation-state in the process (Bosworth and Guild 2008, p. 715).

Increased vigilance has thus been placed by the state on national borders and their control to prove the state's continued importance to citizens and foreigners alike (Guild 2009). At the same time, the borders that traditionally demarcated the edge of sovereign power have been transformed as a result of globalization from static lines delimiting territory to mobile (spatially and temporally) and personalized borders (Weber 2006). Once an asylum seeker crosses national borders, these remain affixed to their body, identifying them as a foreigner whose status is determined by legal and social identifiers of their extraneousness to the host society (Sciurba 2009). New and bolstered internal borders shape the experience of asylum seekers in the host country, policed by an ever-expanding web of agents—police, hospitals, schools and workplaces (Weber 2011). Yet the extraneousness that a foreigner personifies is most often useful to the prevailing modes of capital accumulation and the hegemonic political demand for flexibility in terms of wage reduction, de-unionization and diminished social and political rights among the labour force (Harvey 2005). Schierup et al. (2016) argue that increased economic informalization does not mean diminished regulation per se. On the contrary, what is called 'deregularization' is a re-regularization of market relations of production in other terms, wherein the state intervenes to defend and privilege the capital markets by eliminating the obstacles to the recommodification of labour, money and nature (Harvey 2005).

The humanity and rights of asylum seekers are thereby affected. Lewis et al., in Chap. 8 of this book, argue that asylum seekers' illegal or otherwise inferior status, and their immiseration and socio-spatial confinement in unliveable conditions, can be ascribed to state regulation of migratory inflows for economic purposes. Given the limited assistance they often enjoy against the protracted time they live in their host country pending a determination of their case, asylum seekers are forced to engage in unlawful economic activities, access to which is only possible given their exploitable status. In such a space, asylum seekers must often make decisions while deprived of the means to avoid triggering legal and media condemnation of such decisions. This impacts their agency and access to citizenship, and supports the prevailing restrictive mechanisms of immigration control and humanitarian assistance, perpetuating their position at the bottom of the national and global social pyramid (Landolt and Goldring 2010). It is here that the entrapment of asylum seekers is most visible, whereby different processes entangle to institutionalize a stereotyped category of the asylum seeker as both victim and threat, whose usage in modern society appears to be increasingly and opportunistically relied upon across the world.

Entrapment, Agency and Resistance

Largely based on qualitative research data, this book provides an interdisciplinary, although primarily criminological attempt to disassemble the complex architecture that functions to entrap asylum seekers in precarious and often immiserated lives. The book analyses the processes that generate entrapment, and how agents mediate, augment or shape the risks asylum seekers must take to exercise their right to seek asylum and conduct a normal life. It is at once an analysis of asylum seekers' agency and micro-level lived experience, paired with a structural and contextualized understanding of the macro-level factors that are brought to bear on that experience.

On this, it is notable that Núñez and Heyman (2007) use the framework of 'morality of risk' to interpret how those who are entrapped take significant risks to ensure or continue their mobility or stay, or to counter the policies shaping their pain and immobility (Haugen 2012). The 'morality of risk' refers to 'different sociocultural frameworks for evaluating courses of action amid serious risks' (Núñez and Heyman 2007, p. 357). It translates, for example, into the decision to avoid medical care for fear of raising the ire of law enforcement, and the 'near-permanent sense of liminality' experienced by asylum seekers. However, entrapment processes also provide 'regions of refuge'. As Núñez and Heyman write, this term was first used by Gonzalo Aguirre Belttran (1979, in Núñez and Heyman 2007, p. 356) to illustrate how marginalized groups cope with processes of domination 'by sheltering in marginal but protective geographies'. In this regard, entrapment processes are multilayered and dynamic. They are a site of contestation and need to be seen through the prisms of agency, security and resistance.

In reflexively examining the agency of asylum seekers and their interaction with processes of entrapment, we use the fluid approach provided by Giddens's (1981) structuration theory. Giddens is critical of the two main approaches to analysing the relationship between the individual and society that have one dominating the other. Giddens's work advocates a break from this dualism to focus on 'studying the modes in which such systems, grounded in the knowledgeable activities of situated actors who draw upon rules and resources in the diversity of action contexts, are produced and reproduced in interaction' (Giddens 1984, p. 25). This application enables us to observe the operation of both individual and structural factors as simultaneously present, and to recognize the agency of individuals in adapting to their context. Employing a multilevel analysis assists in establishing contextually grounded research advocated for by postcolonial scholars (Mohanty 2003). Giddens's structuration theory thus positions the everyday experiences of asylum seekers within a broader structural context.

The value of a contextualized approach in irregular and asylum migration research is well established (Anderson and Ruhs 2010; Bloch and Chimienti 2011, p. 9; Castles 2003; Koser 2006). For example, Anderson and Ruhs (2010) underscore the importance of embarking upon structural analysis—by considering labour market regulation and segmentation, for example—in conjunction with a focus on individual agency in research on irregular migration, because examining the resistance and coping mechanisms adopted by irregular migrants avoids oversimplified perceptions of this diverse population as either victims of exploitation or potential law-breakers.

Within this setting, in deploying the concept of entrapment, we are guided by its legal definition as exists in several common law countries, in which it is used as a defence to a crime, the basis to exclude evidence or to stay proceedings if an abuse of process can be proved. As a strictly legal concept, entrapment refers to the 'deliberate action by a police officer or other law enforcement agent to induce a person to commit an offence' (Mann 2015, p. 276). The concept emerged in the nineteenth century and coincided with the advent of official professional police forces (Chambliss 2011). The essential element in the concept is that the person 'would not have committed the crime or would have been unlikely to commit the crime, had the induction not occurred' (*R v Sloane* (1990) 49 A Crim R 270, 272–3). Historically, entrapment existed as a defence in the United States (US) and to some extent arose also through the constitutional guarantee of due process: see *Sorrells v United States* 287 US 435 (1932). No such defence exists in the United Kingdom (UK) (*Sang [1980] AC 402; (1979).* However, in the UK and Australia, the evidence can be excluded if it amounts to an abuse of process.

The premise of the entrapment defence is an intriguing one that lays the foundation for this book. In a traditional legal sense, the prohibition on law enforcement using tactics of arrest that amount to entrapment effectively provides checks and balances on covert and overt law enforcement operations. In entrapment cases, the law is supposed to protect those who are induced by the state and its agents to commit acts that are regarded as illegal. For asylum seekers, refugee law ought to provide the same protections and remedy any illegality. The international refugee law framework provides a mechanism for the legal arrival of asylum seekers and their legal access to rights and entitlements. We know from our research with asylum seekers that their assumptions about the Global North prior to arrival in a destination country are often based on claims by those countries to uphold human rights (Gerard 2014; Vecchio 2015). They assume that they will be offered sanctuary, have their human rights met and that the rule of law will apply. However, the reality that greets them upon arrival in the destination country is very different and is captured in this conversation with an asylum seeker that took place in the southern European Union (EU) member state of Malta:

> I come from the conflict-prone Congo, where the EU are and are actively promoting human rights and peacebuilding. Yet when I arrive here in the EU there is no such protection. Where are the human rights now? (Asylum Seeker 9—Malta)

Asylum seekers arrive in the destination country expecting to find safety, security and respite. Instead, they endure the consequences of policies akin to criminal justice practices that seek to deter and incapacitate asylum seekers, whether in the community or in detention centres.

In an obvious limitation and point of departure in entrapment cases at law, criminal liability arises where the person intends to commit and does commit a crime. For law enforcement agents, of course, where they are authorized by law then their conduct is not deemed criminal. The same provision would prevent an entrapment case from gaining ground in asylum seeker cases, as government agencies are clearly backed by a sophisticated legal apparatus that prescribes restrictive border security policies and minimal assistance. So, criminal liability would not arise. Nevertheless, there needs to be a way of protecting asylum seekers from the manufacture of their criminal liability by the state. This is a central premise advanced by this book.

In this book, we draw on asylum seeker experiences of and resistance to policies of deterrence, immiseration and forced destitution to inscribe new conceptualizations of the entrapment process. We trace entrapment to a wide range of agent provocateurs. These agents include law enforcement agencies, non-governmental organizations, employers and asylum seekers. Identifying these many actors represents an important challenge. It is critical to exposing the connectors and dividers that affect asylum seeker experiences and mobility. And with identifying new agents and practices of entrapment comes a pathway to dismantling such entrapment. As Weber (2015) writes, just as the previously significant parish borders in England have become progressively insignificant, it is not impossible to envisage that the mobile borders that appear impermeable and unshakable today will also become a thing of the past. After all, entrapment fractures the human security of us all.

Our lives have changed considerably over the past two to three decades as a result of the arrival of asylum seekers and their characterization as a threat and an unwanted social group whose humanity has been questioned or concealed. Butler (2004) discusses at length how certain lives are grievable, while the suffering or loss of life experienced by other subjects is less prone to evoke emotions in 'us'—spectators of a reality that is shaped by exclusionary processes that ultimately determine who is normatively human, and whose lives are therefore grievable. For example, the agency of asylum seekers is interpreted within the parameters of their exclusion, and notions of asylum seekers, whereby they engage in 'asylum shopping' like consumers, are an affront to the public of the host country (Moore, 2013). Further, an emergent body of literature is evaluating the exclusionary processes embedded within specific refugee policies enacted by agencies either contracted or mandated to provide humanitarian aid and protection to asylum seekers. The Chap. 4 by Elisa Pascucci in this book offers one such example relating to public perceptions of aid workers shaping asylum seeker agency. The often-cited works of Harrell-Bond (2002) and Agier (2011) are critical here, as they cast light on how asylum seekers' choices and expectations are formed and performed through the management of refugees by humanitarian agencies. These processes influence the decision-making and livelihoods of asylum seekers as well as public discourse as the media and public opinion delimit what is sayable by governing the domain in which knowledge is produced (Moore 2013).

As Butler (2004, p. 11) argues, 'conditions do not "act" in the way that individuals do, but no agent acts without them.' It is undeniable that the social, legal and economic processes underpinning precarity generate the boundaries wherein individuals' existence and exercise of their agency are possible. Asylum seekers in Hong Kong frame their choices and evaluate the consequences of their actions in accordance with their resources and the amount and kind of information available to them (see Francesco Vecchio in Chap. 10 of this book). When denied legitimate opportunities to survive or improve their livelihoods, asylum seekers find themselves bound to people with whom they share similar liminal conditions of duress, which in turn exposes them to norms, values and strategies that increase their risk of being exploited and policed. Ironically, the means by which asylum seekers choose to ameliorate their individual circumstances may confirm the suspicions and incur the scorn of the public. Conforming to judgements about their deviant character or illicit behaviour turns asylum seekers into non-citizens and 'non-persons', enabling the criminalization that further reduces the scope of legal activities available to them.

About This Book

This book is loosely divided into three sections that bring together contributions from several regions across the globe. The first part critically investigates the structure that shapes or otherwise supports the entrapment of asylum seekers in precarious livelihoods, and how this entrapment may impact the agency of the people who deal with this population, revealing consequences that affect not only asylum seekers but us all. Emphasis is placed on the social processes by which asylum seekers are constructed and defined as a problem. Rather than solely focusing on the politics and policies that are at the core of research concerned with asylum seeker rights and their violation, this section sheds light on the matrix of cultural and socio-political factors that affect the politics of asylum, and the practices that fashion the entrapment of asylum seekers in precarious livelihoods.

The Chap. 2, by Olga Jubany, analyses the daily experiences of immigration officers in the UK during the period of training that prepares them for their future border protection duties. An argument is made that the negative representation of asylum seekers in our society is related to a 'subculture' of refusal and rejection that goes beyond legal definitions of asylum to coalesce with discourses of abuse and otherness that have a dangerous influence on the work of the immigration authority. Through the narratives of her research participants, Jubany evidences how the discourses of border protection and human rights entangle, and how the latter most often succumbs to the former via a slow yet progressive acquisition by new recruits of the official and informal meta-messages that guide their training and deployment in the field. A truth of convenience is thereby constructed—one that supports disbelief and mistrust in asylum seekers. The chapter helps conceptualize the entrapment of asylum seekers, as it argues not only that the stories of asylum seekers, their trauma and experiences become irrelevant in the face of official status determination procedures, but also that these interpretations may and, in this circumstance, do permeate several strata of society, such as the case of young professionals recruited in law enforcement progressively altering their views of asylum over time. Through ethnographic research, Jubany explores immigration officers' attitudes to asylum seekers and the correlation of these attitudes to public discourse.

If Jubany's chapter explores a two-way downward entrapment cycle, the Chap. 3, by Pierluigi Musarò, furthers insight into Jubany's metalanguage of disbelief and suspicion by developing understanding of the spectacle of the humanitarian border—another site where the modern representation of asylum seekers as cheats and threats is fashioned, and where their representation as agentic individuals is ignored. The border that in Jubany's chapter is enforced by authorities for security and identity reasons is here similarly shaped and reproduced by the media's uncritical representation of emergencies that form an imaginary of migration that does little to improve understanding of the root causes of migration. In fact, media coverage often depicts unprecedented levels of migration as a mass casualty and a shared suffering that inspires instinctive but limited empathy. Further, news reports create an impression of deaths at sea as 'business as usual', while military personnel are deployed in response, the heroic rescue and tragic sacrifice of whom engender the strongest emotions. They are grieved and awarded the highest honours, as heroes who needlessly succumbed to the risks of their jobs—risks that we are not given to critically question in the face of the gravity of performances of courage that make us all prideful citizens of a generous, albeit under siege, civilization.

The Chap. 4, by Elisa Pascucci, examines the role of humanitarian agencies in the establishment of the macro settings of governance that influence dominant representations of asylum seekers. The chapter offers a critique of the distance that humanitarian agencies, mandated to protect asylum seekers, put between them and their alleged beneficiaries. It describes how fear is augmented by forms of urban restructuring that emphasize the use of gates, walls and restricted access. These forms of urban architecture create uneasiness and prevent humanitarian agencies from getting to know the needs and wants of asylum seekers. In turn, asylum seekers' understanding of humanitarian work, and the people who are supposed to assist them, is impacted, putting them at a distance from humanitarian workers. This exacerbates their frustration, uncertainty and precariousness, and fuels expressions of agency that foster stereotyping and misunderstandings. In turn, this reinforces aid workers' perceived need to protect themselves with mechanisms of restricted access such as gates and walls.

The second section explores the human impacts of the practices discussed above and draws together both the collective and individual survival strategies of asylum seekers caught within and between borders. It endeavours to capture the experiences and everyday lives of the people engulfed by walls of compliance and arbitrary sociological categories of race, gender and wealth. The entrapment of asylum seekers emerges from the robust evidence of the increasing securitization of migration, citizenship and belonging. The resistance of asylum seekers to such entrapment is examined to reveal the forces and practices that asylum seekers and their sympathizers face and contest, at times generating conflict that may not always resolve in the best interests of asylum seekers, but is nonetheless indicative of their legitimate expression of agency.

This section starts with a Chap. 5 by Alison Gerard that draws on qualitative research conducted with a diverse sample of female asylum seekers in Hong Kong to reveal the gendered consequences of entrapment. The chapter outlines how women perceive their own legal categorization and manage the precarious livelihoods that ensue from 'doing time' in this 'global' city. Complex structural economic, social and political factors influence the arrival of women asylum seekers in Hong Kong. These factors give rise to both dynamic and blurred legal categories that the government's recently established 'unified screening mechanism' for all humanitarian protection claimants has sought to disentangle. Processes aimed at sorting women into palatable legal categories permeate the daily lives of asylum seekers in Hong Kong and govern their interactions with government and non-government agencies alike. Gerard extends the analysis of entrapment by actors beyond police and state agencies by examining the role of non-government agencies in entrapment. The gendered analysis of entrapment generated by focusing on women's experiences elucidates the varied contradictions that women's resistance to entrapment may produce, in turn revealing the heterogeneity in women's attitudes to conditions of precarity and the strategies they adopt to resist the securitization of migration that results in their entrapment.

Frances Webber's Chap. 6 presents a compelling argument about the need for and use of litigation by asylum seekers and their support people to wrestle policies aimed at confining the agency of asylum seekers. In so doing, the chapter illustrates the limitations of the judicial review process which, even when successful, 'cannot reverse decisions on their merits but can only demand that the decision-maker re-make the decision lawfully'. This limitation constitutes one impediment to dismantling the central and peripheral walls erected to delimit asylum seeker agency in the UK, and allegedly aimed at preventing the arrival of others in their footsteps. Webber speaks of a sense of engagement that is engendered by litigation that does not end with the final outcome of the litigation itself. However, the chapter evinces that a sense of fatigue might eventually result, as significant efforts are put into legal battles that are nullified by power exercised both within and outside courtrooms, whereby temporary victories in the former may become the catalyst for government and parliament to form more stringent rules, regulations, policies and laws in the latter.

Finally, in this section Gabriella Sanchez depicts, through vivid ethnographic examples, the successful border-crossing of Mexican migrants, and increasingly asylum seekers, through one of the most militarized borderlines in the world. According to a large body of research, asylum seekers often remain grateful to smugglers who may have cost them dearly but deliver them to safety, whether or not in the destination country of their choosing (van Liempt and Doomernick 2006). In this chapter, it is similarly confirmed that the services of smugglers do allow certain people to successfully cross the US–Mexico border. And yet an argument might be made that, while agents may be reliable and thanked for their intervention which allows migrants to defeat the state, a further process of entrapment is also at play. The chapter reveals that the border-crossing of these migrants may further broaden state objectives that arguably hinge upon border porosity, such as migrants acquiring an illegal status as a consequence of their illegal entry; their families requiring extensive disposable incomes to provide for their border-crossing, safety and shelter; and the financial and economic pressures facing these families ultimately containing them at the lower rungs of society, where they are forced to work hard in sectors of the economy in which their labour is highly exploitable.

The third section explores, in broader terms, this process of interlocking economic exploitation and asylum seeking, whereby the latter appears suspiciously useful when spaces of socio-legal marginalization, or exception (Agamben 1995), and predatory globalization (Falk 1999) meet and merge. This is compounded by the paradoxical intertwining of the politics surrounding asylum seeking, increasingly stringent border controls and the conveniently concealed socio-economic advantage that emerges when asylum seekers and their families are forced to live in poverty at the margins of society.

Chapter 8, by Lewis et al., examines the structural context of asylum seekers falling prey to exploitative conditions of work. In this chapter, asylum seeker narratives evidence how their livelihoods are reduced to a condition of hyper-precarity resulting from diminished access to immigration, banking, housing, health and legal aid services, wherein asylum seekers and other migrants may face 'no real or acceptable alternative' but to submit to forced labour and the associated abuses. In Chap. 9, Michele Manocchi explores the social condition of asylum seekers living in a former industrial city of North-West Italy from the privileged position of a researcher and collaborator with several non-governmental organizations, thereby obtaining access to case files as well as opinions and views of caseworkers and asylum seekers alike. In this chapter, deep contradictions within the Italian system of reception and integration of asylum seekers are brought to light. The chapter examines how the agency of asylum seekers and their intentions and outcomes are often misrepresented by caseworkers who are hard pressed to follow bureaucratic procedures for the disbursement of funds. As this chapter analyses, these funds involve placing asylum seekers in training programmes that do not meet their needs. Their economic integration is thereby hindered by the same organizations that are mandated to provide for their long-term well-being.

In the Chap. 10, Francesco Vecchio examines the entrapment of a group of asylum seekers in Hong Kong through a consideration of their motivation to live in slums that are unlawfully built, unsafe and unhygienic. An argument is made that the deterrent policies and politics aimed at the exclusion of asylum seekers produce their socio-legal and spatial banishment, which they negotiate by creating a community upon which to rely in times of difficulty and emergency. Such a community is supported by their untenured legal status and foreign ethnicity, which shape their vulnerability. Vecchio demonstrates that entrapment is here fashioned when asylum seekers' condition effectively defines an identity that revolves around the slums, to produce an integrative supporting mechanism that shapes asylum seeker engagement with income-generating activities that raise suspicion about the reasons why asylum seekers travel to Hong Kong. In turn, this influences asylum seeker policies and politics, while asylum seekers' work and residence in slums channel resources to local employers (Vecchio 2015).

The chapters in this book engage directly and indirectly with the concept of entrapment. However, they all provide compelling evidence of the processes that determine the space within which asylum seeker agency is exerted and the extent to which this organizes asylum seekers and our social world.

References

Aas, K. F. (2011). "Crimmigrant" bodies and bona fide travelers: Surveillance, citizenship and global governance. *Theoretical Criminology, 15*(3), 331–346.

Aas, K. F., & Bosworth, M. (Eds.). (2013). *The borders of punishment: Migration, citizenship, and social exclusion*. Oxford: Oxford University Press.

Agamben, G. (1995). *Homo sacer: Il potere sovrano e la nuda vita* [The sovereign power and bare life]. Torino: Einaudi.

Agier, M. (2011). *Managing the undesirable: Refugee camps and humanitarian government*. Cambridge: Polity Press.

Agnew, R. (1992). Foundation for a general strain theory of crime and delinquency. *Criminology, 30*(1), 47–87.

Anderson, B., & Ruhs, M. (2010). Researching illegality and labour migration. *Population, Space and Place, 16*(3), 175–179. doi:10.1002/psp.594.

Bauman, Z. (1998). *Globalisation: The human consequences*. New York: Columbia University Press.

Black, R. (1993). Refugees and asylum seekers in Western Europe: New challenges. In R. Back & V. Robinson (Eds.), *Geography and refugees: Patterns and processes of change*. London/New York: Belhaven Press.

Bloch, A., & Chimienti, M. (2011). Irregular migration in a globalising world. *Ethnic and Racial Studies, 78*, 1–15.

Bosworth, M., & Guild, M. (2008). Governing through migration control. *British Journal of Criminology, 48*(6), 703–719.

Butler, J. (2004). *Precarious life: The power of mourning and violence*. London: Verso.

Castles, S. (2003). Towards a sociology of forced migration and social transformation. *Sociology, 37*(1), 13–34. doi:10.1177/0038038503037001384.

Chambliss, W. (2011). *Police and law enforcement*. London: Sage.

Cohen, R. (2006). *Migration and its enemies: Global capital, migrant labour and the nation-state*. Aldershot: Ashgate.

Coutin, B. (2010). Confined within: National territories as zones of confinement. *Political Geography, 29*, 200–208.

Crisp, J. (2007). Vital distinction. *Refugees, 148*, 4–14.

Dauvergne, C. (2008). *Making people illegal: What globalisation means for migration and law*. Cambridge: Cambridge University Press.

De Genova, N. P. (2002). Migrant "illegality" and deportability in everyday life. *Annual Review of Anthropology, 31*, 419–447.

Falk, R. (1999). *Predatory globalization: A critique*. London: Polity Press.

Freeman, G. P. (1994). Can liberal states control unwanted migration? *The ANNALS of the American Academy of Political and Social Science, 534*(1), 17–30.

Gerard, A. (2014). *The securitisation of migration and refugee women*. Abingdon: Routledge.

Gibney, M. J. (2004). *The ethics and politics of asylum: Liberal democracy and the response to refugees*. Cambridge: Cambridge University Press.

Gibney, M. J., & Hansen, R. (2005). Asylum policy in the west: Past trends, future possibilities. In G. J. Borjas & J. Crisp (Eds.), *Poverty, international migration and asylum* (pp. 70–96). Houndmills/New York: Palgrave Macmillan.

Giddens, A. (1981). *A contemporary critique of historical materialism, vol. 1: Power, property and the state*. Berkeley: University of California Press.

Giddens, A. (1984). *The constitution of society*. Berkeley: University of California Press.

Goodwin-Gill, G., & McAdam, J. (2007). *The refugee in international law.* Oxford: Oxford University Press.

Guarnizo, L. E. (2012). The fluid, multi-scalar, and contradictory construction of citizenship. In M. P. Smith & M. McQuarrie (Eds.), *Remaking urban citizenship: Organizations, institutions, and the right to the city* (pp. 11–35). London: Transaction Publishers.

Guild, E. (2009). *Security and migration in the 21st century.* Cambridge: Polity Press.

Haddad, E. (2008). *The refugee in international society: Between sovereigns.* Cambridge: Cambridge University Press.

Hammar, T. (2001). Politics of immigration control and politicisation of international migration. In M. A. B. Siddique (Ed.), *International migration into the 21st century: Essays in honour of Reginald Appleyard* (pp. 15–28). Cheltenham: Edward Elgar.

Harrell-Bond, B. (2002). Can humanitarian work with refugees be humane? *Human Rights Quarterly, 24*(1), 51–85.

Harvey, D. (2005). *A brief history of neoliberalism.* Oxford: Oxford University Press.

Haugen, H. Ø. (2012). Nigerians in China: A second state of immobility. *International Migration, 50*(2), 65–80.

Huot, S., Bobadilla, A., Bailliard, A., & Rudman, D. L. (2016). Constructing undesirables: A critical discourse analysis of "othering" within the Protecting Canada's Immigration System Act. *International Migration, 54*(2), 131–143. doi:10.1111/imig.12210.

Huysmans, J. (2006). *The politics of insecurity: Fear, migration and asylum in the EU.* London: Routledge.

Johansen, N. B. (2013). Governing the funnel of expulsion: Agamben, the dynamics of force, and minimalist biopolitics. In K. F. Aas & M. Bosworth (Eds.), *The borders of punishment: Migration, citizenship, and social exclusion* (pp. 257–272). Oxford: Oxford University Press.

Joppke, C. (1998). Why liberal states accept unwanted immigration. *World Politics, 50*(2), 266–293.

Kapoor, I. (2013). *Celebrity humanitarianism: The ideology of global charity.* Abingdon: Routledge.

Keely, C. B. (2001). The international refugee regime(s): The end of the Cold War matters. *International Migration Review, 35*(1), 303–314.

Khosravi, S. (2010). *'Illegal traveller': An auto-ethnography of borders.* Houndmills: Palgrave Macmillan.

Koser, K. (1997). Social networks and the asylum cycle: The case of Iranians in the Netherlands. *International Migration Review, 31*(3), 591–611.
Koser, K. (2006). Irregular migration. In B. Marshall (Ed.), *The politics of migration: A survey*. London: Routledge.
Landolt, P., & Goldring, L. (2010). *The long term impacts of non-citizenship on work: Precarious legal status and the institutional production of a migrant working poor*, viewed 15 August 2012. http://www.yorku.ca/raps1/events/pdf/Landolt_Goldring.pdf
Loescher, G. (1993). *Beyond charity: International cooperation and the global refugee crisis*. Oxford: Oxford University Press.
Malkki, L. H. (1995). Refugees and exile: From "refugee studies" to the national order of things. *Annual Review of Anthropology, 24*, 495–523.
Mann, T. (2015). *Australian law dictionary*. Sydney: Oxford University Press.
Mohanty, C. T. (2003). *Feminism without borders*. Durham: Duke University Press.
Moore, K. (2013). "Asylum shopping" in the neoliberal social imaginary. *Media, Culture & Society, 35*(3), 348–365.
Mountz, A. (2010). *Seeking asylum: Human smuggling and bureaucracy at the border*. Minneapolis/London: University of Minnesota Press.
Muus, P. (Ed.). (1997). *Exclusion and inclusion of refugees in contemporary Europe*. Utrecht: ERCOMER.
Núñez, G. G., & Heyman, J. M. (2007). Entrapment processes and immigrant communities in a time of heightened border vigilance. *Human Organization, 66*(4), 354–365.
Pickering, S. (2005). *Refugees and state crime*. Sydney: The Federation Press.
Polanyi, K. (2001). *The great transformation: The political and economic origins of our time*. Boston: Beacon Press.
Sassen, S. (1996). *Losing control? Sovereignty in an age of globalization*. New York: Columbia University Press.
Schierup, C. U., Alund, A., & Likic-Brboric, B. (2016). Migration, precarization and the democratic deficit in global governance. *International Migration, 53*(3), 50–63. doi:10.1111/imig.12171.
Sciurba, A. (2009). *Campi di forza: percorsi confinati di migranti in Europa* [Force fields: Migrant confined paths in Europe]. Verona: Ombre Corte.
Squire, V. (2009). *The exclusionary politics of asylum*. Houndmills: Palgrave Macmillan.
Stein, B. N. (1986). The experience of being a refugee: Insights from the research literature. In C. Williams & J. Westermeyer (Eds.), *Refugee mental health in resettlement countries* (pp. 5–23). Washington, DC: Hemisphere Publications.

Tyler, I. (2013). *Revolting subject: Social abjection and resistance in neoliberal Britain*. London: Zed Books.

UNHCR. (2010). *Convention and protocol relating to the status of refugees*. United Nations High Commissioner for Refugees. Available at: http://www.unhcr.org/3b66c2aa10.html

UNHCR. (2016). Global forced displacement hits record high. *UNHCR News*. Available at: http://www.unhcr.org/en-au/news/latest/2016/6/5763b65a4/global-forced-displacement-hits-record-high.html

Van Hear, N. (1998). *New diasporas: The mass exodus, dispersal and regrouping of migrant communities*. London: UCL Press.

Van Hear, N., & Crisp, J. (1998). Refugee protection and immigration control: Addressing the asylum dilemma. *Refugee Survey Quarterly, 17*(3), 1–27.

van Liempt, I., & Doomernick, J. (2006). Migrant's agency in the smuggling process: The perspectives of smuggled migrants in the Netherlands. *International Migration, 44*(4), 165–189.

Vecchio, F. (2013). La promessa e la realtà dell'asilo in Asia. In I. S. M. U. Fondazione (Ed.), *XIX Rapporto sulle Migrazioni 2013* (pp. 203–213). Milan: FrancoAngeli.

Vecchio, F. (2015). *Asylum seeking and the global city*. Abingdon: Routledge.

Webber, F. (2012). *Borderline justice: The fight for refugee and migrant rights*. London: Pluto Press.

Weber, L. (2006). The shifting frontiers of migration control. In S. Pickering & L. Weber (Eds.), *Borders, mobility and technologies of control* (pp. 21–44). Dordrecht: Springer.

Weber, L. (2011). *Policing non-citizens*. Abingdon: Routledge.

Weber, L. (Ed.). (2015). *Rethinking border control for a globalizing world: A preferred future*. Abingdon: Routledge.

Weber, L., & Pickering, S. (2011). *Globalization and borders: Death at the global frontier*. London: Palgrave.

Zetter, R. (2007). More labels, fewer refugees: Remaking the refugee label in an era of globalization. *Journal of Refugee Studies, 20*(2), 172–192.

Zizek, S. (2016). *La nuova lotta di classe: rifugiati, terrorismo e altri problemi coi vicini* [Against the double blackmail: Refugees, terror and other troubles with the neighbours]. Milano: Ponte alle Grazie.

2

Unmasking the Cultural Construction of Asylum Screening at the Border

Olga Jubany

The Technocratic Fallacy of Asylum Screening

I think the whole issue is about immigration officers just being sort of human beings, you know? Often I think that the kind of human element just gets overlooked. (Chief Immigration Officer[1])

Beyond the transposition of rules, asylum screening entails a complex process of decision-making, grounded on the cultural constructions of the actions and interactions of the actors involved. As this process has developed at borders, distinct expressions of power emerge within the reticent spaces of the state's apparatus. Fostered on this premise, which challenges essentialist accounts of the state (see Gill 2010), this chapter argues that bureaucratic state institutions, and notably asylum screening at borders, must be understood as the 'powerful sites of symbolic and

O. Jubany (✉)
Department of Social Anthropology, Universitat de Barcelona,
Barcelona, Spain

F. Vecchio, A. Gerard (eds.), *Entrapping Asylum Seekers*, Transnational Crime, Crime Control and Security, DOI 10.1057/978-1-137-58739-8_2

cultural production' that they are (Ferguson and Gupta 2008, p. 105; see also Mountz 2010; Fassin 2013).

Drawing parallels with law enforcement debates (Gill 2010; Prokkola and Ridanpää 2014; Loftus 2015), this chapter analyses and exposes the transposition of law into practice as a complex socio-cultural construction of border control (Marston et al. 2005). To address these practices, the chapter explores the ways in which officers embody their roles and actively engage in making borders 'real', in a current context in which both the securitization of border control (Horii 2012) and the deconstruction of asylum (Hollifield 2000; Lazaridis 2015) play powerful roles. Considering the closed circuits of state bodies, the chapter pays particular attention to how decisions are made within the context of the shifting grounds of social acceptance and rejection of asylum seekers and refugees.

Stemming from the understanding that subjective meanings give rise to an apparently objective social world, the arguments presented here delve into the construction of asylum as a profoundly cultural process within the professional world of border control. This allows us to understand the extent to which officers working in border control rely on racialised and androcentric constructions that are reproduced in everyday norms and practices. What is more, it shows how profound stereotypes (Pilivain and Briar 1964; Werthman and Pilivain 1967; Martin Cassares 2007) shaped as social stigmas (Goffman 1963; Becker 1973), which breed prejudice and racialised stereotypes, through the application of unshakeable labels (Matza 1969; Schur 1971; Rosenhan 1973; Solomos 1993), become engrained in the cultures of border control. The border as a 'site' is understood as a context where persons, objects and ideas come together in a constantly unfolding space 'always folded into the object-order, literally as part of the context and the relata' (Marston et al. 2005, p. 426). As this chapter demonstrates, it is through the ethnographic approach that these sites bare themselves to foster the existence of subcultures which, when unchallenged, reflexively recreate the worlds in which they exist.

Grounded on an unprecedented ethnographic investigation,[2] this chapter explores the quotidian actions and interactions of immigration officers to unravel how these are largely unaffected by legal and policy regulations, as they reveal themselves to be 'quieter registers of power'

(Allen 2011, p. 291). By tracing new recruits' experiences, from formal training through to socialization in the field, the significance of subscribing to a worldview specific to border control becomes evident. This deep incursion into the world of the officers exposes the distortion of asylum as a right and the complicity of the state in consolidating this fallacy, ensuring its impact on border control. As the chapter goes on to illustrate, officers come to rely on a corpus of values, norms and common actions that replace legal definitions of 'asylum seeker' or 'refugee'. From this point, asylum seekers are measured against standards that, outside the immigration service subculture, embody a range of common ethno- and androcentric stereotypes largely built on discrimination, racism and moral panics. Yet, as the chapter reveals, this process is perceived by officers as professional knowledge, disguised through the social reproduction of border spaces and rationalized by the meanings, labels and categories they ascribe to this 'reality'.

As the relationship between asylum seekers and host countries has transformed from one of trust to mistrust, asylum seekers have been increasingly depicted as social threats (Daniel and Knudsen 1995; Bigo and Guild 2005; Lazaridis 2015). Building on this assumption, officers are tasked with playing a more active role in reducing the numbers of asylum applicants. To this aim, the asylum screening interview has become the space where officers embody their social control role, consolidated through the 'site of the border' assumptions of suspicion and distrust. This is revealed not as a gathering of individualized subjective beliefs, but as an assemblage of core values assumed and shared by immigration officers as a group, and is the core learning outcome that emerges from formal and informal training.

Later on, the chapter illustrates how the transfer of knowledge and skills, such as interview techniques and credibility training, represents a further step in the legitimation of officers' 'professional knowledge'. This is shown to further obscure the labelling process as officers socially reproduce a subcultural world that not only corresponds to the state's goal of reducing immigration, but is also rationalized as 'professional knowledge', ensuring its preservation.

In the final considerations, the chapter denounces the state's approach to asylum screening at the border illustrating how determined policy and legislative frameworks give way to the immigration service subcultural principles, norms and practises. This is a debate that underwrites the construction of border processes and asylum screening practices beyond the institutional fallacy that portrays them as undeniable, revealing them to be complex subjective cultural constructions. Furthermore, this highlights how current international laws, protocols and commitments related to asylum can be recognized and socially constructed as irrelevant, leaving officers to establish their own systems and standards for uncovering the 'truth'. This, in turn, shows the extent to which the granting of asylum in contemporary societies is not just a matter of administrative citizenship but a very significant cultural construction of social acceptance or rejection.

Impenetrable Professional Worlds and Meta-narratives

> *Why do we have a UK immigration control system? One, to prevent terrorists and other unacceptable people; two, to protect the resident work force; and three, to control the rate of immigration.* (Immigration Officer[3])

The anthropological tradition of ethnography, drawn from the paradigms of social constructionism and symbolic interactionism, has proved essential to understanding how knowledge is constructed, internalized and institutionalized in social settings shaped by organizational and policy values. In the context of this research, this means understanding how the performances of border agents relate to specific narratives, building on their social construction of specific 'truths'. To uncover the construction of professional worlds involves an immersion into the site, unravelling how 'truths' and 'facts' are consolidated as 'professional knowledge', through symbolic interaction processes. From its beginnings in the 1960s, law enforcement debates focused on controlled organizational frames and professional worlds, 'traditionally characterised by a concern to expose the culture and practices of operational police work' (Loftus 2015, p. 119). Uncovering the practices of labelling that existed behind the bureaucratic shield, this debate exposed the role of law enforcement officers in the subjugation of populations living on the "margins of society". In this regard, much of the long tradition of the study of law enforcement (see Reiner 1997) is analogous with that of immigration officers' 'realities'.

Despite the evident parallels with immigration control, few attempts have been made to look at the world of immigration officers from this social control approach, although this is essential to understand the foundations of 'professional knowledge' (Becker 1973). The precedents established within subcultural studies, identifying 'fundamental assumptions about the nature of being and comprehensible forms of action' (Heyman 1995, p. 265), illustrate the extent to which organizational values and processes of socialization determine agents' roles (Goffman 1961). At state borders, officers' training and socialization processes serve to transmit the 'ideology' of the site (Cohen 1985, p. 101), while also providing tools that serve to rationalize their role in the process (Foucault 1988).

Immigration officers also rely on the development and rationalization of their own knowledge and skills, and a shared 'way of thinking and acting' (Bigo 2014) within the context of the border 'site'. This raises the issues of reflexivity and consciousness guiding trainers as they establish the 'routinisation of communication' (Riggins 1990) when transmitting to new officers what is expected of them in their role. As officers are trained, these expectations are often transmitted as complex and contradictory meta-messages (Bateson 1955), constantly reinterpreted within the context of the site, and the relationships between the officers and those directing them. It is in this process that the joint actions of the Home Office and immigration officers are guided by establishing shared meanings (Blumer 1969) which come to constitute the 'truths' and 'facts' about the world they work in. As these 'truths' are established, officers' roles are shaped during training against the backdrop of the 'site', and build on the deconstruction of asylum as a right through explicit messages and meta-messages about social threats, welfare abuse and moral panics (Cohen 2002). Thus, training constitutes the undertaking of a 'process of perception', whereby officers come to socially reproduce the world around them based on their expectations about the people they will meet and the stories they will hear (Lippmann 1946).

In exploring the relationship between the actors' views and their responses to the organizational demands placed on them, the 'site' becomes a complex assemblage, imbued with deposits of power and knowledge: 'At each level – ideas, organizations, professionals and political economy, these deposits take the form of descriptions (stories) and causal theories, which are drawn upon and leave behind real forms of power … [which] draw upon existing social, political and economic arrangements (as well as previous ideas) and then, in turn, leave behind their own deposits which are drawn up to shape later changes, reforms and policies' (Cohen 1985, p. 89). The border 'site' is thus recognized as a construction comprised of *longue durée* features deposited and accumulated over time (see Fassin 2013; Jubany 2017), and the daily unfolding of information as a source of change and reinterpretation (Deleuze and Guattari 1987).

To unravel how the worlds of social control are socially reconstructed through officers' daily actions requires an ethnographic lens, characterized by a deep immersion into the 'site'. Yet, borders as subjects of study present a great challenge as they epitomize state fortresses, of a highly politicized and confidential nature (see Hofstede 1980; Tayeb 1988; Lane 1989). Thus, this ethnographic infiltration discloses much about the character of these restricted sites.

Despite receiving official support from the United Nations High Commissioner for Refugees (UNHCR) and a formal letter of approval from the UK border control, the research was dissuaded by the Home Office from accessing the field, with no clear reason provided. Two years after receiving the initial letter granting access, the UNHCR was 'advised' by the Home Office to 'lessen' its support for the research. Far from discouraging the research, the eventual withdrawal of all formal support highlighted the need to concentrate on informal routes. To this aim, a number of line managers were contacted individually and, over three years after commencement of the access procedures, the first positive response arrived from a senior port officer willing to be interviewed on an anonymous basis. Once I had gained access to the field, the number of research participants snowballed and eventually officers from all grades were interviewed: senior immigration officers, immigration officers and assistant immigration officers. Furthermore, the opportunity to take part in the six-week training programme for new recruits emerged during the fieldwork, allowing continued participant observation in formal training scenarios, job shadowing, mentoring and role-plays. Unquestionably, the participant observation[4] provided a unique insight into this concealed world.[5] The difficulty of gaining access to the site highlighted the importance of exploring the human significance of borders. The Home Office's efforts to deter access underlines the resistance of state bodies to allow an outside reading of borders, while the unique access gained through the kindness and interest of the individuals involved highlights the discord between official approaches to asylum processing and the practices officers undertake. Ultimately, access to the site was in the hands of the officers themselves, and not only did they decide to provide such access, but they also felt the need to make themselves heard (see Jubany 2017).

It is by entering the field and drawing 'attention to the intimate and divergent relations between bodies, objects, orders and spaces' (Marston et al. 2005, p. 424) that we can define how 'truths' are negotiated at the border, permeated by the meta-message of disbelief and denial that obscurely shapes the context. As will be shown in subsequent sections, this subcultural background determines how immigration officers are expected to act towards asylum seekers, outlining and developing their role as social control agents through the communication and normalization of asylum 'truths' in the screening process.

Learning to Disbelieve: Categorization, Skills and Credibility

> *I remember my first day in the job when they told me how I'd have to refuse, I thought I was joining a job where I just stamped passports. I didn't know we actually sent people back and things like that. I remember thinking that, you know, how on earth am I going to tell them that? So it is quite, quite a terrifying prospect.* (Immigration Officer[6])

Border agents who join the immigration service have little idea about what immigration officers do when they begin their induction training programme.[7] The way in which their roles are introduced during the course is crucial in transmitting how they should behave and what is expected of them. From the beginning of the training the messages of deterrence and control determine the development of 'prior knowledge', reflecting the cultural setting and the state's goals on asylum and immigration.

These messages are implicit in key pieces of information, such as those transmitted in the glossary of acronyms and jargon, introduced from day one. Many terms such as 'Watch House' and 'Suspect Index' carry clear meanings about how immigration officers are to understand their role (to safeguard) and how they should envisage asylum seekers (to suspect). The guide to these specialist terms, not included in the official handbook, exposes the existence of a subcultural life (Gelder and Thornton 1997) at the border. Initially, the core content of the course suggests that professional learning will take place in the classroom, yet, as the course develops, it is the informal situations, such as job shadowing and role-play, that promote learning in an informal and convivial way, and emerge as key to knowledge transfer. Furthermore, from the beginning of the course trainers reinforce that specialist knowledge is required to perform the officers' roles by underpinning the need to learn in the field. It is the 'off the record' learning experiences, where officers shadow experienced officers on port visits and are assigned mentors to guide them through their initial experiences, that the skills transmitted in the formal training scenarios become irrelevant. These exercises do not imply learning or applying skills as such, but in learning to adopt certain perspectives necessary to become 'true officers', already established through the meta-messages of denial and disbelief.

Essential to establishing this early definition of the role is the presentation of asylum as a channel for abuse and a security risk, rather than as a right. Simultaneously, through the presentation of 'evidence' for this, new recruits are frequently introduced to anecdotes and stories that portray asylum seekers as deceitful and dishonest, rather than subjugated, abused or at risk. Thus, this is a key message established from the beginning of training, introduced in formal and informal ways as the course moves between the classroom and the applied learning contexts in the field. In all these scenarios, officers are trained to approach asylum seekers with suspicion and told that they will be lied to; however, they are not instructed at any stage of their training on how asylum seekers may exercise their rights. Nor are documents like the UN Handbook on Procedures and Criteria for Determining Refugee Status[8] offered as a frame for processing asylum seekers:

> Not only do we not know about it [the handbook] but we're not really interested in it. Because it's, well it's not for us. I mean, you know? Our management could give us copies or they could put a copy in the library or something but they don't. And I certainly don't think many people would read it anyway. (Immigration Officer[9])

While the convention definition of an asylum seeker is introduced to the recruits, it is immediately redefined within the working parameters of the immigration service, always related to credibility of the asylum seeker:

> Another aspect to question is if that fear is strong enough not to send them back to their country, regardless of the situation in the country. The situation of the person is what counts, their personal fear and it has to be 'well founded'. If someone says that they are afraid for their life, you need to discuss further and assess if what they are telling you is credible or not. (Senior Training Officer[10])

These 'clarifications' are commonplace as trainers instruct new officers on what documents and concepts 'really' mean within the context of the immigration service. Fundamental concepts such as 'asylum' are subject to 'clarifications', as trainers complicate the categorization of asylum seekers and refugees by engaging with wider societal debates about 'bogus refugees' and 'economic migrants':

> This distinction has been in the news a lot because of bogus refugees. The convention excludes economic migrants so you need to look very closely at why they need to leave the country. An asylum seeker has to convince the country where they apply with documentary evidence and a credible account to establish a well-founded fear of persecution. (Training Officer[11])

By all accounts, the interpretations that new officers receive are to induce the refusal rather than protection of refugees. This message is conveyed in different ways—for example, in the fallacy that connects asylum with welfare exploitation, crime and security—and is inherent in almost every official declaration related to asylum policy:

> The government's sort of unofficial policy is that the asylum system is being exploited for immigration purposes. They'll never say that in public but that's definitely the line, the policy is to refuse as many applications as possible. I'm not necessarily saying it's the right policy but it's the policy that's been followed by each government of whatever political persuasion for a long time. (Immigration Officer[12])

In this way, when basic explanations of key concepts like asylum are provided during officer training, additional messages always filter through. This process occurs in both formal and informal training scenarios, as officers learn from their experienced colleagues in job shadowing exercises, as well as in the classroom. Through these 'clarifying interpretations', a negative connotation is always attached to asylum seekers, such as 'bogus refugees' and 'economic migrants' or 'potential terrorists', providing grounds for excluding rather than protecting applicants.

Furthermore, with reference to public debates, the concept of asylum seeker is diluted and mixed with other meta-messages, legitimating the alienated image of the asylum seekers as 'other', welfare cheat and potential terrorist. By engaging with these debates, the image of the folk-devil (Cohen 1972) is introduced to allude to refugees and asylum applicants. Fundamentally, the officer embodies the role of protector of the border, while potential asylum seekers appear as the threat. Another important definition that is reconceptualized within immigration language relates to the term 'persecution'. New recruits are taught that refugees are victims of 'injustice but not of justice'. In other words, if asylum seekers have been prosecuted rather than persecuted they do not fit with the concept of refugee:

> They think that if they have committed an offence and the police are looking for them for punishment for common law offences in the country, they are persecuted, but they are not, they are being prosecuted, so they are not refugees. (Training Officer[13])

In describing these scenarios, the trainer refers to 'prosecution' in general terms, while the event that asylum seekers may be fleeing state violence—often sustained by the normative of the law, is never discussed in a critical way. While trainers highlight the diversity of potential scenarios, the ambiguities of different contexts are not addressed nor are officers instructed in how to develop a nuanced approach to uncovering the 'truth' in these scenarios. The only underlying assumption is that asylum seekers may be criminals and offenders themselves. They are not only 'others', but also a potential threat. This perspective is further consolidated when trainers ask new recruits to deliberate on the reasons why asylum seekers may be detained at the border, encouraging trainees to apply a securitized mind-set to their roles:

Trainer: Who do you think should be detained?

- Criminals
- Violent people
- People who have been refused previously
- Previously absconded
- Non or forged documented
- Terrorists

Participant Observation Diary: Training Sessions[14]

In this way, officers are introduced to 'professional' techniques to categorize asylum seekers outside the frames of reference of the convention, instead grounded on wider social anxieties (Bauman 2007). Behind this, the state's goal remains, as the meta-message encourages officers to rationalize decisions with the belief that the majority of asylum seekers are potential security risks or an economic drain on the nation. This has direct implications for those applying for refugee status as 'moral panics' (Cohen 2002) influence the ways in which officers conceive asylum seekers and make their decisions.

While the official line establishes the bureaucratic nature of the officers' job, their roles are made clearer through the unofficial approaches that trainers present as personal perspectives and stories, instructing trainees on the ideal attitudes they should assume in their role as immigration officers. Officers are told that they are investigators whose initial attitude towards all applicants should be one of suspicion and disbelief, and whose function is to find the truth about the narratives presented by asylum seekers, while always assuming that the applicant's story is deceptive. Once again, the message of mistrust is driven by the wider meta-message of disbelief underpinning the state's political discourse:

> Your role as immigration officer is to allow them [asylum seekers] to give you the full account of the case. You have to be objective and sensitive but don't forget that you are there to challenge any inconsistencies. You have to challenge the credibility of the individual as well as the actual case. (Training Officer[15])

Rationalizing Refusal

> *The immigration officer's duties involve mostly interviewing, so again we will cover the fundamentals of immigration legislation, the immigration service, what it does, its place in the whole migration issue and then focus in on various interviewing skills. Interviewing is a big part of the job so we have very many sessions on the different interviewing skills.* (Immigration Training Officer[16])

In spite of the prevalent official line which maintains that officers' bureaucratic role implies that they are merely collecting information, the unofficial story and everyday practices contradict this account, as is clear from the fact that the investigative element forms the core of officers' training course. Interviews are presented to new officers as the essence of their work and the basis on which they will make decisions. However, even prior to the introduction of investigation techniques, the course is geared to instruct officers on strategies for determining and deciding on asylum cases. The key elements in these strategies are the narratives, anecdotes and role-plays that establish the importance of officers' roles as a line of defence against security and other threats, whilst establishing the deceitful profile of asylum seekers.

These perspectives are further consolidated as the main interviewing methods introduced follow a well-known police interrogation technique used to obtain 'criminal evidence': the PEACE model (Prepare and

Planning, Engage, Account, Closure and Evaluation). In this scenario, asylum seekers are regarded as 'suspects' and border agents as 'investigators'. The correlation between asylum seekers and offenders is recurrent throughout the course, reinforcing the imperative to mistrust individuals during the interview. PEACE provides trainees with a rational and proven strategy for obtaining information to make judgments and, as students are told, 'to highlight the discrepancies in the story'. Trainers suggest that students look at the Home Office records and files to 'get ideas' about the questions they need to prepare, but the technique proposed as the best is 'to sit down with a colleague and talk through what you are going to say'.[17] By focusing on the need to highlight discrepancies, a consistent message emerges, which not only reinforces officers' roles in 'safeguarding' borders, but also tells officers to be suspicious of all narratives:

> Credibility is estimating the evidence, bringing out the real reasons, testing the evidence. You must give them a chance to say what they need to say and afterwards you test what they have actually said. Point out the discrepancies and find out discrepancies, that's your job. (Training Officer[18])

Trainers tell students to search for and uncover any discrepancies in the applicant's stories, always assuming that every asylum seeker's narrative is full of discrepancies. To this aim officers are instructed to engage openly with asylum seekers and present themselves as approachable during the interview, in order to gather more information to be tested. For instance, through the use of 'cognitive and conversational models' asylum seekers are obliged to recount all the details of their story backwards, as a technique to double check and verify the story when presented in an unstructured, non-linear way.

New officers are trained to do this reflexively by constantly returning to their initial interview plan and focusing on the areas of the asylum seeker's narrative that they can use to highlight and tease out inconsistencies. To this end, officers are encouraged to ask open-ended questions that encourage asylum seekers to talk more, thus providing them with more information that can be tested and used to assess an asylum seekers 'credibility':

> You should ask yourself – would this story be reasonable to myself, would it be reasonable to do so? This is what credibility is about. It is credible if it is reasonable … look at the whole picture and ask yourself if it is reasonable, if it is credible. (Training Officer[19])

The credibility of the narrative becomes crucial in framing and rationalizing asylum decisions and is presented as objective knowledge. Yet, in this context, credibility is a concept grounded in the meta-message of disbelief, constructed within the subcultural language to meet the aims of the officers' work. As officers are trained and begin to shadow experienced officers in the field, establishing credibility in an interview becomes their main objective. While credibility is presented to new recruits as an objective estimation of an asylum seeker's narrative, determining the veracity of the narrative requires a more complex negotiation 'between what is told and what really occurred' (Fassin 2013, p. 40). The notion of 'what really occurred' is always determined by those in a position of power; hence this is intrinsically linked to officers' own experiences and beliefs, and the subcultural principles. Moreover, as Fassin (2013) would argue, this does not occur against a backdrop in which the Convention represents an immutable object, but rather in a context in which legal definitions of asylum and social acceptance are transformed through public, legal and political debates.

Rendering credibility as synonymous with 'truth' has implications for the ways in which officers internalize the 'skills' they are taught. The messages about credibility become the essence of the interviews, so that officers' primary 'task is to test the credibility of the claim'.[20] The 'investigation techniques' they are taught rely on the need to establish credibility, check 'facts' and 'challenge the truth'. Thus, to officers, credibility becomes indistinguishable from truth and is perceived as an objective estimation of the facts, rather than the result of culturally determined interpretation. Within the immigration service, subculture credibility is not perceived as an idea constructed by an individual but an objective interpretation of a group, essential to performing officers' roles:

> The first thing that you evaluate is the story. To me the story is fundamental, the credibility of the story I mean. (Immigration Officer[21])

Thus, although credibility is not a quality inherent to an individual or story, but rather a quality that officers attach to them, it is still a synonym for the truth that they must uncover. In other words, officers decide whether or not something is credible, although in most cases this is presented as something determined once an officer has the requisite experience:

> With all your knowledge, more or less theoretical and also a lot of the practical, well, you go on to establish what we call credibility. (Training Officer[22])

It is only when the decision about credibility is made that the rest of the narrative will be examined. While the interview techniques appear to be a rationalizing tool, the ambiguous nature of 'credibility' leads trainers to constantly remind officers of the need to learn professional knowledge and 'common sense' in order to perform their roles:

> Much of it is common sense. You will have the opportunity to try out your skills. Next Thursday you will be interviewing real asylum seekers. (Training Officer[23])

On these lines, upon entering the field, officers' ability to perform their new role quickly becomes contingent on their ability to perform within the parameters of the immigration service subculture and adopt its values. While the training teaches officers skills that they believe they will use throughout their careers in the immigration service, in time it is mainly the meta-message that remains, revealing itself as the most important learning outcome of the training course.

The Taciturn World of Bureaucratic Decisions

> *The first thing is to establish general credibility, something more ethereal, more general, you know? So that you think, "this thing he is telling me is impossible".* (Chief Immigration Officer[24])

Beyond the purpose of communicating both the formal and informal professional procedures, an essential function of immigration training is to ensure that new recruits start the job with a specific viewpoint about the immigration officers' role, and about the purpose of the immigration service as a whole. Yet it is mainly through the initial socialization process, part of which takes place during the training sessions, that officers' roles are fully defined. In their initial incursions into the field, recruits see immigration officers as alien to them: they do not know them personally, their practices seem rather far removed from the 'right procedures', and they often feel pessimistic about the job. In addition, they are overwhelmed by the number of 'unexpected' elements of the job they encounter first-hand.

However, this gap between recruits and officers blurs as the training advances and newcomers spend more time at ports. Their impression that immigration officers do not apply 'correct procedures' fades as they begin to see that officers use 'practical procedures', grounded on 'professional knowledge' that emerges from experience in the field. By the end of the training course the initial fears and criticisms of 'cynical' officers given by new recruits have been overturned as they come to empathize with those they observe in the field. Furthermore, in many cases these experienced officers present their viewpoints and explain the 'alternative' procedures, which often openly contradict the content delivered in the formal training:

Recruit II: We had a man who said that he was here only for two days but when we searched his luggage he had four pairs of shoes so it was very suspicious.

Recruit I: In a search I found a piece of evidence that proved that he had been in another country when he wasn't supposed to be.

Trainer: Well done. Any other interesting thing?

Recruit IV: I was with an IO, and I started writing things down on a landing card. He asked me what was I doing and I explained that I was reporting what was happening on the landing card as I had been told in the training. He said that in that shift I didn't need to do that at all.

Participant Observation Diary: Training Session[25]

The weight given to 'experience' over training is highlighted throughout the induction process and becomes more evident in the field, where the formal teaching is fused with the 'off-the-record' approach communicated by officers as 'professional knowledge'. As new recruits become fully immersed into the organizational subculture, the formal skills based around interview techniques are left behind, while the meta-messages of disbelief and denial become clear factors in establishing 'prior knowledge' in determining claims. In this distancing process, the gap between the official discourses about what officers do and what new officers see in the field is made explicit. This begins with the most fundamental official fallacy that officers are there to collect information systematically, and do not legally make decisions on asylum cases.[26] This fallacy is reinforced by the official messages which maintain officers play no substantial role in the bureaucratic process, despite formal training focussing on interview skills, credibility and decision-making. Furthermore, it is the unofficial approaches characterized by the meta-message of suspicion, distrust and denial that contribute to the culture of disbelief (Jubany 2011, 2017) accentuating the ambiguity officers 'feel' about the significance of the roles in the process:

> I don't feel perhaps completely responsible but I feel that I'm relevant to their claim. (Immigration Officer[27])

In addition, once officers understand that their function is to decide on the 'truth', and therefore who is deserving and who is not, no official guidelines on how to make these judgements are provided, leaving a gap which officers are encouraged to fill with 'professional common sense' guided by the 'site' meta-narratives as the rule. Officers are left to establish their own criteria, based on their own experiences and prejudices, guided by what they see in the field, in performing their role at the border. The clearest guidance is the shared goal of uncovering lies and deceits in the interviews. The subcultural socialization reveals itself through the training on how to construct, or deconstruct, applicants' credibility:

> What happens is that sometimes this common sense appears to have a bad reputation, it seems that common sense has to be synonymous with pure simplicity in its worst meaning, but it is not like that. (Immigration Officer[28])

It is through the socialization process that officers gather their 'stock of knowledge', referring to the cumulative experience of the group or so-called professional knowledge (Cicourel and Knorr-Cetina 1981). These are not written rules, but rather are considered factual norms and values, and thus they go unchallenged within the context of border control. Yet it is within this 'professional knowledge' that we find the values that officers use to decide on asylum cases. The bases of these criteria are neither in the handbooks provided during the training nor in any public manual, although they become more relevant than any other directive.

Most of the labels, criteria and categories that officers use in assessing applicants stem from general ethnocentric and racialised constructions of categories such as gender, religion, country of origin and level of education. The cumulative labelling process leads officers to attribute characteristics to individuals which, much like common social prejudices (Gilbert 1951), they then use to classify asylum seekers as deserving or undeserving. Their 'interpretations' are substantively grounded on subcultural understandings and expectations about factors such as assumed human behaviour and social stereotypes, and play a significant role in decision-making. To officers, the application of these categories requires what they consider 'professional knowledge', known only to those with experience in the job.[29] Furthermore, the application of these criteria is articulated to allow officers to draw on their stock on knowledge and rationalizing also the group knowledge. For instance, an applicant's country of origin does not provide officers with information that someone from a specific country has more or less grounds to apply, but it informs them of the set of features that members of that country are believed to share:

> It's like all the Turks who've been beaten up so many times, you know? Or not so much the women, but the men, every time they go out they seem to have been beaten by the police. I don't believe it. You know, I just don't believe it happens quite that much. (Immigration Officer[30])

This is also the case with labels linked to the sex-gender roles, as per contemporary Western heteronormative constructions (Rosaldo and Lamphere 2001), that officers expect to be fulfilled by applicants:

> I went through a phase where particularly the Kenyan girls would say they'd been raped, and I didn't believe it. Looking at it from a woman's point of view, something like that must be so terrible that maybe people cope with things differently but I'm sure however they cope with it, they will be able to convey the horror because, because it will be a lasting horror to them. And these girls just used to say it as, almost as if it was, 'oh and by the way, I was raped, and then I was raped by six men' or whatever, you know? Please, I don't believe them. And someone once said to me, 'oh perhaps in their culture it's not that bad'. That's bollocks, if you'll pardon my French. Rape is always rape. I don't believe there is a single culture which accepts being taken in that way by force as the norm. (Immigration Officer[31])

When the officer cited above justifies her views as being 'from a woman's point of view', this is understood as coming from a specific androcentric perspective, very much informed by her socio-cultural upbringing wherein the lack of emotion, particularly in a woman, is read as a sign of deception. This is a common connection officers establish, by incorporating expected demeanour and expression of emotions in judgements of the applicant's credibility, as this officer does not 'believe' this applicant because of the lack of anticipated emotions. What is more, when this officer suggests that the asylum seeker's lack of emotion could be justified by cultural differences, this is immediately dismissed, reinforcing the centrality of the officers' views and the notion of 'professional knowledge'. Thus, the significance of the applicant's socio-cultural context is denied, and the potential for different gender role constructions dismissed. In this way, officers correlate what they 'know' with the expectations they apply to Western sex/gender constructions, Explicit behaviours, performances or even appearances are expected from men and from women by the officers as per the sex-gender identities formed by the ethno-androcentric views of the West (Butler 1990). Through this, they come to concur that there are certain 'truths' that must be present within a narrative to enable them to establish the plausibility of a story:

> There are things that can't be, and if they can't be, they can't be. (Immigration Officer[32])

Such things that 'can't be'—in the eyes of officers—will make them doubt the whole story. Officers apply heteronormative gender labels to construct the personal characteristics which define what they perceive as a 'normal' display of emotions. When performances fall outside of the 'normal' limits set by the officers this becomes a reason to suspect the narrative.

A fundamental element of all of the criteria used to judge an applicant's credibility is that they invariably begin from a position of suspicion and distrust. This is particularly evident in relation to the provision of formal documentation. If an applicant arrives with too many documents, they may be treated with suspicion, as it is assumed that their documents are likely to be forgeries. Yet if the applicant arrives with no documentation, there will also be suspicion and doubt about their nationality and thus the veracity of their story:

> Proof can have a good or a bad influence, it can be good or bad, it depends on the country, it depends if it is fabricated, it doesn't necessarily help. (Chief Immigration Officer[33])

The fragility of the concept of credibility is most evident in cases of rape or torture, where officers may deny that alleged events could have taken place, usually because of pre-attached labels—for example, if an applicant fails to display the expected level of emotion in recounting their story—and thus these accounts are considered in a negative light. Even in cases where physical evidence is presented to support the claims of abuse,[34] officers' 'logic', 'coherence' and 'common sense' prevail in determining credibility:

> Can you establish that it is genuine? Because in certain locations, certain countries, official looking documentation can be produced at the drop of a hat. It's very difficult to say what is genuine and what's not genuine. (Chief Immigration Officer[35])

The specific criteria against which asylum seekers' credibility is measured are used to rationalize decisions, yet these criteria are related to officers' 'prior knowledge'. This is established in the understanding of asylum geared towards denying rather than protecting asylum applicants. It is through the socialization process that the fears and anxieties about migration and asylum seekers are legitimized within the subculture. To officers, this is objective information rather than constructed preconceptions, to the extent that officers may appear oblivious to the labelling process that they themselves apply:

> Youngsters from Africa do not present a very articulate story because it is the one they have been provided with. Maybe if they presented their real story, although it would be much more incredible, well, I don't know but probably it would be better. (Immigration Officer[36])

In the same way that this officer categorizes 'youngsters from Africa', a socially constructed set of expectations and norms becomes 'the knowledge' of the immigration officers. Furthermore, it is an officer's ability to identify lies and deceits that signifies them being a 'true' group member (Gardner 1994) and is functionally relevant 'to adopt[ing] the group norms' (Snyder and Miene 1994, p. 37). This leads to the development and application of further labels emerging from officers' socio-cultural assumptions:

> You have the Somalis who I would say are all European residents and I can only imagine they're coming over here for benefits or whatever but I don't see them as asylum seekers anyway. You can't take those people seriously, we see the way they're dressed when they arrive, they haven't just come from Mogadishu, not by the way they're dressed. (Immigration Officer[37])

The construction, development and application of such criteria are not only significant in providing officers with a systematized and coherent method to screen asylum seekers, but also insofar as they stand in for what the official line does not provide. By ensuring that credibility remains ambiguous officers are encouraged to fill in the blanks which, in turn, creates a sense of cohesion in the group as they are left to establish common standards (Wright 1984). What's more, the establishment of these standards becomes the determining factor for becoming 'legitimate labellers' (Mercer 1973), in their own eyes and that of their subculture.

Behind the Screen

> *I genuinely believe that my prejudices are born of experience rather than prejudice.* (Immigration Officer[38])

When thinking about bureaucracy, the prevailing images that often come to mind are of pencil pushers, paperwork and queuing. This depiction, however, would rarely align with a critical evaluation of police activities; yet somehow it remains uncritically associated with the image of state border management regimes. As the evidence presented here demonstrates, the bureaucratic application of very specific criteria in order to process asylum requests obscures the reality of the decision-making processes. States are often criticized for using 'push-back' techniques and legal protocols, such as Dublin I and II, as means to shirk their responsibilities towards asylum seekers as signatories of the Convention. Yet, as this chapter has shown, these criticisms should go beyond the legal shell to condemn how states look to efface asylum seekers not only through legal protocols, but also through tacit involvement in socializing denial and disbelief among immigration officers.

Throughout this chapter, the importance of the meta-messages that are communicated to officers has been shown. As soon as officers join the border service, and progress into the field, the 'ideology' of the site serves as a frame of reference that constantly reminds them of the state's goals in relation to immigration and asylum policy (Cohen 2002). The messages of 'control', 'prevention' and 'safeguarding' replace any idea of protecting asylum seekers, setting the tone for the continued development of officers' 'professional knowledge'. These messages become the essence of the immigration service subculture ensuring officers respond to the political goals, whilst downplaying the moral and humanitarian commitments of the state as signatories of the *Geneva Convention* and the *European Charter on Human Rights.* While the state is vague in telling officers exactly how to perform their roles, the meta-messages make it clear what is expected of them in their jobs.

Through training and socialization into the subculture, officers come to see the concept of asylum itself as a 'pattern of immigration',[39] and arc relentlessly encouraged to find inconsistencies, irregularities and lies in applicants' stories, which they use to rationalize their denial of the fundamental right of asylum. What is more, the meta-message serves as a frame that not only tells officers that they are expected to 'say no', but also reinforces the idea that officers should not feel responsible for asylum seekers. The meta-message becomes the bridge between the goals of the Home Office and officers' roles, producing a working environment that at once appears detached from political inference, and perfectly serves the political goals of the state. By maintaining a degree of detachment between the political narratives and the quotidian activities of immigration officers, autonomous self-sufficient spheres are promoted on both sides (see also Fugerlud 2004). As Simmel points out, it is this conflict, whereby officers see politicians as detached and clueless despite having some influence over their work, that helps promote internal cohesion and defines the group boundaries (Simmel 1966).

Moreover, establishing moral distance and limiting responsibility is not only ensured by the system but is also tied to officers' professional roles and development, which promotes 'the rational pursuit of self-interest over moral concerns' (Gill 2016, p. 45). This process is geared towards establishing governance structures, such that officers are compelled to embody policy through their social control role, rather than to simply enact it. Asylum seekers are constructed through policy narratives as deviants, justifying the removal of moral responsibility for those on the frontline.

Regardless of the empirical evidence presented here, the official and legal line that denies that immigration officers perform any decision-making role remains, perpetuating the fallacy that asylum screening is a mere technocratic process. Officers do not need to justify actions that they are not supposed to be performing and for which they will not see the direct results. Their narratives of accountability are constructions that are ordinarily transmitted as part of the subculture (Cohen 2001). Officers' limited sense of accountability, as Cohen explains, reflects an acceptance by the majority of their apparently bureaucratic role in the process:

> I do not feel responsible because I must do my job to comply with very specific procedures that are determined by the law, by the normative. I mean, I am sorry I am such a 'soviet', such a bureaucrat, but I only feel responsible to the law. (Immigration Officer[40])

There is thus a wholesale denial built into the immigration service that is actively encouraged and reproduced by the state, and which serves to present immigration decisions as bureaucratic representations of 'natural justice'. As evidence shows, the decision-making process is much less about the application of the rule of law, and more closely related to officers' ability to make decisions about asylum seeker narratives. This is a point similarly established by Fassin in the context of French asylum courts, whereby the truth is not negotiated in a political vacuum but in a 'social environment in which public discourses stigmatize refugees while officially defending the doctrine of protection' (2013, p. 60). This 'truth' about asylum, 'the way it is permanently transformed through international debates and national jurisprudence and by the daily work of officers' (Fassin 2013, p. 40), plays a powerful role in the ways in which border agents come to understand and embody their place at the border (Weber and Bowling 2004).

The subcultural development of criteria and ways of categorizing asylum seekers reveals itself to be the backbone of the majority of asylum screening decisions. The fact that officers are directed to base their decisions on credibility, but are given no guidelines as to how they should do this, highlights the degree of autonomy with which the immigration service subculture is permitted to establish its own labels and criteria when processing asylum requests. As has been shown in this chapter without reservations, in many cases the basis for these labels is often nebulous and does not take into account the circumstances of individual cases, resulting in poor decisions based on racialised identities, stereotypes and prejudice:

> You tend to see people as stereotypes and that affects everything you do in the job, particularly with asylum. (Immigration Officer[41])

Just as officers construct asylum seekers' narratives within the subcultural milieu of the immigration service, as Cohen (2001) illustrates, individuals also rationalize their behaviour within the ordinary cultural transmission of the border subculture.

Nonetheless, as officers assume their role they come to believe that it is they who hold the moral high ground in the interaction with asylum seekers, as it is they who are protecting the nation from a threat and uncovering lies and deceits. This performance is thus related to the unquestioned 'banality of evil' (Arendt 1963), as officers do not see the tragedy resulting from the cumulative outcomes of their actions as they reproduce the fallacy that they play an insignificant role in a bureaucratic process. Adopting these perspectives is central to officers' performance of their role; and, once this role is embraced, it is unlikely that they will express any doubt about the handling of asylum claims. The exemption of immigration officers' actions is assured both legally and through the narrative that deconstructs asylum. Despite this, the human side remains and officers do still express reservations about their role in the process:

> So in that context, I mean it's not fair on the refugees really 'cause they won't get a fair shot. And there's even, it gets to a state where people have competitions to see who can finish their interview quicker. Which is another reason it seems to me why we should do away with interviews altogether. And the onus should be put entirely on the asylum seeker, do you know what I'm saying? (Chief Immigration Officer[42])

Even in such expressions of concern about the screening process at the border, however, the meta-messages remain, as does the code that the truthfulness of asylum seekers must be established beyond the narrative. It is the cultural setting on asylum and the subculture, and not the formal regulations, that guides officers to seek to reduce asylum entries and rationalizes their role in 'protecting' the country from asylum seekers as the embodiment of social threats, even though they are, undeniably and empirically, amongst the most vulnerable members of our contemporary society.

Notes

1. DI/V-UK6-AR00-CIO: In this, and all subsequent quotes, there is a code that indicates that it is empirical material from immigration officers, expressed either as extracts from in-depth interviews (indicated as I/V) or from notes from participant observation (indicated as P/O). Part

of the code also indicates the category of the person interviewed: HMI—Her Majesty's Inspector; CIO—Chief Immigration Officer; IO—Immigration Officer; AIO—Assistant Immigration Officer; TO—Training Officer; and NR—new recruit. The rest of the code is for data management purposes only. The codes do not follow a clear pattern so confidentiality and anonymity are assured.

2. Acknowledgement and thanks to the UK Economic and Social Research Council that kindly funded this investigation (Grant: R00429934237). Further thanks to Aidan McGovern for his role in expanding the research and thorough editing work.
3. DI/V-UK-P32:81-208:212-IO.
4. Aside from the training course, participant observation was conducted at six-month intervals at ports: on arrival, in-between interviews and after the interviews.
5. Participant observation of the training was not restricted to formal sessions but included the breaks when new recruits and trainers commented on the content of sessions, often deviating from the official guidelines to relay the informal expectations of the job (see Jubany 2017). The data was gathered from research conducted within the UK border management agency between 1999 and 2002–3, while in 2013 a second main investigation began, to extrapolate the conclusions of this work to a wider framework.
6. DI/V-UK3-AR00-IO.
7. While the empirical grounds for this research were conducted within the now defunct Immigration and Nationality Directorate in the UK, further investigation reveals that the training plans for new recruits remains unchanged, with the focus placed on learning interview techniques towards challenging the applicants' credibility, as is reflected in recent policy and training documents issued by the Home Office (2015a, b). Despite changes to the nomenclature and organizational structures of the UK border control, the messages conveyed by official documents remain strikingly similar and coupled with evidence that continues to highlight the concealed decision-making processes of asylum decisions within the UK (Asylum Aid 2011; Anderson et al. 2014; Souter 2011), and asylum screening continues to be determined by the overarching meta-messages of disbelief and deterrence (Jubany 2017).
8. The aims of the UNHCR handbook are to provide guidelines to determine refugee status and to clarify the definition of the term 'refugee' for

the purposes of the convention. This is specifically addressed 'to those who in their daily work are called upon to determine refugee status' (UNHCR 2011, p. 42), mainly immigration officers. Despite this, since 2002 neither the UNHCR nor the British Refugee Council has had any presence in the UK training course, as the role of officers in protecting asylum seekers' rights has been further obscured within the asylum governance structures.

9. D/I-UK14-AR00-5-IO.
10. P/O-UK-P-UK22/JN00-TA-2-TO.
11. P/O-UK-P-UK12JN00-T2-TO.
12. D/V-UK-P14: 279-478:484-IO.
13. P/O-UK-P39:5-73:75-TO.
14. P/O-UK-20-00-ME-TS.
15. DI/V-PUK22J-T5-TO.
16. DI/V-UK9-MY00-TO.
17. Training Officer—P/O-UK20JN-TO.
18. P/O-UK12J-T3-TO.
19. P/O-TO-UK10JN-T5-TO.
20. Training Officer—P/O-36:81-268:269.
21. DI/V-UK-P2:2-51:70-IO.
22. P/O-2:23-70:79-TO.
23. P/O-UK20JN-TO.
24. DI/V-UK-P2:183:192-IO.
25. P/O-TO-UK07JN-T/S1-TS.
26. The jurisdictional as well as organizational procedures in the UK establish that immigration officers do not have the legal power or duty to decide on asylum seekers' applications. At the time of the research, immigration officers in the UK received and interviewed asylum seekers, before forwarding a report containing their decision to a Chief Immigration Officer at Immigration and Nationality Directorate (IND) headquarters. Here decisions were legally endorsed and the verdict sent to the applicant. This changed under the New Asylum Model (Home Office 2006), which was intended to encourage greater accountability for officers by merging the roles of interviewer and caseworker; yet the process remains the same, with higher-ranked officers in UK Visas and Immigration now approving decisions.
27. DI/V-UK-P:13:179-693:694-IO.
28. DI/V-UK-P6:145-501:504-IO.

29. For further analysis of the criteria used and the ways assumed human behaviour affects asylum decisions, see Jubany (2011, 2017) and Herlihy et al. (2010).
30. DI/V-UK5-17-IO.
31. DI/V-UK5-AR00-IO.
32. DI/V-UK-P19:303-IO.
33. DI/V-P1-349:360-CIO.
34. This is evidenced in relation to the Detained Fast Track (DFT) procedures and the negative rationalization of evidence within the immigration service. In one such case, despite documentary evidence being presented to support that the applicant had been tortured, the caseworker denied that the events took place, noting that the evidence of torture did not prove that the applicant was tortured.
35. DI/V-UK15-AR00-CIO.
36. DI/V-P6-785:792-IO.
37. DI/V-UK-P18-546:560-IO.
38. DI/V-UK-P13:328-536:53-7-IO.
39. DI/V-P13-33:35-IO.
40. DI/V-UK-P6:170-908:913-IO.
41. DI/V-P13:329-546:548-IO.
42. DI/V-UK6-AR00-CIO.

References

Allen, J. (2011). Topological twists: Power's shifting geographies. *Dialogues in Human Geography, 1*(3), 283–298.

Anderson, J., Hollaus, J., Lindsay, A., & Williamson, C. (2014). *The culture of disbelief: An ethnographic approach to understanding an under-theorised concept in the UK asylum system* (Working paper series, No. 102). Oxford: Refugee Studies Centre.

Arendt, H. (1963). *Eichmann in Jerusalem: A report on the banality of evil.* New York: Viking Press.

Asylum Aid. (2011). *Unsustainable: The quality of initial decision-making in women's asylum claims.* London: Asylum Aid.

Bateson, G. (1955). A theory of play and fantasy. *Psychiatric Research Reports, 2,* 39–51.

Bauman, Z. (2007). *Liquid times.* Cambridge: Polity.

Becker, H. S. (1973). *Outsiders: Studies in the sociology of deviance*. New York: The Free Press.

Bigo, D. (2014). The (in)securitization practices of the three universes of EU border control: Military/navy – border guards/police – database analysts. *Security Dialogue, 45*(3), 209–225.

Bigo, D., & Guild, E. (2005). *Controlling frontiers: Free movement into and within Europe*. Aldershot: Ashgate Publishing.

Blumer, H. (1969). *Symbolic interaction*. New York: Prentice-Hall.

Butler, J. (1990). *Gender trouble: Feminism and the subversion of identity*. New York: Routledge.

Cicourel, A., & Knorr-Cetina, K. (Eds.). (1981). *Advances in social theory and methodology: Towards an integration of micro and macro sociologies*. Boston: Routledge & Kegan Paul.

Cohen, S. (1972). *Folk devils and moral panics*. London: MacGibbon and Kee.

Cohen, S. (1985). *Visions of social control: Crime, punishment and classification*. Cambridge: Polity.

Cohen, S. (2001). *States of denial: Knowing about atrocities and suffering*. Cambridge: Polity.

Cohen, S. (2002). *Folk devils and moral panics* (3rd ed.). Oxon: Routledge.

Daniel, E. V., & Knudsen, J. C. (Eds.). (1995). *Mistrusting refugees*. London: University of California Press.

Deleuze, G., & Guattari, F. (1987). *A thousand plateaus: Capitalism and schizophrenia* (B. Massumi, Trans.). Minneapolis University of Minnesota Press.

Fassin, D. (2013). The precarious truth of asylum. *Public Culture, 25*, 39–63.

Ferguson, J., & Gupta, A. (2008). Spatializing states: Toward an ethnography of neoliberal governmentality. *Anthropologies of Modernity: Foucault, Governmentality, and Life Politics, 29*(4), 105–131.

Foucault, M. (1988). *Technologies of the self: A seminar with Michel Foucault*. In L. Martin, H. Gutman & P. Hutton (Eds.). Amherst: University of Massachusetts Press.

Fugerlud, O. (2004). Constructing exclusion: The micro-sociology of an immigration department. *Social Anthropology, 12*(1), 25–40.

Gardner, R. C. (1994). Stereotypes as consensual beliefs. In M. Zanna & J. Olson (Eds.), *The psychology of prejudice*. Hillsdale: Lawrence Erlbaum Associates.

Gelder, K., & Thornton, S. et al. (Eds.). (1997). *The subcultures' reader*. London: Routledge.

Gilbert, G. (1951). Stereotype persistence and change among college students. *Journal of Abnormal and Social Psychology, 46*, 245–254.

Gill, N. (2010). New state-theoretic approaches to asylum and refugee geographies. *Progress in Human Geography, 34*(5), 626–645.

Gill, N. (2016). *Nothing personal?: Geographies of governing and activism in the British asylum system*. New York: Wiley.

Goffman, E. (1961). *Asylums*. New York: Anchor Books.

Goffman, E. (1963). *Behaviour in public places: Notes on the social organization of gatherings*. New York: Free Press.

Herlihy, J., Gleeson, K., & Turner, S. (2010). What assumptions about human behaviour underlie asylum judgments? *International Journal of Refugee Law, 22*(3), 351–366.

Heyman, J. (1995). Putting power in the anthropology of bureaucracy: The immigration and naturalization service at the Mexico-United States. *Current Anthropology, 36*, 261–287.

Hofstede, G. (1980). Motivation, leadership and organisation: Do American theories apply abroad?. *Organisational Dynamics*, (Summer 1980), 42–63.

Hollifield, J. F. (2000). The politics of international migration: How can we "bring the state back in"? In C. Brettell & J. F. Hollifield (Eds.), *Migration theory: Talking across disciplines* (pp. 227–288). New York/London: Taylor and Francis.

Home Office. (2006). *Controlling our borders: Making immigration work for Britain*. Norwich: Her Majesty's Stationary Office.

Home Office. (2015a, January). *Asylum policy instructions: Assessing credibility and refugee status*. Home Office.

Home Office. (2015b, March). *Asylum policy instructions: Asylum interviews*. Home Office.

Horii, S. (2012). It is about more than just training: The effect of Frontex border guard training. *Refugee Survey Quarterly, 31*, 158–177.

Jubany, O. (2011). Constructing truths in a culture of disbelief: Understanding asylum screening from within. *International Sociology, 26*(1), 74–94.

Jubany, O. (2017). *Screening asylum in a culture of disbelief: Truths, denials and sceptical borders*. Oxford: Palgrave Macmillan.

Lane, T. (1989). *The living organisation: system of behaviour*. London: Praeger.

Lazaridis, G. (2015). *International migration into Europe: From subjects to objects*. Basingstoke: Palgrave Macmillan.

Lippmann, W. (1946). *Public opinion*. New York: Transaction Publishers.

Loftus, B. (2015). Border regimes and the sociology of policing. *Policing and Society: An International Journal of Research and Policy, 24*, 115–125.

Marston, S. A., Jones, J. P., & Woodward, K. (2005). Human geography without scale. *Transactions of the Institute of British Geographers, 30*(4), 416–432.

Martin Cassares, A. (2007). *Antropología del género: culturas, mitos y estereotipos sexuales*. Madrid: Cátedra.

Matza, D. (1969). *Becoming deviant*. New York: Prentice Hall.

Mercer, J. R. (1973). *Labeling the mentally retarded*. Berkeley: University of California Press.

Mountz, A. (2010). *Seeking asylum: Human smuggling and bureaucracy at the border*. Minneapolis: University of Minnesota Press.

Pilivain, I., & Briar, S. (1964). Police encounters with juveniles. *American Journal of Sociology, 70*, 2016–2014.

Prokkola, E.-K., & Ridanpää, J. (2014). Border guarding and the politics of the body: An examination of the Finnish Border Guard service. *Gender, Place & Culture, 0524*(October), 1–17.

Reiner, R. (1997). Policing and the police. In M. Maguire, R. Morgan, & R. Reiner (Eds.), *The Oxford handbook of criminology*. Oxford: Clarendon Press.

Riggins, S. (1990). *Beyond Goffman: Studies on communication, institutions and social interaction*. Berlin: Mouton de Gruyter.

Rosaldo, M., & Lamphere, L. (2001). *Women, culture and society: Theoretical overview*. Stanford: Stanford University Press.

Rosenhan, D. L. (1973). On being sane in insane places. *Science, 179*, 250–258.

Schur, E. (1971). *Labelling deviant behaviour: Its sociological implications*. London: Harper and Row Publishers.

Simmel, G. (1966). *Conflict*. New York: Free Press.

Snyder, M., & Miene, P. (1994). On the functions of stereotypes and prejudice. In M. P. Zanna & J. M. Olson (Eds.), *The psychology of prejudice: The Ontario symposium* (Vol. 7, pp. 33–540). Hillsdale: Lawrence Erlbaum Associates.

Solomos, J. (1993). *Race and racism in Britain* (2nd ed.). London: Macmillan.

Souter, J. (2011). A culture of disbelief or denial? Critiquing refugee status determination in the United Kingdom. *Oxford Monitor of Forced Migration, 1*(1), 48–59.

Tayeb, M. H. (1988). *Organisations and national culture: A comparative analysis*. London: Sage Publications.

UNHCR. (2011). *Handbook on procedures and criteria for determining refugee status*. Geneva: UNHCR.

Weber, L., & Bowling, B. (2004). Policing migration: A framework for investigating the regulation of global mobility. *Policing and Society, 14*(3), 195–212.

Werthman, C., & Pilivain, I. (1967). Gang members and the police. In D. Bordua (Ed.), *The Police*. New York: Wiley.

Wright, C. (1984). *Construction of deviance in sociological theory: The problems of commensurability*. New York: University Press of America.

3

Beyond the Border Spectacle: Migration Across the Mediterranean Sea

Pierluigi Musarò

Introduction

We live in a world on the move. The history of humanity is a history of migration. Since the beginning of human existence, humankind has had both the reason and the means to travel from one place to another (Castles and Miller 2009). In the words of the United Nations (UN) Special Representative on Migration, Peter D. Sutherland, 'Migration – when it is safe, legal, and voluntary – is the oldest poverty-reduction and human-development strategy.'[1]

Nevertheless, with more than 20,000 people dying during their high-risk journeys through the Mediterranean Sea in the last two decades, Europe has become the deadliest migration destination in the world (Brian and Laczko 2014). Further, given the clandestine nature of these crossings and the lack of reliable data, the real number may well be higher (Aalberts and Gammeltoft-Hansen 2014).[2]

P. Musarò (✉)
Department of Sociology and Business Law, University of Bologna, Bologna, Italy

F. Vecchio, A. Gerard (eds.), *Entrapping Asylum Seekers*, Transnational Crime, Crime Control and Security, DOI 10.1057/978-1-137-58739-8_3

In 2013, the European Parliament President, Martin Schulz, said that Europe's migration policy had 'turned the Mediterranean into a graveyard', referring to the number of drowned refugees in the region as a direct result of the policies. During a visit to Lampedusa, following the tragic shipwreck of 3 October 2013, when 366 migrants died, European Commission President, Jose Manuel Barroso, said that he was 'profoundly shocked' by the victim's coffins he witnessed. On the same occasion, Italian Prime Minister Enrico Letta described the shipwreck as 'a European tragedy'.[3] On 11 October 2013, another big shipwreck occurred between Malta and Lampedusa that brought the death toll to over 600 in that incident. In those days right after the incident, as the world watched in horror the images of migrants who had lost their lives while attempting to swim to the shores of the Italian island, the European Commission started to mobilize its member states to create the Mediterranean Task Force.[4]

On 18 October 2013, on the wave of the diffused shock felt across Europe, the Italian authorities declared a day of national mourning for the tragedies at sea, gave honorary Italian citizenship to the dead and independently launched operation Mare Nostrum—a military–humanitarian operation in the Mediterranean aimed at rescuing migrants and arresting smugglers.[5]

It is important to note that Mare Nostrum (translated as 'our sea') was the Roman name for the Mediterranean Sea, picked up by Italian dictator Mussolini to frame fascist propaganda about the 'Italian lake'. As the (ambivalent) name indicates, the possessive 'our' projects the Mediterranean as a European space of care and control, while it ambiguously connotes both Italy and Europe.

Furthermore, it is interesting how the Italian Government neither mentioned that the survivors of the shipwreck were automatically charged with the criminal offence of illegal entry—despite their eligibility to apply for asylum—nor that they were being detained on the island's holding centre. At the same time, the Italian media failed to report that the Sicilian captains and shipcrews, who helped during the rescue, were to be prosecuted on the charge of assisting illegal immigration, and even human trafficking. Neither did the government mention the mobility restrictions of the visa regime in place at the time, which forced people to take a boat and risk their lives crossing the Mediterranean.[6]

Drawing upon this peculiar co-existence of the securitization of the border and the progressive discursive and legal articulation of responsibilities for vulnerable groups (Aas and Gundhus 2015), this chapter focuses on the context of Mediterranean migrant tragedies with the aim of investigating the effect of the media on public understanding of the migration and refugee crisis. In particular, it explores how migrants are represented in the contexts of humanitarian aid, on the one hand, and border control, on the other, highlighting the contrasts between the two perspectives, but also how they influence each other.

Although, in many ways, both migration studies and media studies are implicitly interlinked and mutually constitutive, rarely have the overlaps between the two fields been explored with the aim of critically bridging some of the gaps between media and migration research. While scholars and activists have widely denounced the securitization and militarization of borders today (Mezzadra and Nielson 2013; Bigo 2002), there has been far less consideration of the visual means through which media and state actors present the border as a space of humanitarian government. Thus, to analyse how humanitarian discourse has gained prominence in the media and political debates on migration in the European Union (EU), this chapter focuses on the humanitarian socio-visual field (Kurasawa 2015).

The media are viewed here as institutionalized means of symbolic production, transmission and circulation, as well as practices, performances and human activities aimed at circulating representations of common life (Silverstone 1999; Couldry 2010). Media, in this account, do not only report on the world 'out there' but also constitute the very meaning of this world, producing hierarchical classifications of 'us' (European citizens) versus 'them' (African migrants), via at the course of news, documentaries or fictional narratives.

The chapter begins with a discussion of the historical and political constitution of the humanitarian narrative in the management of migration. More specifically, it considers the discursive practices enacted by the European Agency for the Management of Operational Cooperation at the External Borders of the Member States of the European Union (or Frontex), and cultural objects—such as images, video and films—produced by Marina Militare and Guardia Costiera, both of which are responsible for search and rescue (SAR) operations at sea, during the military–humanitarian operation Mare Nostrum. These are considered not only as material or digital artefacts but also as institutional nodes in the European public sphere and actants whose visibility shapes public discourse and collective ways of thinking about the world.

This is followed by an analysis of the configuration of 'the military–humanitarian border spectacle', intended as an emotional and physical setting in which fears and insecurities can be used for both progressive and regressive purposes. By focusing on the intimate link between the 'borderization' and the 'spectacularization' processes, the chapter conceptualizes this spectacularization of the border in two different ways. On the one hand, it can be seen as part of the humanitarian imaginary: 'a configuration of practices which use the communicative structure of the theatre in order to perform collective imaginations of vulnerable others in the West, with a view to cultivating a longer-term disposition to thinking, feeling and acting towards these others' (Chouliaraki 2013, p. 45). On the other hand, it can be viewed as 'a constellation of images and discursive formations, which repetitively supply migrant "illegality" with the semblance of an objective fact' (De Genova 2013, p. 1).

The chapter concludes with remarks on the current state of humanitarianism in liberal democracies. While reaffirming our cosmopolitan solidarity through the rescue of lives and the language of compassion towards those people rescued who are seen as part of our common humanity, the spectacle of increasingly militarized and securitized borders created around Europe filters human mobility, by categorizing humanitarian subjects as worthy or unworthy, desirable or undesirable, deserving or undeserving.

The Growing Migrant Crisis

Europe's 'migrant crisis' is a very recent and human-made phenomenon, constituting a policy domain that frequently stirs strong emotions and controversies. It is a policy area where economic, political, humanitarian, cultural and legal points of view often clash with particular force.

In the early 1990s, a radical and widespread migration policy change emerged, followed by an alarming media coverage that highlighted the large numbers of 'boat people' arriving from North African countries into southern European states, represented as a significant problem to be managed in terms of a wider social, cultural and political 'crisis' (Jeandesboz and Pallister-Wilkins 2014).

During the 1990s, the need for intra-European cooperation in the field of migration control came to be recognized, leading to the acceptance and gradual implementation of the Schengen Agreement of 14 June 1985, which paved the way towards the legislative and political foundation of Europe's more recent coordinated defensive approach on migration (Gelatt 2005). The Mediterranean became the southern external border of a new area without borders. In 1990, the first six founding members (Germany, France, Italy, Belgium, Luxemburg and the Netherlands) signed the Schengen Convention in order to put the common area into practice. One after the other, all European states implemented the Schengen Agreement, and 'Europe' as a political entity transformed from its initial nucleus of six countries into the present EU with 28 member states (2015). But this was not a policy without costs: some level of mutual trust on immigration and asylum policies was required, meaning that new legislation and substantial investments in border control and migrant detention, as well as the reception of asylum seekers, had to be implemented. Largely preoccupied with questions of border policing and migration control, national migration policies shifted from a positive emphasis on the recruitment of foreign labour, to a negative focus on the stemming of migratory flows. The 'European internal security field' (Bigo 1994) shaped by the new national migration policies created a tight nexus of discourses and policies concerning transnational issues of crime, law and disorder. In solidifying this securitized conception of migration, European members generated a cognitive and administrative template for the regulation of migration, key elements of which subsequently found their way into the EU (Walters 2010). This was the first step towards what would become the Dublin Convention, which supplanted Schengen with similar rules in 1997, and the Treaty of Amsterdam, which formally incorporated Schengen into the framework of the EU as Schengen acquis.

In parallel to the evolution of European policies on migration and border control, the obligation to conduct SAR services is upheld both by moral tradition and international maritime law. The latter includes the 1974 *International Convention for the Safety of Life at Sea* (SOLAS), the 1979 *International Convention on Maritime Search and Rescue* (SAR), the 1982 UN *Convention on the Law of the Sea* (UNCLOS), the 1989 *International Salvage Convention* and the reg. EU 656/2014 that defines the norms for the surveillance of external sea borders. Nevertheless, this complicated set of rules and conventions signed by European states has not prevented the occurrence of tragedies at sea. A key example is the 'Porto Palo' shipwreck that occurred on Christmas Eve 1996, in which around 300 migrants from Pakistan, India and Sri Lanka died while attempting to reach Italian shores (Bellu 2004)—an incident that, sadly, is not isolated.

To understand how, in the last two decades, more than 20,000 migrants have lost their lives trying to cross the Mediterranean, we should pay attention to the ways in which the governments of Mediterranean countries have repeatedly argued over their respective obligations regarding migrants lost at sea, and several claims have been made that neighbours have deliberately abandoned boats in danger in foreign SAR regions, while regular testimonies by survivors tell of both commercial and navy ships ignoring their pleas for help (CIR 2007).

Far outstripping any real 'migration crisis' is the public anxiety surrounding migration in Europe, which is increasing in part due to the distorted and unfair media coverage of migration and the rhetoric of politicians, who describe Europe as besieged by people fleeing conflict or seeking a better life. Indeed, across the West, the media representation of migration often reflects a repetitively negative narrative. In European countries, irregular migration from Africa to Europe has also increasingly been defined as a security problem associated with international crime and terrorism.

Sensational media reportage and popular discourses give rise to an apocalyptic image of 'floods' of 'clandestine immigrants' approaching our shores. A 'tide' of 'desperate' Africans fleeing poverty at home in search of the European 'el Dorado', crammed into long-worn ships barely staying afloat, is an all-too-familiar image conjured by the media (Pastore et al.

2006). Hence, the perceived 'solutions' to what has been defined as a 'migration crisis' (Moore et al. 2012) focus on 'fighting' and 'combating' illegal migration through a crackdown on trafficking and smuggling networks in combination with an intensification of border controls. As a consequence, an increasing amount of resources are being dedicated to preventing migrants from entering without authorization, and enforcing the return of irregular migrants.

Yet, in terms of numbers, we must note that Europe's 'migration crisis' is vastly inflated in the public debate (Musarò and Parmiggiani 2014). We usually forget that only a small fraction of all immigrants in Europe today have entered by sea, and the majority of Europe's irregular migrants are visa overstayers, having entered by air. Even as numbers of maritime arrivals have sharply risen since the Syria and Libya conflicts, reaching more than 750,000 in 2015—some 627,527 people reached Greece's shores, and around 141,100 arrived in Italy—in the whole of 2014 the number of people arriving by sea was only 219,000. This should be contrasted with the 3.4 million migrants entering EU member states each year, and with the world's 51 million forcibly displaced people, the vast majority of whom are hosted by poor nations, not by rich Western states (IOM 2015).

The prominence of Europe's southern external borders in European media and political debates obscures the fact that the 'crisis' appears to reflect Europe's 'response' to irregular migrants and asylum seekers, including the EU's ability to keep people safe and secure. The approach to migration adopted by the EU, national political actors, non-government organizations (NGOs) and the media is usually focused on the securitarian and humanitarian side of the phenomenon, emphasizing framings of irregularity, 'illegality', security and humanitarian crisis.

If we focus on the economic and political instrumentalization of migrant flows, it is clear that, as argued by Mountz (2010, pp. xvi–xvii), 'on islands, in airports, at sea, and in offshore detention centres where authorities and migrants encounter each other, states perform crises and develop proper narratives to manage the geographical margins of their sovereign territory'.

These migration crisis narratives are closely related to the national interests of states and the powers they are able to exercise in controlling undesirable immigration. At a policy level, for example, crisis-mode responses may either reflect or break with predominant modes of governing migration; and the crisis narratives are adopted by governments to legitimize the orientation of their policy strategies. Since the 'war on terror', in particular, state powers have reformulated their priorities away from the (welfare) protection of citizens towards integration within a global economy and source of global capital, opening a defensive modality of politics that Hage (2003) identifies as the expression of 'paranoid' forms of nationalism.

For example, on 12 February 2011, as a response to the 'invasion' of 5000 'clandestine migrants' in the wake of the Arab Spring, Italy declared a 'state of emergency' until the end of the year. It was renewed on 6 October 2011 to last until the end of 2012, prompting the issuing of thousands of six-month 'humanitarian' temporary residence permits by ministerial decree and the subsequent 'warehousing' of thousands of people in reception centres. A key consequence of these emergency measures, which are predictable consequences of a lack of legal entry routes for those forced to flee, is that migrants' human rights have been sidelined by the focus on temporary remedies instead of long-term solutions.

Considering the emotional reactions of the European leaders to the Lampedusa 'tragedies' and their silence on EU immigration policies, we should ask: what do we know about this 'crisis' in terms of its seriousness and the allocation of responsibility for it? What types of solutions do we consider possible: fighting smugglers, rescuing people or changing EU policies?

The Humanitarian Discourse

In order to unveil the instrumentalization of the humanitarian discourse—that is, the subordination of other-oriented aim of saving lives and changing societies to the self-oriented imperative of protecting Europe and its identity through border control—the chapter now considers the recent strengthening of humanitarian rhetoric in migration governance within the visual economy of Western humanitarianism.

If we intend humanitarianism as 'a historically specific articulation of cosmopolitan solidarity, which acts directly on the Global South through specialized institutions, yet seeks legitimacy in the West through a communicative structure that disseminates moral discourses of care and responsibility' (Chouliaraki 2013, p. 27), how is our moral attitude towards helping vulnerable strangers affected when the spectacle of suffering is performed at home? Whose humanity is included in recent invocations of humanitarian discourses of care and responsibility, and whose is not?

While we usually define humanitarianism as a moral imperative to reduce distant suffering (Calhoun 2008), recent events and media attention on the migrant tragedies at sea have intensified humanitarian discourses in the context of borders and migration. Subjects, policies and mechanisms related to mobility have played a crucial role in the spatial and symbolic reshaping of Europe that has characterized the last two decades. Since the restrictive policy change in the asylum regime enacted in the early 1990s, migration and asylum have been high on Europe's agenda and a major cause for concern for European citizens, alarmed by the levels of 'illegal' migration as well as concerned by the humanitarian duty of safeguarding the rights of people who are attempting to cross the borders (Mezzadra and Neilson 2013).

The key position that 'humanitarian reason'—intended as a compassionate mode of governance that concerns populations in precarious situations (Fassin 2012)—occupies in the contemporary moral order illustrates how the establishment of such narrative conventions for the representation of suffering was historically central to the emergence of the humanitarian project, broadly construed as the mobilization of sympathy for humans in severe distress as well as the development of measures aimed at preventing needless suffering. As a consequence of these representational conventions, moral sentiments have become an essential force in contemporary politics: they nourish its discourses and legitimize its practices, particularly where these discourses and practices are focused on the disadvantaged and the dominated, whether at home (the immigrants) or farther away (the victims of war or natural disaster) Fassin and Pandolfi (2010).

The chapter focuses on Frontex[7] and the Italian military–humanitarian operation Mare Nostrum, here understood as 'frame sponsors' (Gamson et al. 1992, p. 385) that contributes towards shaping irregular migration in Europe.

Frontex was established in 2004 as a 'compensatory measure' to Schengen (Vaughan-Williams 2008, p. 66). Its overall mission is to promote and coordinate the management of the EU's external borders, and it does so through common risk analysis, the training of border guards and, most visibly, expansive joint return, sea and land border operations. It has approximately 300 employees stationed in its headquarters in Warsaw, and a much larger pool of personnel and equipment at its disposal from member states for potential operations (Neal 2009). It receives funding mainly from the European Commission, in addition to funding from some member states, such as the Schengen signatory countries. The agency's budget has grown from EUR 6.2 million in 2005 to EUR 119. 2 million in 2013,[8] exceeding that of Europol. How does Frontex's public communication explain and legitimize its actions and the increasing investment in border control to the citizens of Europe and the national politicians of EU member states?

According to Horsti (2012), through the media, Frontex discursively assures the public that there are security concerns and border problems that the agency needs to 'combat'. For example, it reinforces official security initiatives through its language and practice of risk analysis. As we can see in its assessment, 'Most risks associated with document fraud were assessed as high. Indeed, document fraudsters not only undermine border security but also the internal security of the EU'[9]; implicit in this type of risk is a view of the border as 'vulnerable', while the people crossing it are construed as a threat.

On the other hand, in recent years, Frontex has also been embracing the discursive strategy of humanitarianism, based on saving migrant lives—a direct response to complaints by human rights activists and NGOs about its mission to protect 'Fortress Europe' without respecting minimum human rights standards. For example, the prevention of migrants from reaching their 'illegitimate' destination is described as a humanitarian action, or 'saving lives'. In these joint operations with member states, Frontex prevents migrants from continuing their journey and forces them to return. At the same time, since the security discourse focuses on the trafficking and smuggling of humans, migrants are typically described as 'victims' of these criminals, and therefore those 'detected' in surveillance operations are 'protected'.[10]

Is the humanitarian discourse simply a smoke screen for a repressive practice, as a critical observer might be tempted to conclude? Investigating this conflicting and ambiguous position of human rights and humanitarian ideals in the policing of European borders, Aas and Gundhus (2015) analyse the complex role of humanitarian thinking and the human rights discourse in Frontex operational activities. Based on interviews with Frontex officials and border guard officers, and the analysis of relevant policy documents and official reports, they reveal that the emotive narratives of compassion and humanitarian assistance feature prominently in the agency's internal discourse, training standards and self-presentation. This type of paradoxical policing—termed by the authors 'humanitarian borderlands'—is 'often conducted simultaneously with, against and through humanity. The mission is framed and legitimized through the language of humanitarianism and human rights, officers are partly required to perform their tasks as humanitarian agents, at the same time as they find themselves complicit and practically involved in deeply inhumane conditions' (Aas and Gundhus 2015, p. 14).

A similar integration of humanitarian and security responses within a common emergency frame is evident in the public communication produced by the Italian Navy and Italian Coast Guard during the operation Mare Nostrum.

While, until October 2013, the public received limited news on dead migrants in the Mediterranean and the few images circulating in the media only portrayed rescued people on Italian shores, during this military–humanitarian operation, the Italian Navy and Italian Coast Guard produced media briefs, interviews, pictures and videos about their high sea operations, which were immediately distributed by the European newspapers or television news.

Assuming the 'social imaginary' (Taylor 2002, p. 106) to be a space of popular practices of representation through which war is imagined as a 'normative resource for the distinction and relation between civic and military virtue' (Frazer and Hutchings 2011, p. 58), we can see how in the institutional communication produced by the Italian Navy, border control is redefined within a moral imagination that emphasizes human vulnerability. Depicting the high sea as a new battlefield, images and videos have thus functioned to reframe border control through practices and discourses of care, aid and assistance.

As it is clear in the official video of Mare Nostrum—which opens with shocking images of desperate people drowning in the high sea, hundreds of coffins and the trembling voice of the Pope denouncing 'It is a shame!' and ends with the smiling eyes of two rescued grateful children with a signboard on which they have written, 'Thank you Italya'[11]—we are presented with an intensely moralistic context within which a military–humanitarian operation is depicted as humanitarian benevolence.

This is also particularly evident in an Italian docudrama produced by the Italian Navy and broadcasted on 6 October 2014 by the Italian national television channel (RAI): *Catia's Choice: 80 miles south of Lampedusa.*[12] Catia Pellegrino is the 36-year-old first female captain of the Italian vessel, *Libra*. She is the protagonist of this 92-minute docudrama, which chronicles the rescuing of refugees crossing the border in small boats, while showing the positive influence of Catia's strength and empathetic nature in serving others and maintaining vigilance in keeping the seas safe on her watch. Catia is thus portrayed as the candle that helps conquer some of the darkness of our world, lighting a path of hope to those in need. It is through a lens of humility that we begin to see this blossoming story.

In *Catia's Choice*, the asymmetrical relationship between heroes and victims can be understood within the context of what Boltanski (1999) calls the 'topic of sentiment'—a mode of representing human suffering that evokes gratitude towards the benefactors and tender-heartedness towards the beneficiaries of the exchange.

Through their efforts to assist vulnerable others and rescue lives at sea, humanitarian soldiers are thus portrayed as performing the empathetic ethos of contemporary Western armies, which acquire their legitimacy not from the defence of the nation but from their efforts to help civilians, to reduce the number of victims on the ground and to protect human life, through collaboration with aid and humanitarian forces (Chouliaraki 2013).

This compassionate attitude is also vibrant in the ways in which the Italian Navy team based in Lampedusa describes its new task as a 'humanitarian operation'. As an Italian seaman stated: 'after all, people choose to live in extremely dangerous conditions and consequently their life cannot be saved other than by highly equipped forces as only the army is. We operate in some way as a ferry-boat for migrants.'[13]

The military migration ferry-boat is ultimately part of what Tazzioli (2015, p. 140) calls '*the exceptionality of (migrant) mobility*'[14]: more than positioned within a frame of security or on a continuum of threat, 'unauthorized migrations are envisioned as mobility to the limit, namely, people moving in exceptionally dangerous conditions and, as a consequence, requiring the mobilization of military forces'. However, if we look beyond the official humanitarian discourse, we realize that almost nothing has changed in terms of techniques of surveillance and monitoring with the commencement of the operation: the radars and methods of patrolling are the same as those used before Mare Nostrum. Rather, the 'military–humanitarian' logic has recast already existing technologies and operative tools by displacing the issue of human rights on saving lives instead of securitizing them.

Finally, during UN Secretary-General Ban Ki-moon's visit to the Italian Parliament on 15 October 2015 it was clear that the humanitarian discourse of assistance and protection was integral to border and migration governance. He paid homage to the Italian soldiers 'who saved thousands of human lives in the Mediterranean', and thanked 'the Italian population for the efforts made to welcome and assist migrants'. After his speech, to highlight the positive Italian attitude towards the current Mediterranean crisis, Italian Prime Minister Matteo Renzi said: 'Italy that welcomes you is the country of the Italian officers who become nurses to deliver babies in the ships on the Mediterranean. It is an Italy of which we are proud.'[15]

The Military–Humanitarian Border Spectacle

The mediated performances of Frontex and Mare Nostrum exemplify how the connection between the combat against 'illegal migrants' and the moral imperative to rescue migrants and refugees ('victims' of human smuggling and perilous, often fatal forms of border crossing) is dramatized by constant TV and newspaper reporting of the 'border spectacle'

(Cuttitta 2014; De Genova 2013). For two decades, the Mediterranean border has been the theatre of operations—in the military and literal sense—enacted by media, nation-states and supranational non-governmental actors. This representation of 'migrant crisis' is a ritual: it consists of symbolic behaviour that is socially standardized and repetitive. As with every ritual, it is a formulaic and dramatic performance that involves symbolic communication and is typically enacted in places and times that have themselves symbolic meaning (Kertzer 1989, p. 9).

The question of 'borders' (how to think of them or figure them out, how to define them and their institution) is central when we reflect on the EU and EU citizenship, and, more generally, on political association. Exploring how this question is performed is fundamental: it is intimately intertwined with the ways in which contemporary mediated representations construct, deconstruct and reconstruct both the nation as a symbolic category of belonging, and ourselves, as cosmopolitan citizens.

Assuming, with Simmel (1983, p. 467), that the border 'is not a spatial fact with sociological effects, but a sociological fact that takes a spatial form', and following Debord's (1995, p. 19) framing of the spectacle as 'a social relationship between people that is mediated by images', it is noteworthy how the border is not just the mirror-like reflection of the divisions existing in the physical–cultural landscape, but a symbolic and political barrier enacted and performed as 'discursive or emotional landscape of social power', as well as 'technical landscape of control and surveillance' (Paasi 1996, p. 63).

Acting on the official theatrical EU border (the Mediterranean), the fight against clandestine migration (alongside its compassionate spectacularization) has become a sort of meta-issue, capable of condensing a whole complex of political fears and concerns regarding globalization, the loss of sovereignty or the welfare state, terrorism, as well as benevolence, compassion and solidarity. In other words, in the last decade in the Mediterranean there has been one spectacle on show, but one that is understood differently by different publics. Like the different light refractions of the same kaleidoscope, the national spectacle of surveillance, policing and border control is also the cosmopolitan spectacle of rescue and salvation. Frontex and Mare Nostrum speak a different language to different political constituencies: to migrants and citizens, to smugglers and transnational activists, to right-wing government coalition members and NGOs. They speak the language of combating human smuggling and potential terrorists, and of ensuring human justice while rescuing lives and protecting migrants' human rights (Albahari 2015). They perform different dramas in making a vigorous display of their technologies and techniques of exclusion against the human border crossers, as well as of their humanitarian benevolence in rescuing lives and taking care of human bodies.

Analysing how humanitarian discourses have become integral to border and migration governance, we should pay attention to the particular ways in which the border spectacle constructs and positions the EU within the migration field, not as the 'Fortress' that perpetrates a fight against vulnerable human beings on the move, but as the innocent victim of an unprovoked transgression. Framing the EU as an innocent victim that is not active, but only reactive, confers upon this political actor an expectation and a sovereign right to respond emphatically to the transgression. In other words, by framing the EU as a passive bystander whose sovereign territory is violated by the intrusion of an uninvited alien that originates in territories and states bearing an external relationship to Europe, these operations, and the practices they convene, appear as a response to a prior transgression called 'illegal immigration', rather than an intervention that plays a fundamental role in structuring contemporary forms of human mobility and distributing both life and death.

Focusing on the intimate link between the borderization and spectacularization processes, we should note that, through their mediated performances, Frontex and Mare Nostrum contribute towards the creation of what Walters (2011, p. 137) has called 'the humanitarian border': a physical–cultural landscape where life and death are daily performed as 'a way of governing this novel and disturbing situation, and compensating for the social violence embodied in the regime of migration control'.

The idea of a military–humanitarian border might appear counterintuitive or even oxymoronic, but not if we engage humanitarianism as a complex domain possessing specific forms of governmental reason, rather than a set of ideas and ideologies, or simply the activity of NGOs. According to Fassin (2007, p. 151), 'humanitarian government can be defined as the administration of human collectivities in the name of a higher moral principle, which sees the preservation of life and the alleviation of suffering as the highest value of action.' If we consider the operation Mare Nostrum, it is clear how one sees war and humanitarian action, typically presumed to be forces opposed to one another, enter into a tense but mutually supportive relationship.

Examining this border spectacle within the framework of humanitarian government—in terms of programmes, discourses, technologies and interventions that operate as an active and constitutive force that naturalizes a particular 'imagined world'—we can better understand some of the problematic aspects of the kind of bordering at stake in the EU's border protection policy.

Beyond the difficulty of drawing a clear line between the regular and irregular migrant, this aspect of bordering is problematic from two perspectives. It negates the lines of interconnection between the EU and the countries from which these migrants originate: neoliberal trade agreements, geopolitical alliances, arms deals, flows of European capital investment and disinvestment, media, tourism and colonialism. As such, it obscures the fact that 'this supra-national entity is taking place in a world where the territorial notions of "interior" and "exterior" are no longer completely separable, not even in a legal manner' (Balibar 2004, p. 23). This politics depicts Europe as a bounded, self-contained entity, distinct from and confronted by an external world of similarly bounded, but far less well-governed entities. It is within this space that irregular migration comes to be imagined as a potentially chaotic set of forces emanating from the world's most troubled states and regions, converging on Europe. As Walters (2010, p. 74) argues: 'Illegal immigration is at once a major symptom of this asymmetry in governance capacity, and a source of justification for Europe to involve itself in attempts to remake the world beyond it in the image of the well-governed, territorial state. In short, anti-illegal immigration activity is more than a branch of migration management. It is nothing less than state-making in a new form.'

This politics of decontextualization—rooted not in geographical lines, but in an act of political imagination—shapes a naturalization of borders that serves to produce the difference between a state's putative inside and outside, between the presumably proper subjects of a state's authority and those mobile human beings branded as different, foreigners, aliens.

Establishing a notion of 'European citizenship', 'extra-communitarian residents' are no longer foreigners in a simple legal sense, but 'absolutely strange' or 'aliens'. They are transformed into subjects and objects of fear, at once experiencing the fear of rejection and elimination and inspiring fear in the resident populations. As a consequence, Balibar (2004, p. 17) asserts, 'the category of the "national" (or the self, of what it requires to be the same) also becomes split and subject to the dissolving action of "internal borders" which mirror the global inequalities.' And in a context where global inequalities widen, potential global mobilities increase and states are pouring more money into the control over borders than ever before, it is comprehensible that the humanitarian terminology is often used to describe migration in contexts of crisis and to obscure questions of political responsibility.

Conclusions

Faced with the rapidly growing number of migrants and refugees entering the EU, the rich EU states, instead of dealing with what most experts have called a 'manageable problem', through a form of 'organised irresponsibility' have contributed to the contemporary 'migrants crisis': first, by framing certain kinds of migration as a risk; second, by transferring this risk to states less equipped to deal with them; and, third, by exporting the idea of migration as a security problem, negatively impacting existing mobility dynamics.

Once a problem is framed and adopted in terms of security crisis or humanitarian emergency, an agent claims a need for and a right to address it by extraordinary means (Calhoun 2010). As Edelman (1977) argues, 'any regime that prides itself on its capacity to manage crises will find crises to manage.'

This scenario is both a challenge and a blessing for the several crisis response agencies involved worldwide in the management of migration. It is a challenge in the sense that, of all the actors in the crisis network, these agencies are held to the highest standards of preparedness, speed of mobilization, smooth communication and coordination, and effective service delivery. On the other hand, a crisis also presents a welcome opportunity to demonstrate relevance and confirm performance capacity.

Europe's 'fight against illegal migration' has created a worrying mechanism for controls to keep on growing indefinitely. The past two decades have seen the consolidation of such an 'industry', involving actors such as European security forces and their African counterparts; NGOs, humanitarian groups and international organizations, often working closely with police; and multinational defence and outsourcing companies. With each new migration 'crisis', this system grows further. Yet, as Andersson (2014) argues, this industry is not the 'solution'; it is a fundamental part of the problem.

What role do media play in this growing 'industry'? As previously shown, moral panics and anxiety produced by daily news coverage maintain a public perception of perpetual crisis underpinning immigration policies and social problems. This promotes a 'commonsense' hostility that has sedimented in dominant media and policy discourses surrounding asylum seekers in the West (Sassen 2009), which is emphasized by some political actors who engage in 'business-as-usual' discourse, downplaying extreme migration experiences, especially where acknowledgement of them would undermine these actors' legitimacy and credibility. This crisis rhetoric is useful to position national security as a primary concern in the dominant public discourse of wealthy European countries. In this context, anguish born of uncertainty and, more specifically, fear play an important ideological role, as support for the claims of leaders to take political action against 'external enemies'. As Bauman (2007, p. 85) suggests: 'the latent function of the barriers at the borders, ostensibly erected against "false asylum seekers" and "merely economic" migrants, is to fortify the shaky, erratic and unpredictable existence of the insiders.'

Created as a spectacle on behalf of missing politics, the military–humanitarian border becomes a powerful dispositif to displace citizens' attention from the internal problems of national states and the divisions within EU. Assuming that 'the identity a person lays claim to is often based, in reverse, on that of his enemy' (Maalouf 2000, p. 14), the nationalism embedded in the humanitarian narratives of border control coincides with a process of rendering inferior other societies.

As discussed above, framing migrants both as enemy and victim, the border spectacle creates a space that posits a radical conflict between 'us' and 'them'. Placing the 'them' beyond the pale, outside the space of political dialogue, EU-mediated performances of migration management do not simply represent a response to a self-evident problem but rather a political, moral and conceptual intervention that actively shapes the social world encountered, including the very meaning of migration.

In line with the moral discourse of global compassion, historically emphasized by media and aid agencies, this dramatization has been discursively dislocated from the context of humanitarian action and philanthropy onto the context of border control. Following decades of humanitarian organizations overly concerned with raising funds, thus turning suffering into a spectacle for consumption, dominant media and political discourses nowadays tend to depict extreme poverty, war and environmental degradation amalgamated into a single stereotypical image of 'African misery' as the root causes of this migration. This neocolonial vocabulary (Musarò 2011) typically accompanies the portrayal of African migrants as passive victims of poverty and war, as desperate and hopeless people (de Haas 2007). As for the passive and voiceless victims portrayed in most of the West's humanitarian fundraising appeals, this politics of pity dehumanizes migrants, denies their agency and reduces them to numbers, bodies, 'bare life' (Agamben 1998), 'non-persons' (Dal Lago 1999). They have no speaking part to play in the political process.

Although humanitarian action is 'quintessentially cosmopolitan' as it represents an effort to relieve the suffering of strangers (Calhoun 2008, p. 73), the border spectacle socializes us to adopt a minimalist version of humanitarianism, here intended as the obligation to save human life, or what Chouliaraki defines as 'solidarity as salvation' (2013, p. 10). From this perspective, the link between humanitarianism and the migration management regime reveals the asymmetry of power between the comfort of spectators in their living rooms and the vulnerability of sufferers on the screen. Mirroring the articulation of European migration policies, this 'dark side' of humanitarianism reflects the tension between inequality and solidarity, between a relation of domination and a relation of assistance. Rather than positively promoting solidarity in the name of human dignity, these military-humanitarian narratives certify the complex ontology of inequality that gives specific hierarchical value and meaning to human life. As is often the case in other instances of humanitarian government, care and control fuel and feed off each other, supporting a 'compassionate repression' (Fassin 2012) that fails to bridge the gap between 'us' and 'them'. On the contrary, this distorted use of humanitarian narratives risks to provide support to the neoliberal global governance in establishing a *moral geography of the world*: an asymmetry of power (in terms of both agency and dignity) that portrays the North as a wealthy, ordered and compassionate entity, a natural performer of a civilizing mission in/towards the underdeveloped, dangerous and voiceless South (Musarò 2013).

Even though politicians continue to claim a proud history of cosmopolitanism and human rights for European identity, publicly describing Western countries as welcoming societies by tradition and conviction, in the last two decades the idea of human rights has been repoliticized and rearticulated as a 'failed', or 'naïve', liberal policy responsible for social and national vulnerabilities, insecurities and potential conflicts over sovereignty. This contradiction invites us to reflect on the clash between our cosmopolitan solidarity and our sense of national belonging and identity. If we usually take for granted that our cosmopolitan solidarity can be expressed properly when we decide to donate money to support victims in refugee camps or to adopt a child at a distance, this moral attitude is challenged by the category of migrants. As soon as these mediatized 'poor victims' decide to move and try to reach our countries, making their way across borders into our cities, they become the concern of the national and international community precisely because of the risks they purportedly pose. Perceived as a threat, at least to the European population's well-being and lifestyle, the victims we were supposed to help through our compassionate solidarity change their status, becoming dangerous, unwanted and criminalized.

The European paternalistic protection spectacularized through military–humanitarian representations darkens the exclusionary mechanism of the visa system and migration policies. The law that illegalizes migrants remains largely invisible, as do the discriminatory politics of citizenship that are institutionalized in immigration law.

The great challenge in the future of Europe as a 'community of citizens' depends on whether, and to what extent, the citizens of Europe will exchange the representation of the 'other' as enemy or alien for a representation of the 'other' as a human interlocutory, whose 'difference' is problematic but also a resource. Only by developing alternative frames around opportunity and rights, rather than threat scenarios, can Europe turn the 'migrant crisis' into an economic and political opportunity, in addition to ensuring the dignity of those migrating to Europe.

Notes

1. http://www.un.org/en/development/desa/population/migration/partners/srsg.shtml, viewed 19 October 2015.
2. One caveat is in order. I am aware that there is a crucial legal difference between 'migrant' and 'refugee', and as a consequence throughout the chapter I use both terms. At the same time, it is worth noting that in the media the terms are often used interchangeably, depending on the period and its public sentiment (according to Google Trends data, throughout 2015, searches for 'refugee' remained slightly higher than those for 'migrant', but searches for 'refugee' spiked in early September, around the time that distressing photos of three-year-old Syrian refugee Aylan Kurdi were circulating). Moreover, although the legal and political separation between refugees, asylum seekers and migrants is ever present in the communitarian discourse and agenda-setting, the difference—upon which not everybody agrees, and which has received criticism by the double standard it imposes upon people in need, producing a selective recognition of suffering—is much more blurred in practice. Particularly interesting in this regard is the announcement by Al Jazeera English that it would stop using the term 'migrant', as it 'is no longer fit for purpose when it comes to describing the horror unfolding in the Mediterranean.' See http://www.newsweek.com/refugee-vs-migrants-whats-right-term-use-371222, viewed 6 November 2015.
3. UN Secretary-General Ban Ki-moon declared to be 'deeply saddened to hear reports of the loss of lives' and called on the international community to protect the rights of migrants and take action to prevent such

tragic incidents occurring in future. See http://www.thenational.ae/world/europe/eu-leaders-vow-to-end-deaths-of-mediterranean-migrants; http://www.un.org/apps/news/story.asp?NewsID=46255#.VqTr7lLon5d, viewed 8 February 2015.

4. The performance of crisis through spectacular interventions such as Mare Nostrum, Frontex's Joint Operation Triton and EUNAVFOR/Operation Sophia, or the absence thereof such as in the case of people arriving on the Aegean islands of Greece, is part of the European migration management.
5. During this period, two other permanent missions coordinated and financed by Frontex and Italy operated in the Mediterranean: Hermes for border control along the Italian coast, implemented by the Military Navy and Coast Guard, and Aeneas for the control of migrant flows. Mare Nostrum simply represented a strengthening of these operations with a broader and more specific twofold objective: to safeguard life at sea and bring migrant smugglers to justice.
6. Today it is virtually impossible to migrate to Europe in a legal and safe way. As the EU Commissioner, Cecilia Malmström, acknowledged: 'migrants are forced to put their lives in the hands of traffickers and smugglers who are making huge profits by exploiting their misery and despair.' See http://ecre.org/component/content/article/70-weekly-bulletin-articles/849-one-year-after-lampedusa-ngos-call-for-eu-action-to-prevent-further-deaths-at-sea.html, viewed 12 January 2015.
7. The Berlusconi government used the 'state of emergency' as an ad hoc measure to bypass ordinary political procedures and release public money. During the North Africa Emergency, which delegated extraordinary powers to the Italian Civil Protection (a Department that coordinates the response to natural disasters, catastrophes or other events that should be faced with extraordinary powers and means) to manage the situation, over €1.5 billion was allocated to fund makeshift reception centres and hotel accommodation distributed across Italy for 21,000 asylum seekers. See http://espresso.repubblica.it/attualita/cronaca/2012/10/15/news/chi-specula-sui-profughi-1.47304.
8. As Amnesty International denounces: 'The EU's priorities regarding migration policy have focused on sealing its borders rather than its human rights obligations. This can be clearly seen in expenditure on constructing "Fortress Europe" as compared with the funding given for supporting asylum procedures and the needs of refugees.' See http://www.amnesty.ch/de/themen/

asyl-migration/europa/dok/2015/Die-Kampagne-SOS-Europa/bericht-the-human-cost-of-fortress-Europe, p. 9, viewed 7 December 2015.

9. Frontex, Annual Risk Analysis Units, 2013: http://frontex.europa.eu/assets/Publications/Risk_Analysis/Annual_Risk_Analysis_2013.pdf, p. 7, viewed 4 November 2015.
10. As the Deputy Executive Director Gil Arias Fernandez argues: 'Facilitators lure these desperate people with the promise of an easy crossing and a better life, and charge up to USD 7,500 for a trip from Afghanistan. This is not always the case. Tragically, since the beginning of the year 41 people lost their lives trying to cross the Evros river or the sea in the area of Alexandropouli, many more die as a result of the dangerous forms of transport used by unscrupulous smugglers, others still end up victims of trafficking for the sex trade or in forced labour' (quoted in Horsti 2012, p. 13).
11. https://www.youtube.com/watch?v=H7LWma67WAA, viewed 9 November 2015.
12. https://www.youtube.com/watch?v=0MJWdxuG0Qo, viewed 6 November 2015.
13. Interview with the Italian seaman, Lampedusa, 30 January 2014, quoted in Tazzioli (2015, p. 140).
14. Emphasis in original.
15. http://www.tgcom24.mediaset.it/mondo/renzi-onu-ha-bisogno-del-cuore-dell-italia-crisi-migranti-ban-ki-moon-elogia-roma_2138575-201502a.shtml, viewed 6 November 2015.

References

Aalberts, T. E., & Gammeltoft-Hansen, T. (2014). Sovereignty at sea the law and politics of saving lives in mare liberum. *Journal of International Relations and Development, 17*, 439–468.

Aas, K. F., & Gundhus, H. O. I. (2015). Policing humanitarian borderlands: Frontex, human rights and the precariousness of life. *British Journal of Criminology, 55*, 1–18.

Agamben, G. (1998). *Homo sacer: Sovereign power and bare life*. Stanford: Stanford University Press.

Albahari, M. (2015). *Crimes of peace: Mediterranean migrations at the world's deadliest border*. Philadelphia: PENN.

Andersson, R. (2014). *Illegality, inc.: Clandestine migration and the business of bordering Europe*. Oakland: University of California Press.

Balibar, E. (2004). *Europe as borderland*. Alexander von Humboldt Lectures in Human Geography, Institute for Human Geography, Univeriteit Nijmegen, viewed 4 November 2015. http://www.ru.nl/socgeo/colloquium/Europe%20as%20Borderland.pdf

Bauman, Z. (2007). *Consuming life*. London: Polity Press.

Bellu, G. M. (2004). *I fantasmi di Porto Palo*. Milano: Mondadori.

Bigo, D. (1994). The European internal security field: Stakes and rivalries in a newly developing area of police intervention. In M. Anderson & M. Den Boer (Eds.), *Policing across national boundaries*. London: Pinter.

Bigo, D. (2002). Security and immigration: Toward a critique of the governmentality of unease. *Alternatives: Global, Local, Political, 27*(1), 63–92.

Boltanski, L. (1999). *Distant suffering: Morality, media and politics*. Cambridge: Cambridge University Press.

Brian, T., & Laczko, F. (Eds.). (2014). *Fatal journeys tracking lives lost during migration*. Geneva: IOM.

Calhoun, C. (2008). The imperative to reduce suffering: Charity, progress, and emergencies in the field of humanitarian action. In M. Barnett & T. Weiss (Eds.), *Humanitarianism in question: Politics, power, ethics*. New York: Cornell University Press.

Calhoun, C. (2010). The idea of emergency: Humanitarian action and global (dis)order. In D. Fassin & M. Pandolfi (Eds.), *Contemporary states of emergency*. New York: Zone Books.

Castles, S., & Miller, M. J. (2009). *The age of migration: International population movements in the modern world*. Basingstoke: Palgrave Macmillan.

Chouliaraki, L. (2013). *The ironic spectator*. Cambridge: Polity Press.

Consiglio Italiano per i Rifugiati [CIR]. (2007) *Report Regarding Recent Search and Rescue Operations in the Mediterranean* (online report), viewed 19 September 2015. http://www.europarl.europa.eu/hearings/20070703/libe/cir_report_en.pdf

Couldry, N. (2010). *Why voice matters: Culture and politics after neoliberalism*. London: Sage.

Cuttitta, P. (2014). Borderizing the island: Setting and narratives of the Lampedusa border play. *Acme: An International E-Journal for Critical Geographies, 13*(2), 196–219.

Dal Lago, A. (1999). *Non-persone: l'esclusione dei migranti in una società globale*. Milano: Feltrinelli.

Debord, G. (1995). *The society of the spectacle*. New York: Zone Books.

De Genova, N. (2013). Spectacles of migrant "illegality": The scene of exclusion, the obscene of inclusion. *Ethnic and Racial Studies, 36*(7), 1180–1198.

de Haas, H. (2007). *The myth of invasion: Irregular migration from West Africa to the Maghreb and the European Union* (IMI research report). Oxford: University of Oxford.

Edelman, M. (1977). *Political language: Words that succeed and policies that fail.* San Diego: Academic Press.

Fassin, D. (2007). Humanitarianism as a politics of life. *Public Culture, 19*(3), 499–520.

Fassin, D. (2012). *Humanitarian reason: A moral history of the present.* Berkeley: California Press.

Fassin, D., & Pandolfi, M. (2010). *Contemporary states of emergency.* New York: Zone Books.

Frazer, E., & Hutchings, K. (2011). Remnants and revenants: Politics and violence in the work of Agamben and Derrida. *British Journal of Politics & International Relations, 13*(2), 127–144.

Gamson, W. A., Croteau, D., Hoynes, W., & Sasson, T. (1992). Media images and the social construction of reality. *Annual Review of Sociology, 18*, 373–393.

Gelatt, J. (2005). *Schengen and the free movement of people across Europe.* Migration Policy Institute, viewed 30 July 2015. http://www.migrationpolicy.org/article/schengen-and-free-movement-peopleacross-europe

Hage, G. (2003). *Against paranoid nationalism: Searching for hope in a shrinking society.* Sydney: Pluto Press.

Horsti, K. (2012). Humanitarian discourse legitimating migration control: FRONTEX public communication. In M. Messier, R. Wodak, & R. Schroeder (Eds.), *Migrations: Interdisciplinary perspectives* (pp. 297–308). Vienna: Springer Science & Business Media.

IOM. (2015). *Mediterranean migrants and refugees: Latest arrivals and fatalities,* viewed 8 November 2015. http://www.iom.int/news/mediterranean-migrants-and-refugees-latest-arrivals-and-fatalities

Jeandesboz, J., & Pallister-Wilkins, P. (2014). Crisis, enforcement and control at the EU borders. In A. Lindley (Ed.), *Crisis and migration: Critical perspectives* (pp. 115–135). London: Routledge.

Kertzer, D. I. (1989). *Ritual, politics, and power.* New Haven: Yale University Press.

Kurasawa, F. (2015). How does humanitarian visuality work? A conceptual toolkit for a sociology of iconic suffering. *Sociologica,* il Mulino, *9*(1), 1–59.

Maalouf, A. (2000). *In the name of identity: Violence and the need to belong.* New York: Penguin Books.
Mezzadra, S., & Neilson, B. (2013). *Border as method, or, multiplication of labor.* London: Duke University Press.
Moore, K., Gross, B., & Threadgold, T. R. (Eds.). (2012). *Migrations and the media: Global crises and the media.* New York: Peter Lang.
Mountz, A. (2010). *Seeking asylum: Human smuggling and bureaucracy at the border.* Minneapolis: University of Minnesota Press.
Musarò, P. (2011). Living in emergency: Humanitarian images and the inequality of lives. *New Cultural Frontiers, 2*, 13–43.
Musarò, P. (2013). "Africans" vs. "Europeans": Humanitarian narratives and the moral geography of the world. *Sociologia della Comunicazione, 45*, 37–59.
Musarò, P., & Parmiggiani, P. (2014). *Media e migrazioni: etica, estetica e politica della narrazione umanitaria.* Milano: FrancoAngeli.
Neal, A. W. (2009). Securitization and risk at the EU border: The origins of Frontex. *Journal of Common Market Studies, 47*, 333–356.
Paasi, A. (1996). *Territories, boundaries and consciousness.* Chichester: Wiley.
Pastore, F., Monzini, P., & Sciortino, G. (2006). Schengen's soft underbelly? Irregular migration and human smuggling across land and sea borders to Italy. *International Migration, 44*, 95–119.
Sassen, S. (2009). Bordering capabilities versus borders: Implications for national borders. *Michigan Journal of International Law, 30*(3), 567–597.
Silverstone, R. (1999). *Why study the media?* London: Sage.
Simmel, G. (1983). *Schriften zur soziologie.* Frankfurt: Suhrkamp.
Taylor, C. (2002). Modern social imaginaries. *Public Culture, 14*(1), 91–124.
Tazzioli, M. (2015). *Spaces for governmentality, autonomous migration and the Arab uprisings.* London: Rowman & Littlefield International.
Vaughan-Williams, N. (2008). Borderwork beyond inside/outside? Frontex, the citizen–detective and the war on terror. *Space and Polity, 12*(1), 63–79.
Walters, W. (2010). Imagined migration world: the EU and the discourse of anti-illegal immigration. In M. Geiger & A. Pecoud (Eds.), *The politics of migration management* (pp. 73–95). Houndmills: Palgrave.
Walters, W. (2011). Foucault and frontiers: Notes on the birth of the humanitarian border. In U. Bröckling, S. Krasmann, & T. Lemke (Eds.), *Governmentality: Current issues and future challenges* (pp. 138–164). New York: Routledge.

4

Seeking Asylum in Neoliberal Cairo: Refugee Protests and the Securitization of Humanitarianism

Elisa Pascucci

Introduction

On 26 July 2016, Asli Nure, an Ethiopian asylum seeker belonging to the Oromo ethnic group and mother of two small children, died in a Cairo hospital as a result of serious, extended burns. In the following days, announcing the temporary closure of its Cairo office via its social media accounts, the UN High Commissioner for Refugees (UNHCR) referred to her death as the result of a regrettable 'violent incident' that had taken place near its premises. For Oromo asylum seekers and activists in Cairo, however, her death was almost an act of self-immolation: Asli Nure had died while helping two other Oromo asylum seekers who had tried to set themselves ablaze. Her death was linked to the repeated public protests through which Oromo communities in Egypt had contested UNHCR policies and operational decisions. Long waiting times for refugee status determination (RSD) procedures, insufficient direct assistance and limited

E. Pascucci (✉)
Faculty of Management, University of Tampere,
Tampere, Finland

F. Vecchio, A. Gerard (eds.), *Entrapping Asylum Seekers*, Transnational Crime, Crime Control and Security, DOI 10.1057/978-1-137-58739-8_4

options for resettlement to third countries were among the issues against which Ethiopian Oromo—as well as other groups among Egypt's large population of 'urban refugees', mostly from Eastern Africa, the Horn of Africa and the Middle East—had frequently rallied.

Refugees' and asylum seekers' political mobilization in Egypt has a relatively long history, one that preceded, and somewhat anticipated, the 2011–13 uprisings (Pascucci 2017). Sit-ins in front of the UNHCR building in Cairo have been happening at least since 2004. In the last months of 2005, a protest encampment set up by Sudanese refugees in Mustapha Mahmoud square, in the neighbourhood of Mohandeseen, Giza, where the UNHCR's offices were then located, became in less than three months one of the biggest protest camps in the history of independent Egypt. After several failed attempts at negotiation between the Sudanese groups and the UNHCR, Egyptian security forces violently evicted the protestors. Over 30 people were killed, and hundreds arrested (Moulin and Nyers 2007; Pascucci 2017).

In reports by non-government organizations (NGOs) and local researchers, as well as in the rare accounts found in the Egyptian press, the spatial practices of the UN office are often regarded as an important element in explaining refugee protests. The UNHCR's reaction to the 2005 Mustapha Mahmoud sit-in was criticized for consisting exclusively of rampant securitization,[1] and greater separation of its staff from asylum claimants. Many NGO workers and refugees in Cairo described the UNHCR as a 'fortress', while a group of local researchers described the office's attitude as one of handling refugees 'at arms' length' (FMRS 2006).

Similar depictions of refugee aid in UN operations are not rare, nor are they limited to the Cairo case. A growing body of work, across disciplines, is exploring the spatial arrangements of contemporary humanitarianism—in particular, its growing tendency towards securitization and 'enclavism' (Duffield 2010; Hyndman 2001; Smirl 2008, 2015; see also Jennings and Bøås 2015). This chapter builds on this literature to explore the relation between the spaces in which refugee aid is delivered and the emergence of refugee protests in Cairo. It shows how, while the protests are motivated by broader demands for more efficient and inclusive asylum policies and procedures, their spatial dynamics often involve the contestation and renegotiation of the boundaries between asylum seekers and refugees, on the one hand, and the practitioners that are supposed to assist them, on the other. In doing so, the chapter describes what can be defined as a spiralling pattern of securitization and contestation. In this context, asylum seekers' frustration and repeated requests for more and better assistance are perceived as a threat by the Cairo UNHCR office, and met with enhanced security and the foreclosure of spaces of interaction, which in turn leads to further grievances and protests. However, humanitarian workers, it is shown, do not always embrace the risk-averse and securitized spatial organization that characterizes the work of the UNHCR. Although the extent to which they benefit from the protection afforded by security procedures and gated architectures is significantly different, both local and international UNHCR staff often consider such measures as excessive and counterproductive, and engage in attempts at limiting their negative impact. Nevertheless, securitization shapes most of their interactions with asylum seekers and refugees. In Cairo, it is suggested, these dynamics display similarities with the socio-spatial polarization that characterizes what has been classified as the city's neoliberal development (Denis 2006; Bayat 2012). The exclusion experienced by asylum seekers and refugees in their daily interactions with aid agencies thus mirrors the marginalization of the urban poor that characterize Cairo (Ayeb and Bush 2012).

The analysis is based on nearly two years of ethnographic fieldwork conducted in Cairo between 2011 and 2015, involving interviews and observation with both aid agencies and asylum seekers. The chapter draws on interviews with UN officers, as well as ethnographic notes collected during repeated visits to two protest encampments held by refugees and asylum seekers in March and April 2011, and April and May 2012. These include informal conversations with protesters, local residents and, occasionally, security officers guarding the UN premises.

The chapter proceeds as follows. First, it provides some background on refugee migration and refugee policies in Egypt and introduces recent critical literature on the spatialities of international humanitarianism. Drawing on analyses of the neoliberal city (Bayat and Biekart 2009; Peck et al. 2009; Fawaz 2009), it highlights the relation between the aid industry's built environment and urban development in the Global South, focusing, in particular, on gated architectures (see Duffield 2010; Smirl

2015). It then moves on to explore the spatialities and cultures of security that characterize the work of UNHCR Cairo, discussing the impact of working 'behind fences and walls' on aid workers. The last section focuses on refugee and asylum seeker protests. In particular, it describes the occupation of the spaces surrounding the UN premises where applicants are supposed to 'wait' for assistance. In doing so, the chapter discusses the extent to which these forms of 'encroachment', through which people expose and contest their state of social and material precariousness, constitute a manifestation of spatialized political agency in a neoliberal urban context (Bayat 2012).

Refugee Aid and Neoliberal Urbanity in Cairo

As of 2016, the Greater Cairo Metropolitan Region (GCMR) had a population of approximately 17 million, with an annual growth rate of over 2 per cent. At least 7 million of its inhabitants were considered to be living in informal—and more or less poor—areas, a number that was estimated to reach 50 per cent of the total population by 2025 (Osman et al. 2016). 'The population of today's GCMR', it has been highlighted, 'has grown since 1950 to be 2.4 million in 1975, 6.4 million in 1986, 12.5 million in 1996, and 17 million in 2006' (Osman et al. 2016, p. 2). This remarkably fast development, it has been observed, is to be attributed not only to the urbanization of rural populations, but also to the real estate speculation favoured by both the hasty process of privatization of state-owned land, and financial deregulation implemented as part of International Monetary Fund–led structural adjustment programmes (Mitchell 2002; Denis 2006).

In the context of this staggering pattern of urban growth, the number of migrants settled in the Cairo region remains relatively low. Egypt has historically been and continues to be mainly a country of emigration. Nevertheless, since its independence, the country—particularly the main urban areas of Cairo and Alexandria—has been home to lively communities of Sudanese and Palestinian exiles, Southern European diasporas, and students from South-East Asia, the Indian subcontinent and Sub-Saharan Africa (Grabska 2006; Gorman 2015). As the product of relatively unconstrained patterns of inter-African and inter-Mediterranean mobility, as well as of Egypt's prominent political and cultural role in the early postcolonial Arab world, the presence of these migrants has left a significant mark on the country's urban life.

It is only since the mid-1990s, as a result of the flows of refugees caused first by the Sudanese civil war and then by the US-led invasion of Iraq, that the UNHCR operation in the country has expanded. Migration from Africa and the Middle East to Egypt thus came to be framed almost exclusively as a humanitarian issue (Pascucci 2017). Yet, and in spite of it being one of the few Middle Eastern and North African countries to have signed the 1951 Geneva Refugee Convention and its 1967 protocol, the Egyptian state has remained largely uninvolved in asylum and refugee reception policies. The Memorandum of Understanding it signed with the UNHCR in 1954 delegates RSD and assistance operations entirely to the UN office. As Kagan (2012) aptly summarizes, the UNHCR functions in Egypt, as it does in other North African and Middle Eastern countries, as a de facto 'surrogate state'.

This 'quasi-sovereign' status is reflected in the urban geographies and built environment that characterize the work of the UN office in Cairo. While asylum seekers and refugee communities are scattered throughout the city's middle-class, lower middle-class and poor informal areas, over the years the UNHCR premises have become increasingly secluded and segregated from the rest of the city. Concrete fences, CCTV cameras, private security and limited staff mobility around the office area are among the visible signs of this predicament. It is the office location, however, which is the most significant element of this pattern of segregation. Until 2007, the UNHCR had its home in a building in the densely populated, semi-central area of Mohandeseen, in the Giza governorate. At the end of that year, however—less than two years after the tragic end of the Mustapha Mahmoud protest camp—the office was relocated to a compound around 30 kilometres south-west of Cairo's city centre, in the Seventh District of Sixth of October City.

Precipitated by the crisis that followed the violent eviction of the 2005 refugee protests, this process of progressive withdrawal and segregation is the product of a number of intertwined factors. According to most of the UN officers and NGO workers interviewed in Cairo for this research, the decision to relocate was made because of the pressure exerted by the Egyptian state Security Investigations (SSI) apparatus.[2] In the officers' accounts, it was explicitly requested that the office relocate to the outskirts of Cairo, far from the overpopulated city centre, mostly in order to prevent and minimize the visibility of possible future protests. The role of Egyptian authorities in the relocation should not come as a surprise. The grip of governmental control and security surveillance on development, aid and civil society work in pre and post-revolutionary Egypt is well documented, and extends well beyond refugee governance (El Ibrashy 2011; Tadros 2012). Moreover, the UNHCR's problematic status in negotiating its protection mandate with hosting governments is also widely recognized (Verdirame and Harrell-Bond 1995; Duffield 2010).

Another major factor that influenced the choice of Sixth of October City was the need to comply with UN field security requirements. In this regard, a brief outline of the role of the UN MOSS (Minimum Operating Security Standards) guidelines is in order. Introduced in the early 2000s, the MOSS has marked what has been defined as a 'security and risk-management turn' in UN field operations at a global level, institutionalized in 2004 through the establishment of the UNDSS (Department of Security and Safety; see Duffield 2010). Integrated a few years later with the newly introduced MORSS (Minimum Operating Residential Security Standards, which regulate the security of UN workers beyond their workspace), the MOSS covers areas spanning the architecture of UN compounds to aid workers' mobility and use of vehicles, including training requirements for national and international staff. In the case of UNHCR Cairo, according to the staff interviewed the building that had hosted the agency until 2007 was classified as non-MOSS compliant, both in terms of its physical premises and its location. Moreover, there was a need to revise the contract with the private company in charge of security services, which in 2007 was already over 10 years old. Although aimed at establishing basic security requirements in a standardized and centralized manner, the MOSS guidelines are calibrated on the 'security phase' of each specific country, or part of the country, and can therefore vary geographically. In their application to specific field operations, both MOSS and MORSS classify urban areas as either safe or unsafe. Areas designated as safe are mostly those that are situated far away from city centres, less populated and characterized by the highest concentration of wealth.

Recent studies have highlighted the role of security and risk-management policies in the merging of aid work 'with international trends towards urban splintering and, reflecting the appearance of elite gated communities, the privatization of space' in cities of the Global South (Duffield 2010, p. 471; see also Grant and Thompson 2013; Jennings and Bøås 2015; Smirl 2015). The aid industry contributes to these emerging forms of segregated urbanism in two main ways: by establishing the offices and residences, and limiting the mobility, of international workers within the boundaries of economically privileged and securitized suburban areas; and by adopting the gated compound as its architectural paradigm. Both these elements are at work in the case of UNHCR Cairo. However, as will be demonstrated, dynamics related to the specific modalities of protection and assistance delivery are also at play, and securitization and bunkerization work in more complex and contradictory ways than those described in most of the existing literature, which examines predominantly post-conflict settings (Smirl 2008, 2015; Duffield 2010; Grant and Thompson 2013).

Debates on 'splintering', 'wounded' or 'pathological' urbanism (Graham and Marvin 2001; Lees 2004; Duffield 2010) and 'fortress architectures' (Murray 2011) resonate strongly with the now substantial body of work on Cairo as a 'neoliberal city' (Kuppinger 2004; Denis 2006; Bayat and Biekart 2009; Bayat 2012). Broadly defined as cities whose spatial and social organizations, as well as structures of governance, are driven by market forces, neoliberal cities are more specifically identified through two opposite and complementary socio-spatial formations. These are the presence of enclosed, gated architectures for wealthy elites; and the concomitant production of a surplus humanity (Bauman 2004), whose spatial discrimination is made visible by the sprawling of shanty towns (Brenner and Theodore 2002; Hackworth 2006). However, the labelling of the phenomena of gated urbanism, informal settlements, segregation and growing spatial inequalities as 'neoliberal urbanity' or 'neo liberal urbanism' poses several problems. Atkinson and Blandy (2005), among others, have warned against generalizations that do not adequately account for the existence of gated architectures beyond the geographies of neoliberalism. As Asef Bayat (2012, p. 116) puts it, 'in reality cities have almost always been marked (and defined by Lefebvre among others) by differentiations, diverse life-styles, and spatial units juxtaposed in close proximity' (see also Parakash and Kruse 2008). These cautions notwithstanding, evidence of the association between neoliberal economic development and the spreading and sharpening of segregation and gated urbanism is robust, in Cairo as well as in other cities (Caldeira 1996, 2000; Mitchell 2002; Fawaz 2009; Murray 2011).

Sixth of October, the suburb to which the UNHCR relocated in 2007, is an example of one of the 'safe areas' designated by the UN MOSS, while at the same time illustrating some of the characteristics of neoliberal urban development in Egypt. Created in the early 1980s as part of the Anwar Sadat government's industrial policies, the satellite city itself was originally the result of large-scale, state-led developmentalist projects (Stewart 1996; Wahdan 2012). However, in its first years the city only attracted a limited number of industries, and had almost no residential or commercial areas. It was mostly starting from the 1990s, simultaneous with the implementation of structural adjustment policies, that the city experienced 'investment surges, with private real-estate developers, encouraged by legal stipulations and the money remitted from Egyptians in Gulf countries, engaged in land speculation and development of expensive residential complexes' (Wahdan 2012, p. 115), particularly highly securitized 'gated communities'.

The UNHCR: Gated Architectures and Security Practices

Although different from the architectures of humanitarian aid in post-interventionary settings—for instance, it does not contain residential units for international members of staff—the UNHCR building in Cairo has many of the characteristics of a gated aid compound. Removed from the street, as requested by the UN security guidelines, the front of the building is isolated by mobile concrete barriers. At the time when research for this paper was conducted, all contact between UNHCR staff and asylum seekers was strictly limited and regulated. In circumstances other than formal meetings, including the early stages of registration, such contact consisted mostly of brief encounters at the external desk, where practitioners and clients were separated by bulletproof glass. In the waiting area, applicants queued, often for hours, under the steel-plate roof of an annex to the building situated to the left of the main entrance, closer to the street. The unwelcoming external appearance of the building was mitigated only by sparse multi-lingual signs and information leaflets on registration procedures, and by short counselling and information sessions held by local staff and interpreters approximately once a week in the waiting area.

Some of the recurrent adjectives used by both UN workers and clients in my research to describe the UNHCR office include 'cold' and 'unwelcoming'. As a young Egyptian aid worker stated while recalling the first time he visited the UNHCR for a job interview, 'they keep you waiting forever, and once you enter you find the inside is just as disempowering and ugly as the outside'. Another worker, a locally recruited administrative assistant, described her office in the basement of the building as 'isolated and isolating, it makes you feel like you are protected, but also completely unaware of what's happening outside'. Isolation was more than just a perception: access to UN buildings is severely restricted. At the time when the research for this chapter was conducted, security guards in uniform controlled both the IDs and personal belongings of all visitors. Asylum seekers and refugees could not access the premises unless they had an appointment for an interview—mostly for status determination or resettlement—usually scheduled months in advance.

There are significant similarities between aid organizations' compounds and residential gated communities (Smirl 2008, 2015). Atkinson and Blandy (2005) define the latter as a 'housing development that restricts public access, usually through the use of gates, booms, walls and fences. These residential areas may also employ security staff or CCTV systems to monitor access' (Atkinson and Blandy 2005, p. 177; see also Smirl 2008, 2015). The impact of such 'defensive living' on residents' perceptions and behaviour has been widely explored, with fear and experiences of isolation playing a central role. According to Low's (2003) analysis on the narratives of residents of gated compounds in the United States (US), living 'behind walls' is motivated by and reinforces fear of the external world. Petra Kuppinger's (2004) work on Cairo has also posited fear as the central driver behind the exponential growth of gated communities, showing how advertising by Egyptian real estate companies mobilizes the affective sphere of danger and mistrust when marketing this kind of housing.

As revealed by the recurrent use of the adjectives 'cold' and 'unwelcoming', both local and international staff at UNHCR Cairo held highly critical views on the office's gated architectures. The perception that these were 'imposed from above' was sharp, as was the feeling that such architectures cause or reinforce—rather than contain and mitigate—fear. Limited opportunities to interact with clients and, more generally, the external world led to uncertainty and confusion as to the actual risks faced by staff, particularly in relation to the behaviour of asylum claimants who stationed outside the office, and the protests they often engaged in. One of the complaints most frequently reported by people working in the compound was that 'we do not know what happens outside', as one informant put it with reference to the groups of people often squatting near the building, and their frequent scuffles with security guards. Many workers, particularly internationals, were quickly escorted inside the building upon their arrival in the morning (most of the people interviewed travelled to work on a private bus provided by the UN) and, in some cases, remained inside until the end of their working day. This meant that it was difficult for them to have an accurate idea of the reasons for and dynamics of the altercations and protests occurring outside. Yet this lack of first-hand experience was precisely what caused fear and uncertainty. These findings resonate with Low's (2003) analysis of gated communities in the US and suggest some degree of convergence between the spatial practices of the aid sector and the experiences of affluent residents in neoliberal cities (Duffield 2010; Smirl 2015). However, the fear experienced by UNHCR staff was not simply the anxiety about an external environment of generalized infrastructural and political insecurity, described by authors like Duffield (2010) in their analyses of aid compounds. Rather, it was also related to specific, localized dynamics of conflict between the organization and its clients. The generic threat posited by the UN centralized security system materialized in the bodies of the frustrated, shouting and, in some cases, publicly protesting asylum seekers outside the office.

The analysis of the UNHCR staff's ambivalent attitudes towards UN security training confirms this point. Such training includes a basic online course which is mandatory regardless of one's field location ('Basic Security in the Field: Staff Safety, Health and Welfare', UNBSF); and a second, advanced course ('Advanced Security in the Field', UNASF) which is only required for workers assigned to areas classified as Phase I—like Egypt was in 2012—or higher. Both modules 'come on two interactive CD-ROMs that combine voice-overs, video clips and role-play exercises with multiple-choice end of level tests' and 'culminate in a final multiple-choice examination' (Duffield 2010, p. 460). Many of my informants in Cairo—at the UNHCR as well as at other UN offices—reported having followed the courses in a fragmentary and non-systematic way, without 'really pay(ing) attention'. Such a dismissive attitude notwithstanding, most of them still regarded security training as necessary, and as an increasingly important part of their job. Silke Roth (2011) has shown how the disciplined acceptance of security regulations is perceived by aid workers as a marker of professionalism. The need to abide by constantly updated security measures is seen as a fundamental component of their role, and conditions their behaviour deeply. Rather than questioning the need for security training, UNHCR staff in Cairo complained about it being inadequate to the specific dangers faced in their field operation, namely, those arising from the particularly tense relations with clients. Many highlighted their 'worries about becoming a target' of angry beneficiaries, as 'verbal threats can be really violent'. Some staff members described situations in which their colleagues had been exposed to danger. A few months before I commenced the fieldwork for this chapter, an Egyptian UNHCR officer had apparently been punched in the face while walking towards the UN private bus that takes members of staff to their homes in various areas of Cairo. On another occasion, two practitioners were attacked while conducting an information session in the external waiting area. In the last case, the two UN workers—two women—had allegedly been physically assaulted by a refugee woman holding a gasoline can, who then threatened to set herself ablaze. Significantly, these episodes of backlashes from the beneficiaries of aid involved mostly Egyptian members of staff, mirroring a global trend in which the actual delivery of aid 'on the ground' is delegated entirely to local workers, who are far more exposed to danger—including death—than are internationals (Duffield 2010; Jennings and Bøås 2015). Overall, though, violent attacks against aid workers remained limited in number and scope and, with the exclusion of the two Egyptian practitioners mentioned above, all the victims of violent episodes that occurred between 2004 and 2016 near the UNHCR premises were asylum seekers or refugees. Indeed, as the next section will show, asylum seekers and refugees are the primary bearers of the consequences of the securitization of aid in Cairo, and those who, most significantly, try to counter and contest them.

Refugee Protests and the Contestation of Securitized Aid

Between 2011 and 2013, as Egypt was living through an unprecedented wave of popular protests, asylum seekers and refugees in Cairo were also frequently gathering and demonstrating around the UNHCR building. Their presence ranged from small, extemporaneous encampments made up of small groups of people who were experiencing housing difficulties or had specific grievances related to their cases, to larger, well-organized protests, mostly by Oromo communities. The latter usually revolved around broader issues such as lack of safety in Egypt, or perceived racialized discrimination by humanitarian organizations.

The asylum seekers and refugees protesting were of different nationalities, ages, genders and legal statuses—from new applicants to rejected asylum seekers who had been living in Egypt illegally for over 10 years. The protests were led by relatively small groups of people who would spend the night camping near the UNHCR office. During the day, different categories of people could be found hanging out around the encampment. New applicants queuing for registration and families waiting in the adjacent small garden shared the space with groups of organized protesters, exchanging information and help. To be sure, the majority of the people I met while visiting the encampments were not actively participating in protest actions. In the space of a couple of months, I met fewer than a dozen people who had organized to spend the night at the encampment, and who were actively 'campaigning' through slogans and signs. Other people had joined the actions occasionally while they were waiting outside the office. Others, yet, were hanging out near the office to meet friends or seek out information, and clearly stated that they did not agree with the reasons for and modalities of the protests.

Yet, among the people who claimed not to agree with the manner in which the protests were conducted, levels of discontent were also high. Checking the list of appointments for resettlement interviews displayed on one of the gates of the compound, an informant commented: 'Why do they keep us waiting like this? If there is no hope, why they don't just tell us? So that we find peace.' While she had never joined any of the protests herself[3] during her regular visits to the UNHCR 'to check the list', she did have long conversations with the people camping, asking for news and exchanging comments on the work of the organization. For her, as for many others, feelings of frustration originated from what seemed to be an endless experience of 'waiting'—for assistance, but also more comprehensively for a definitive solution to displacement (Hyndman and Giles 2011). In 2012, at the UNHCR Cairo office a team of around ten members of staff in charge of interviews—excluding interns and temporary workers recruited for specific emergencies—had to deal with an average 'caseload' of 15,000 RSD files a year. The average waiting time for asylum seekers to complete RSD procedures was between ten months and one year, and the processing of refugees' resettlement applications—which involves both the UNHCR and embassies of the foreign countries of destination—used to take well over one year.

The reversal of the designated usage of space was a typical pattern in the protests, highlighting the salience of UNHCR spatial practices in their dynamics. Improvised encampments set up by asylum seekers who had to wait long hours to access registration material, or simply to get to talk to UNHCR staff, would become spaces for gathering, exchanging news and, in some cases, voicing common grievances. People camped right where they were supposed to queue, often because, if required to come back the following day, they found it more convenient to simply spend the night in Sixth of October. Paradoxically, although it was meant to prevent protests, by rendering the office much more difficult to access, the relocation de facto caused an increase in the number of people camping outside it.

Informants who lived in the slum of Ezbet el Haggana—locally known as Kilo Arba wa Nuss, and historically home to a large Sudanese community—frequently complained that travelling from their neighbourhood to Sixth of October was too costly and tiring to be manageable more than once a month. When asylum seekers register with the UNHCR for the first time or undergo interviews, all the family members must be physically present—a requirement in effect in most UNHCR field operations, aimed at preventing frauds. For a family of four, a daily trip from the slum at the north-east of Cairo to Sixth of October cost at least 20 Egyptian pounds (US$2.9)—while the average income in places like Kilo Arba wa Nuss was estimated to be between US$1.6 and US$2 a day. It is thus not surprising that some people chose to camp outside the UNHCR premises for days hoping to be received. As a Sudanese refugee I met at one of the sit-ins held in April 2012 put it:

> If I want to talk to someone here, about my case, I need to come at dawn and wait here forever. Then sometimes I don't even get to talk to anyone. I have to go back to Kilo Arba wa Nuss, and back here. Why? I just stay here, better. The Sudanese people in the camp [points to the people distributing leaflets] can help me to find a place if I need to spend the night here.

That the protests worked to expose and contest the spatial order of the UNHCR is all the more evident if we consider the slogans, demands and actions that directly addressed the issue of the distance between aid workers and their clients. Between February and March 2011, during the first phase of the Egyptian uprising that eventually led to the ousting of Hosni Mubarak, a wave of protests was triggered by the UNHCR decision to close its offices and evacuate its international staff. Asylum claimants and refugees saw the decision—made in accordance with UN security guidelines—as a symptom of the unreliability of the office, as well as of the privileged status of UN workers. As many of the people I spoke to remarked, it was a sign that UN workers could afford a degree of protection that was unthinkable for their clients. The following quote, from an interview with an Iraqi asylum seeker who had never taken part in any of the protests, exemplifies this feeling well:

> UNHCR is supposed to protect us. In their images, they portray themselves almost as a mother, as if they really cared. Yet they leave when the situation gets tough. What that means? It means they are very far from us, and they are only preoccupied with themselves and their job. I can't leave, I can't go anywhere from here, apart back to Iraq, and it's surely not safe. But they leave now that we really do not know what is going to happen in Egypt. As far as I can see, the country could draw into the same kind of chaos as Iraq in a few months.

Existing literature considers access to fast and privileged channels of international mobility, one of the most evident spatial manifestations of the gap separating aid workers from the majority of their beneficiaries in the global south (Smirl 2008; Duffield 2010). As the quote above illustrates, also among asylum seekers and refugees in Cairo, aid workers—in particular, but not exclusively, internationals—were regarded as belonging to a mobile transnational elite, completely separate from the 'immobilized' refugee populations they were supposed to help. As already noted, rather than identifying with their international status and segregated living and working conditions, many of the UN staff interviewed were acutely aware of the negative effects of securitization on their clients. Some even expressed sympathy for asylum seekers' grievances about the office's lack of accessibility. As one of them commented: 'It is just nonsensical to have moved here to Sixth of October. It made us far removed, inaccessible, almost impossible to reach for the most destitute among our applicants.' Yet the structural conditions that determined their increasing physical remoteness proved very difficult to alter.

Asylum seekers' and refugees' experience of the social gap separating them from aid workers (Pascucci 2016) points to the need to understand the contestation of the spatial boundaries of aid in the wider context of the politics of Egyptian urban development. One of the most widely used sentences in the signs I observed in 2011 and 2012 was a simple question:

'Where is the UNHCR?' Another sign, shown to me in April 2012, read: 'I am right here, I sleep in the street, and I face many problems by myself: where are you instead?' The question referred to what was perceived as a lack of meaningful, effective policies of protection and assistance. Yet, in highlighting 'presence' in the public space—'I am here, I sleep in the street'—it also exposed how remote and defensive the UNHCR appeared to those who waited outside its premises. For Asef Bayat (2012), the highly visible presence of the urban poor in the public spaces of Cairo and other cities of the Middle East is a product of what he names the 'inside-out' effect of neoliberal urbanity. Bayat contends that the privatization of space and urban infrastructures that neoliberal 'accumulation through dispossession' (Harvey 2003) entails leads to 'survival through repossession' by the subaltern. 'Survival through repossession', he argues, is not only a struggle around access to basic services—water, housing and electricity—but also, and very visibly so, a form of resistance where 'political and social space' is at stake.

Bayat's (2012) 'survival through repossession', however, does not refer specifically to practices that involve conflict and overt contestation. Rather, the phenomena he considers are the public presence of street vendors, disenfranchised families squatting in public space, groups of urban youths 'wandering', and similar acts of ordinary, gradual and incremental appropriation of public space (Bayat 2013). Refugee protests in Cairo raise the question of whether survival through repossession can also have a contentious side, showing how, in some cases, what Bayat (2010) defines as 'quiet encroachment of the ordinary' (Bayat 2012, 2013) is not necessarily so quiet. The 'ordinary' Cairo asylum seekers were so visibly and sometimes polemically encroaching was made up of not only immobility, prolonged waiting, limited assistance and lack of communication with aid agencies' management. Long queues under the sun, fences, barbed wire, CCTV cameras and frequent encounters with both private security guards and Egyptian police forces were also part of that 'ordinary'—a heavily securitized environment in which coupling presence with active resistance seemed the only way to be seen and heard.

Conclusion: A Secondary State of Exclusion

This chapter has argued that the spatialities and materialities of refugee governance play a central role in the socioeconomic and legal conditions that determine the precarious status of asylum seekers. Focusing on the case of UNHCR Cairo, and building upon a growing body of literature on humanitarian spaces and securitization, the chapter has shown how the growing physical separation of humanitarian workers from asylum seekers and refugees—caused by gated architectures and pervasive security training—has a profound impact on the aid relation. This socio-spatial separation, I have suggested, mirrors broader dynamics at work in what have been classified as neoliberal cities (Denis 2006; Bayat 2012). In particular, the chapter has shown how the UNHCR staff's lack of first-hand knowledge and experience of the identities and grievances of the applicants waiting, squatting and protesting outside their office resonates with the feeling of isolation so common among the customers of the growing market for 'defensive living' described in the literature on residential gated communities (Low 2003; Kuppinger 2004). As expatriates and mobile local elites lead lives that are increasingly segregated from those of the urban poor, so are Cairo's aid workers ever more removed from the highly vulnerable people they are supposed to help. Unfortunately, the awareness of the limits securitization imposes on their work among many of the practitioners interviewed, and the deep sympathy many of them expressed for asylum seekers' frustration at the UNHCR's remoteness were not enough to counter the negative effects of this entrenched physical separation.

The analysis suggests that researchers should focus their attention not only on 'what' asylum regimes and humanitarian aid do, but also on *how* they do it. Specific material tools, spatial arrangements, labour regimes and local micro-economies can determine outcomes that are at odds with the stated objectives and, in some cases, with the very values that are supposed to inform the humanitarian enterprise. While formally operating according to universal principles of shared 'humanity', aid organizations are actors imbued with material power and resources which—as a result of complex transnational arrangements such as the UN security procedures that this chapter has examined—often end up reinforcing, rather than countering, exclusion. Haugen (2012) has defined the condition of migrants who find themselves 'spatially entrapped' in their country of destination as 'a second state of immobility', after the one already experienced in their home country. In a similar way, what asylum seekers experience as a result of humanitarian organizations' securitized architectures and practices could be defined as a 'second state of exclusion', additional to that produced by legal restrictions and socioeconomic marginalization.

The analysis, however, has also shown how this 'second state of exclusion' does not go uncontested. Considering refugees' and asylum seekers' attitudes towards UNHCR spatial practices, the chapter has argued that the production of street politics that characterizes neoliberal urbanity (Ismail 2006; Bayat 2012, 2013) is important in understanding the emergence of protests against the UN office in Cairo. In such hostile and securitized spaces, asylum seekers' claims for safety and protection cannot but be chaotically expressed through a search for public visibility. This amounts to an attempt to be seen and heard beyond the fences and the security measures precluding, quite literally, access to any kind of meaningful, direct engagement with the people in charge of making decisions on their cases. People who have no option but to wait on the sidewalks and in the public gardens surrounding the premises of highly securitized aid agencies reappropriate those spaces, subverting their designated usages and joining forces to express grievances. For asylum seekers and refugees in Cairo, this has often taken the form of well-articulated demands and even organized collective protests. In other cases, however, as evidenced by Asli Nure's tragic death mentioned in the introduction, their state of entrapment does not allow for political expressions other than extreme acts performed on and against their own bodies.

By way of conclusion, some elements emerging from the analysis that deserve further exploration need to be highlighted. Although the socio-spatial distance between aid workers, on the one hand, and asylum seekers and refugees, on the other, appears sharply defined, and seemingly impossible to overcome, the UNHCR Cairo case points to a number of more complex, and more nuanced, aspects of this situation. In particular, the role of locally recruited humanitarian staff, to whom most of the face-to-face interactions with beneficiaries are delegated, should be further explored when studying refugee aid. In Cairo, this category of workers must bear many of the negative consequences of an increasingly securitized humanitarian enterprise. Further research is needed on this localized division of labour, as well as asylum seekers' and refugees' perceptions of this group of aid workers. Along these lines, several Sudanese, Ethiopian and Eritrean asylum seekers remarked how the segregation and 'inaccessibility' of the UN office did not affect all categories of applicants in the same way. According to them, Iraqis and Syrians encountered fewer problems in obtaining appointments for interviews or information about the processing of their case, and were treated better by the private security staff guarding the UNHCR premises. This points to the role racialization plays in the spatial dynamics of contemporary refugee governance, which should also be examined in future research. The case of the UNHCR Cairo office highlights how humanitarian organizations, embedded as they are in complex networks of urban and security governance, can also contribute to the marginalization and entrapment of asylum seekers.

Notes

1. In this chapter, I use 'securitization' in a manner akin to the original definition by the Copenhagen school of international relations (Bouzan et al. 1998), namely, the reframing of a specific subjectivity or relation (refugees expressing frustration and protesting, and their interactions with aid workers) as a security problem. However, I maintain a rather broad definition of the term, encompassing the organization of the physical environment in which aid is delivered and the ways in which issues are problematized in security training, aid workers' narratives and refugees' claims.
2. The agency was renamed 'Homeland Security' after the 2011 uprising.
3. Although the majority of the people involved were men, during my ethnography I did meet women who were actively participating in protests—particularly Ethiopian-Oromo and Sudanese women. In the case of the

person quoted here, an Arab-Iraqi woman, not only gender but also national belonging and chances for improving her legal status might have played a role in explaining why she had never taken part in mobilizations. As highlighted by the quote, in 2011–12, Iraqis, like all other categories of asylum seekers, had to endure prolonged waiting times for the completion of legal procedures. However, access to refugee status and resettlement was much easier for them than for other nationalities, which might explain their general lack of engagement with asylum seeker mobilization.

References

Atkinson, R., & Blandy, S. (2005). Introduction: International perspectives on the new enclavism and the rise of gated communities. *Housing Studies, 20*(2), 177–186.

Ayeb, H., & Bush, R. (2012). Introduction: Marginality and exclusion in Egypt and the Middle East. In H. Ayeb & R. Bush (Eds.), *Marginality and exclusion in Egypt* (pp. 3–13). London: Zed Books.

Bauman, Z. (2004). *Wasted lives: Modernity and its outcasts*. Cambridge: Polity Press.

Bayat, A. (2012). Politics in the city-inside-out. *City & Society, 24*(2), 110–128.

Bayat, A. (2013). *Life as politics: How ordinary people change the Middle East*. 2nd edition. Stanford: Stanford University Press.

Bayat, A., & Biekart, K. (2009). Cities of extremes. *Development and Change, 40*(5), 815–825.

Brenner, N., & Theodore, N. (2002). *Spaces of neoliberalism: Urban restructuring in North America and Western Europe*. Oxford: Wiley-Blackwell.

Buzan, B., Waever, O., & de Wilde, J. (1998). *Security: A new framework for analysis*. Boulder: Lynne Rienner Publishers.

Caldeira, T. P. R. (1996). Fortified enclaves: The new urban segregation. *Public Culture, 8*(2), 303–328.

Caldeira, T. P. R. (2000). *City of walls: Crime, segregation, and citizenship in São Paulo*. Berkeley/Los Angeles: University of California Press.

Denis, E. (2006). Cairo as neo-liberal capital? From walled city to gated community. In D. Singerman & P. Amar (Eds.), *Cairo cosmopolitan: Politics, culture and urban space in the new globalised Middle East* (pp. 47–72). Cairo: American University of Cairo Press.

Duffield, M. (2010). Risk-management and the fortified aid compound: Everyday life in post-interventionary society. *Journal of Intervention and State Building, 4*(4), 453–474.

El Ibrashy, W. (2011). After the universities when will the security leave the unions, parties, mosques, churches, newspapers and satellite TV? *Sout el Umma* (original version in Arabic, English translation), viewed 20 August 2016. http://www.madamasr.com/content/egypt-three-years-state-vs-journalists

Fawaz, M. (2009). Neoliberal urbanity: A view from Beirut's periphery. *Development and Change, 40*(5), 827–852.

Forced Migration and Refugee Studies Program (FMRS). (2006). *A tragedy of failures and false expectations: Report on the events surrounding the three-month sit-in and forced removal of Sudanese refugees in Cairo, September–December 2005*. Cairo: American University in Cairo, viewed 3 August 2016. http://www.aucegypt.edu/gapp/cmrs/reports/documents/report_edited_v.pdf

Gorman, A. (2015). The Italians of Egypt: Return to diaspora. In A. Gorman & S. Kasbarian (Eds.), *Diasporas of the modern Middle East: Contextualizing community* (pp. 138–170). Edinburgh: Edinburgh University Press.

Grabska, K. (2006). Marginalization in urban spaces of the global south: Urban refugees in Cairo. *Journal of Refugee Studies, 19*(3), 287–307.

Graham, S., & Marvin, S. (2001). *Splintering urbanism: Networked infrastructures, technological mobilities and the urban condition*. New York/London: Routledge.

Grant, R., & Thompson, D. (2013). The development complex, rural economy and urban-spatial and economic development in Juba, South Sudan. *Local Economy, 28*(2), 218–230.

Hackworth, J. (2006). *The neoliberal city: Governance, ideology and development in American urbanism*. New York: Cornell University Press.

Harvey, D. (2003). *The new imperialism*. Oxford: Oxford University Press.

Haugen, H. Ø. (2012). Nigerians in China: A second state of immobility. *International Migration, 50*(2), 65–80.

Hyndman, J. (2001). *Managing displacement: Refugees and the politics of humanitarianism*. Minneapolis: University of Minnesota Press.

Hyndman, J., & Giles, W. (2011). Waiting for what? The feminization of asylum in protracted refugee situations. *Gender Place & Culture: A Journal of Feminist Geography, 18*(3), 361–379.

Ismail, S. (2006). *Political life in Cairo's new urban quarters: Encountering the everyday state*. Minneapolis: University of Minnesota Press.

Jennings, K., & Bøås, M. (2015). Transactions and interactions: Everyday life in the peacekeeping economy. *Journal of Intervention and Statebuilding, 9*(3), 281–295.

Kagan, M. (2012). *The UN 'surrogate state' and the foundation of refugee policy in the Middle East* (Scholarly Works Paper 781), viewed 18 August 2016. http://scholars.law.unlv.edu/facpub/781

Kuppinger, P. (2004). Exclusive greenery: New gated communities in Cairo. *City & Society, 16*(2), 35–62.

Lees, L. (2004). The emancipatory city: Urban (re)visions. In L. Lees (Ed.), *The emancipatory city? Paradoxes and possibilities* (pp. 3–20). London: Sage.

Low, S. (2003). *Behind the gates*. New York/London: Routledge.

Mitchell, T. (2002). *Rule of experts: Egypt, technopolitics, modernity*. Berkeley/Los Angeles: University of California Press.

Moulin, C., & Nyers, P. (2007). "We live in a country of UNHCR": Refugee protests and global political society. *International Political Sociology, 1*, 356–372.

Murray, P. (2011). *City of extremes: The spatial politics of Johannesburg*. Durham: Duke University Press.

Osman, T., Divigalpitiya, P., & Arima, T. (2016). Quantifying the driving forces of informal urbanization in the western part of the Greater Cairo Metropolitan Region. *Environments, 3*(2), 13. doi:10.3390/environments3020013.

Parakash, G., & Kruse, K. M. (2008). *The spaces of the modern city: Imaginaries, politics, and everyday life*. Princeton: Princeton University Press.

Pascucci, E. (2016). The humanitarian infrastructure and the question of over-research: Reflections on fieldwork in the refugee crises in the Middle East and North Africa. *Area, 49*, 249–255. in press.

Pascucci, E. (2017). From "refugee population" to political community: The Mustapha Mahmoud refugee protest camp. In G. Brown, A. Feigenbaum, F. Frenzel, & P. McCurdy (Eds.), *Protest camps in international context: Spaces, infrastructures, and media of resistance* (pp. 289-308). Bristol: Policy Press at the University of Bristol.

Peck, J., Theodore, N., & Brenner, N. (2009). Neoliberal urbanism: Models, moments, mutations. *SAIS Review of International Affairs, 29*(1), 49–66.

Roth, S. (2011). Dealing with danger: Risk and security in the everyday lives of aid workers. In A. M. Fechter & H. Hindman (Eds.), *Inside the everyday lives of development workers: The challenges and futures of aidland* (pp. 151–168). Sterling: Kumarian Press.

Smirl, L. (2008). Building the other, constructing ourselves: Spatial dimensions of international humanitarian response. *International Political Sociology, 2*, 236–253.

Smirl, L. (2015). *Spaces of aid: How cars, compounds and hotels shape humanitarianism*. London: Zed Books.

Stewart, D. J. (1996). Cities in the desert: The Egyptian New-Town Program. *Annals of the Association of American Geographers, 86*(3), 459–480.

Tadros, M. (2012). Backstage governance. *Institute of Development Studies Bulletin, 43*(1), 62–70.

Verdirame, G., & Harrell-Bond, B. (1995). *Rights in exile: Janus-faced humanitarianism*. New York/Oxford: Berghahn.

Wahdan, D. (2012). Transport thugs: Spatial marginalization in a Cairo suburb. In H. Ayeb & R. Bush (Eds.), *Marginality and exclusion in Egypt* (pp. 112–132). London: Zed Books.

5

Contesting Entrapment: Women Asylum Seekers in Hong Kong

Alison Gerard

Introduction

This chapter explores the entrapment of asylum seekers in Hong Kong, drawing on qualitative research carried out with a diverse sample of women asylum seekers. These women's narratives illustrate how structural factors, such as the securitization of migration (Gerard 2014), permeate everyday encounters and produce entrapment. Núñez and Heyman (2007) first applied the concept of entrapment to irregular migration. As characterized by Núñez and Heyman, entrapment is a dynamic process whereby state actors impose significant risk on the mobility of irregular migrants. Irregular migrants respond by exerting agency to resist by both 'forgoing travel and covertly defying movement controls' (2007, p. 354). This produces multiple and overlapping barriers that contribute to an experience of liminality for asylum seekers. This chapter expands on this definition by analysing the situation of women asylum seekers in Hong Kong and illustrating the regional variations of entrapment that Núñez

A. Gerard (✉)
Centre for Law and Justice, Charles Sturt University,
Bathurst, NSW, Australia

F. Vecchio, A. Gerard (eds.), *Entrapping Asylum Seekers*, Transnational Crime, Crime Control and Security, DOI 10.1057/978-1-137-58739-8_5

and Heyman envisaged. The chapter makes two significant contributions to the study of entrapment processes. First, the account presented herein extends the analysis of the role played by actors in processes of entrapment beyond that of police and state agencies to include the role of non-government agencies. Second, the gendered analysis of entrapment generated by focusing on women's experiences elucidates the contradictions that women's resistance to entrapment may produce.

For women asylum seekers in Hong Kong, entrapment ensues from the corralling of asylum seekers into rigid legal categories imposed 'from above' that induce poverty and protracted uncertainty around legal status, while they are forced to wait years for determination of their claim for humanitarian protection. Women are forced into these legal categories of torture/non-refoulement claimant, based on which they are only entitled to limited access to accommodation, medical services, education and psycho-social supports. The protracted delays associated with applying for humanitarian protection are seen here as a form of control by the state, or what Hage (2009, p. 101) refers to as 'circumstances that are conspiring to make a total agentless victim and object out of [asylum seekers]'. In contrast to the view of asylum seekers as 'total agentless victims', this chapter explores the varying extremities of precarious livelihoods produced by entrapment and women's strategies to negate their dehumanizing effects. The chapter shows how these strategies may serve to reinforce constructions of asylum seeker illegality and thereby further entrap asylum seekers in the stereotypical corollary applied to asylum seekers as either bogus or genuine.

The entrapment of women asylum seekers by the rigid legal categories imposed on them occurs against a backdrop of the securitization of migration—embodied by the policies, practices and discourses that are based on the assumption that certain migrants, chief amongst them asylum seekers and irregular migrants, pose an unacceptable risk to society (Vecchio 2015; Gerard 2014). Although these strategies are officially designed to deter, their effectiveness in doing so remains unproven. The securitization of migration has made travel and subsistence easier for some migrants but more difficult and dangerous for asylum seekers and irregular migrants as they seek entry through the increasingly narrow pathways available to them to cross international borders (Weber and

Pickering 2011; Pickering and Cochrane 2012). Not only have these border controls led to increased risk-taking by those seeking to enter a country, but they have also reduced circular migration as people are prevented from returning home and are instead compelled to look for permanent resettlement (Massey et al. 2002). In this chapter, the term 'asylum seeker' will be used broadly to denote those with Refugee Convention[1] status, applicants for Refugee Convention status, torture claimants and those successful in their torture claims.

Migration processes are shaped by gender but also reconfigure 'gender identities, roles and ideologies' (Luibheid 2013, p. 99). This analysis probes the gendered consequences of entrapment and how women's agency and resistance to entrapment may either accelerate or reduce exposure to risk, measured in terms of insecurity and vulnerability. Gender is relational and contextual, and women asylum seekers in Hong Kong are not a homogenous group. The differential impact of entrapment is visible primarily through analysis of the politico-legal forces that influence women's asylum seeking. Those who arrive as foreign domestic workers and later apply for asylum are contrasted with women asylum seekers from sub-Saharan Africa, a group much more recognized stereotypically within Hong Kong as 'genuine' asylum seekers. In this, the role of non-government organizations (NGOs) as actors in the entrapment process looms large. Yet, several strategies adopted by women asylum seekers to resist entrapment were facilitated by some of the NGOs that operate in Hong Kong. NGOs provide, in effect, a waiting room for humanitarian protection claimants, and activities and services to support their endurance of entrapment. This provision of services, however, is only available to selected asylum seekers, thus valorizing certain categories of asylum seekers while reinforcing the vulnerability of others.

Putting together a chapter on the experiences of women asylum seekers requires careful reflection on historical context, and the heterogeneity of women's experiences as advocated by postcolonial scholars (Mohanty 2003). This chapter's starting point is to challenge the ahistorical and unexamined assumptions pervasive in conceptualizations of asylum seekers and refugees, such as the assumption that women are passive victims devoid of agency (Malkki 1995). Núñez and Heyman (2007, p. 357) remind us however, that agency for irregular migrants, who often experience a 'near permanent state of liminality' in the borderlands in and around the Global North, should not be overstated. Notwithstanding this, asylum seekers use their agency in ways that resist their entrapment and as a coping strategy. Yet, in doing so, their actions may also reinforce stereotypical understandings of asylum seekers. This analysis is made possible through the diverse sample of qualitative research undertaken with respondents in mid-2014. The participants' countries of origin included: Somalia ($n = 2$), Congo ($n = 1$), Rwanda ($n = 3$), Uganda ($n = 1$), Nigeria ($n = 2$), Indonesia ($n = 2$), Sri Lanka ($n = 3$), Angola ($n = 1$) and the Philippines ($n = 3$). I used purposive sampling to obtain participants. I worked with NGOs and informant recruiters to identify safe spaces in which the interviews could be conducted and to meet participants. In addition to these asylum seeker interviews, I also interviewed ten participants from five NGOs working with asylum seeker populations in Hong Kong. The interviews were recorded and transcribed, and thematic analysis was then used to analyse the narratives therein.

To establish a context for the analysis that follows, this chapter will begin with a background to refugee status determination and the nature of legal categories imposed 'from above' in Hong Kong. It will then analyse the nature of entrapment and its resistance by women seeking asylum in Hong Kong, focusing on four main areas: the politico-legal factors shaping women's asylum seeking and agency, companionship, employment strategies and the role of NGOs as actors in entrapment processes.

Seeking Asylum in Hong Kong

The historical context of Hong Kong's frontier has shaped the public's views of who can claim asylum and the availability of other forms of humanitarian protection. Hong Kong, a Special Administrative Region of China, sits on the edge of the region's largest national economy and is itself a major centre of financial activity and globalization (Vecchio 2015). Migrant labour contributes much to both the formal and informal economy. Statistics are difficult to verify, but, in a somewhat dated analysis, migrant labour has previously been estimated to contribute about 1 per cent of total Gross National Product, representing a contribution of

HK$13.8 billion to the economy (AMC 2004). A significant number of foreign domestic workers provide their labour to satiate the global city of Hong Kong, often from the Philippines, Sri Lanka and Indonesia (Constable 2014). Many of the respondents in my research were former domestic workers who engaged with the informal economy while awaiting determination of their claims for refugee status. A confluence of factors have made the city home to a flourishing informal economy: economic restructuring in Hong Kong that has left jobs clustered around the top and lower ends of the labour market; the collapse of manufacturing and, with it, organized labour through trade unions; and the increase in service sector jobs (see Vecchio 2015). Matthews and Yang (2012) have traced the work of Africans as part of the emerging 'low-end globalization' in Hong Kong and China, whose involvement in illicit trade is often tolerated by the Hong Kong government (see also Mathews et al. 2014). Through the informal economy, asylum seekers in Hong Kong also contribute to the local economy and create new industries (Vecchio 2013). The official government approach to migrant labour in Hong Kong is uneven: some forms of migratory labour are encouraged, facilitated and fostered, while others are tolerated yet officially deterred.

Hong Kong's historical treatment of asylum seekers demonstrates the production of illegality through immigration controls. Hong Kong has a long history of placing asylum seekers in limbo. Britain controlled Hong Kong and the New Territories from the mid-1800s until 1 July 1997. During much of that time, migration was largely circular between Hong Kong and mainland China, and seeking refuge was 'routine' (Madokoro 2012, p. 409). The term 'refugee' was used in the earlier years to describe economic migrants coming from mainland China and migrants who may have been persecuted under the definition within the 1951 Refugee Convention (Vecchio 2015). This stopped abruptly after the commencement of the militarization of Hong Kong's border with China in 1950, which continued until 1967, with the possibility of asylum for migrants from mainland China extinguished from 1967 (Madokoro 2012). At the time, British and Hong Kong authorities were adamant that Hong Kong would not become a transit country for refugees, so both governments refused to recognize refugees and referred instead to migrants as 'immigrants', 'escapees' and 'illegals' (Madokoro 2011, p. 419).

Hong Kong received over 223,302 Vietnamese boat people from early May 1975 (Troeung 2015). Under the Comprehensive Plan of Action of the UN High Commissioner for Refugees (UNHCR), the Hong Kong government forcibly deported thousands of refugees to Vietnam between 1989 and 1997 (Robinson 2004). Those who were not deported were held in Hong Kong initially in open centres and later in closed centres, including converted prisons (Troeung 2015). The last camp was closed in 2000, almost 25 years after the end of the Vietnam War (Troeung 2015). The Hong Kong government has asked the UNHCR to repay Hong Kong for the expenses incurred during this period and has consistently refused to extend the Refugee Convention to Hong Kong (Vecchio 2015). Contemporaneously, the policy of the government towards asylum seekers, refugees and other humanitarian protection claimants is to deter new arrivals (Vecchio 2015). Refugees are viewed as 'economic burdens and troublemakers' (Troeung 2015, pp. 248–9). Nevertheless, many thousands of asylum seekers enter Hong Kong each year to seek asylum, and many engage with the informal economy while awaiting their claim to humanitarian protection.

Refugee Protection Legal Framework in Hong Kong

It is only relatively recently that the Hong Kong government has had chief responsibility for sorting asylum seekers and other humanitarian protection claimants into palatable legal categories. The People's Republic of China is signatory to the 1951 Refugee Convention, and although the government extended the Convention to Macau, they did not do so for Hong Kong (Ramsden and Marsh 2014). While not a signatory to the 1951 Refugee Convention or its accompanying Protocols, Hong Kong is subject to the 1984 *Convention against Torture and Other Cruel, Inhuman or Degrading Treatment or Punishment* (CAT). Article 3 of the CAT also prohibits refoulement, akin to Article 1 of the 1951 Refugee Convention, in cases where claimants would face torture or other inhumane treatment. Moreover, the *International Covenant on Civil and Political Rights*

(ICCPR) and the *International Covenant on Economic, Social and Cultural Rights* (ICESCR) also provide relief to those seeking asylum (Ramsden and Marsh 2014). The Unified Screening Mechanism (USM) was launched in Hong Kong in March 2014 as a single legal mechanism for applying for humanitarian protection. Up until that time, claimants could go through a number of channels to seek humanitarian protection based on the 1951 Refugee Convention, the CAT and the ICCPR and ICESCR, leading to protracted delays and confusion for claimants (Ramsden and Marsh 2014). This research took place before the launch of the USM, when the UNHCR was still the main agency responsible for receiving and determining the claims of asylum seekers.

The Hong Kong government refers to asylum seekers as 'illegal immigrants'. In public discourse, 'asylum seeker' and 'illegal immigrant' are used interchangeably (Vecchio 2015). Under the USM, the Hong Kong government states that:

> any illegal immigrant claiming that he or she would face risks of torture, cruel, inhuman or degrading treatment or punishment or persecution in his or her country of origin is subject to a standardized screening procedure.
>
> If the non-refoulement claims are unsubstantiated, the claimant would be removed to his or her home country as soon as practicable. Even if such claims are substantiated, the claimants must leave when the alleged risks cease to exist, as Hong Kong is not a signatory of the 1951 Convention Relating to the Status of Refugees. (LegCo 2016, p. 1)

As at end September 2016, there were around 11,000 'torture/non-refoulement claim cases' in Hong Kong, just under a third of whom were women (HKSAR 2016). Almost half were categorized as overstayers (43 per cent) and the majority (51 per cent) were classified as 'illegal immigrants' (HKSAR 2016). Their country breakdown is set out below in Fig. 5.1. Most of those making a torture/non-refoulement claim come from Vietnam, India and Pakistan, followed by Bangladesh and Indonesia.

Rates of recognition in Hong Kong are extremely low—see Fig. 5.2. Between late 2009 and September 2016, 10,172 torture/non-refoulement claim cases were determined, but only 65 were granted refugee status

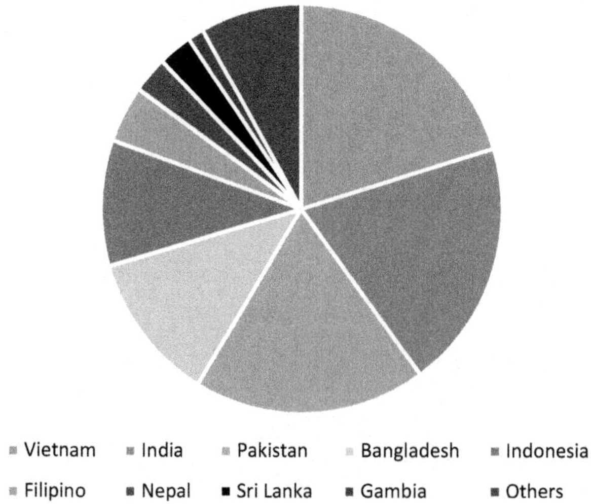

Fig. 5.1 Nationality of torture/non-refoulement claimants in Hong Kong (HKSAR 2016)

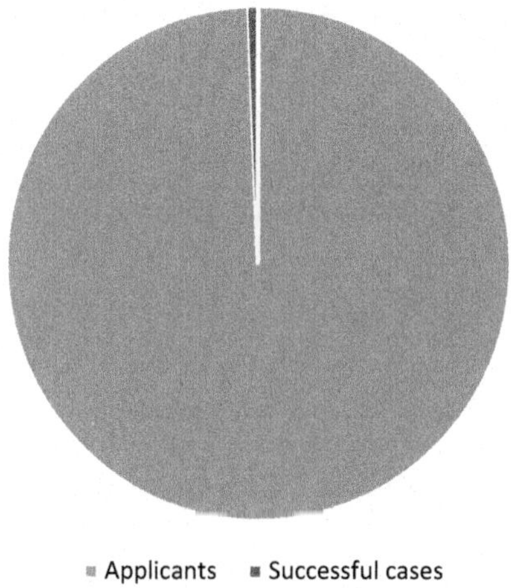

Fig. 5.2 Percentage of successful torture/non-refoulement claims in Hong Kong 2009–16

(HKSAR 2016). It was not possible to source a gendered breakdown of successful cases. Fourteen of those successful were from Sri Lanka. There were no successful cases from Indonesia or the Philippines (HKSAR 2016).

It is estimated that the USM decision-making process runs for 25 weeks. There is an appeals process for torture claimants through the Torture Claims Appeal Board, and determination of appeals may be made without a hearing (LegCo 2016, p. 1). This poses obvious risks to the robustness of the adjudication of the claim for humanitarian protection.

To understand how processes of entrapment are both embedded and resisted within the daily lived experience of women asylum seekers, and the actors involved, I listened to what asylum seekers said about their lives in Hong Kong (see Silvey 2006, p. 71). The next section analyses how the imposition of rigid legal categories impacts the contested spaces of entrapment for women asylum seekers in Hong Kong.

Politico-legal Factors of Entrapment for Women Asylum Seekers in Hong Kong

Multiple individual and structural factors influence the arrival of women asylum seekers in Hong Kong. The women's narratives in this research demonstrate how this complexity on a macro and micro level is met with rigid legal categories for humanitarian protection claimants imposed 'from above', by both the Hong Kong government as well as the UNHCR, at the time of this research.

Entrapped by Stereotypes of Asylum Seekers

Asylum seekers are sorted into legal categories that, on one end, grant refugee protection and, on the other, the status of rejected asylum seeker and/or rejected torture claimant. These legal categories typically valorize those asylum seekers from usual refugee-sending countries such as Somalia and Rwanda although, as explored above, few are granted refugee protection. The legal framework allows for applications from former foreign domestic workers originating from the Philippines, Sri Lanka and

Indonesia, but, apart from the rare case, these claims are dismissed. Yet the legal categories provide opportunity to women asylum seekers to partially regularize their legal status, prolong their stay in Hong Kong while their claims are being determined, and provide some resources for subsistence, albeit minimal.

Through analysis of the lived experiences of women seeking asylum in Hong Kong, the complexity and struggle involved in negotiating the consequences of entrapment and their gendered dimensions become visible. In her seminal work on Canada's Gender Guidelines,[2] Macklin's 1995 research highlighted the inherent tensions that result from sorting women asylum seekers into legal categories. Evaluating progress against Macklin's (1995) original contribution, Labman and Dauvergne (2014, p. 265) write that 'for women in refugee law, the issue has always been fitting into the correct category and, thus, bending the category to fit women'. In this regard, legal concepts, even when the intention is humanitarian, contain inherent limitations (Brown and Schept 2016, p. 7). These tensions are reflected in women's accounts of seeking asylum in Hong Kong and illuminate the forms of entrapment to which these women are subject.

The women I interviewed used a variety of pathways to come to Hong Kong and apply for humanitarian protection. Those from Sub-Saharan Africa tended to come by boat or car from China or flew into Hong Kong from other parts of South-East Asia. As one respondent from Rwanda described:

> I didn't choose to come to Hong Kong. We were going around and arrived in Burundi and we didn't find a visa to Europe so they just give us China and Guangzhou. When we arrived the authorities say you cannot stay here but to go to Hong Kong because they will help you. They say there will be human rights in Hong Kong so then we choose to come here. We arrived by minibus. We were sleeping in a playground for two days with my two-year-old daughter and husband, and then we saw another black man and he was speaking French. He said you cannot stay here you need to go and see the UNHCR. So we go there and then to ISS[3] and they find us an apartment. It's a small room but we are happy as it is security. (AS39)

From this excerpt it is clear that some asylum seekers arrive in Hong Kong without much prior knowledge or planning. Another respondent from Rwanda described how she had to flee with her husband as he was targeted by the Rwandan government. When they fled she was pregnant and her husband had just been released from prison. A friend organized for them to fly to Guangzhou in China and then they made their way to Hong Kong by boat (AS 40). They spent three nights sleeping at the Star Ferry terminal in Hong Kong before another asylum seeker introduced them to ISS and UNHCR. For those arriving in Hong Kong, peer networks are critical to finding basic resources.

Just under a third of the women asylum seekers I interviewed had applied for asylum in Hong Kong after working as a foreign domestic worker. Almost 8 of the 21 women interviewed were former foreign domestic workers—a small sample of the estimated 336,000 migrant domestic workers in Hong Kong, the majority of whom are women (HKJC 2016). Indeed, one in three households with children in Hong Kong employs a migrant domestic worker. Historically, most were from China, but a liberalization of labour laws in the 1970s meant that, since that time, workers have arrived from the Philippines, Indonesia and Thailand, and, more recently, Sri Lanka, Myanmar and Bangladesh (HKJC 2016). Viewed from 'above', foreign domestic workers who become asylum seekers are perceived as a considerable annoyance and cast as deceitful for falsifying their claim to asylum (Constable 2014). As Constable (2014) argues in relation to women foreign domestic workers, Hong Kong wants workers, not 'people', especially those who later apply for asylum.

The confluence of foreign domestic workers, asylum and pregnancy is especially fraught (Constable 2014). Constable argues that foreign domestic workers apply for asylum or make a torture claim as a strategy to stay longer in Hong Kong and to find a way to make more money or return home (Constable 2014). For some former foreign domestic workers, a claim for refugee protection is made once they become pregnant, which is understood by Constable as a strategy for 'good mothering', as explored in later sections of this chapter on companionship and entrapment. In my research, I found that women's reasons for seeking asylum were complex. For one respondent, her experiences of abuse in Sri Lanka were interwoven with the desire to become a foreign domestic worker. However, it is important not to overstate agency here (see Núñez and Heyman 2007), as there are inherent limitations on the lives of liminality experienced by many asylum seekers, a precarious livelihood being almost a pre-condition of seeking asylum in Hong Kong. Certainly, employment conditions for foreign domestic workers can be both inflexible and exploitative, with limited pathways for redress (HKJC 2016). Thus, applying for asylum may become an important strategy for gaining some form of recognizable legal status after ceasing employment as a foreign domestic worker, however partial. Katrina, from the Philippines, came to Hong Kong as a foreign domestic worker and worked for three years. After leaving this employer she then became an 'overstayer' for three years, and filed a torture claim which, at the time of the interview, had been under review for the previous four years. Thus, for Katrina, applying for asylum was a means of gaining temporary security. She spoke about how she was scared of running into police when she was an overstayer, but now that she had applied for a torture claim, she was no longer scared. These legal categories inscribe categories of deservedness or unworthiness. Regardless of the circumstances of the individual asylum seeker, it is clear that these strategies are seen as an abuse of process and an indication of the 'bogus' nature of claims to asylum, which in turn shapes access to services for this population.

Precarious Livelihoods

Whilst asylum seekers await determination of their claims, the economic and social support provided to them is minimal and designed to discourage large numbers of people from settling in Hong Kong. The Hong Kong Social Welfare Department contracts the provision of support to international aid NGO, the International Social Service (ISS). Assistance is provided 'in-kind' through vouchers and rental allowance paid directly to a landlord. At the time that this research was undertaken, rental allowance of HK$1200 was provided per month, and food groceries every 10 days totalling HK$1000 per month (Ramsden and Marsh 2014). Each child attracts an additional amount in rental allowance and food vouchers. Access to education for children is managed on a case-by-case basis, elevating the role of advocates within the system to secure access to basic rights. Claimants are prohibited from working. There is some provision for substantiated torture claimants to apply to work, although no transparent criteria exists on how decisions on such applications are to be made (Ramsden and Marsh 2014).

The focus on temporary support denies the reality that many asylum seekers and refugees will spend up to a decade awaiting determination of their claim. According to the Hong Kong government, the average time a non-refoulement claimant spent in Hong Kong was 2.7 years (LegCo 2016, p. 1). Some women in the present research had been waiting for more than nine years for their claims for humanitarian protection to be resolved (AS34). This was much longer than the times for refugee status determination claimed by the Hong Kong government and points to the confusion caused by overlapping status determination procedures. A Congolese asylum seeker I spoke to described the difficulties of having 'no job, no working, and no money' for this lengthy period of time: 'Hong Kong is not good if you don't have money' (AS22). This respondent could not afford transport, suitable accommodation or resources for her school-age children. For asylum seekers enduring these delays, Hong Kong has been described as a 'prison without walls' (Chiu 2012). Precarity is induced by the minimal provisions provided to asylum seekers during their wait. Others have commented on how this level of precarity has caused asylum seekers to look favourably upon experiences of detention, because at least shelter, food and other provisions are accessible while being detained (Mathews 2014).

There have been many criticisms of the minimal food and accommodation support provided to asylum seekers who have registered with the Hong Kong government and are waiting determination of their claims (Constable 2015; Vecchio 2015; Mathews 2014). In Hong Kong, the in-kind assistance is facilitated by ISS on behalf of the government, thus enlisting this actor in the implementation of its strategy of entrapment. At the time these interviews took place, money was directly paid to landlords and shop keepers who are provided with a lucrative business through these arrangements. In a win for asylum seekers, vouchers are now provided so that groceries up to a certain amount can be obtained from a supermarket. In line with previous research (Vecchio 2015), my respondents also talked about the poor quality of the food, and concerns over their nutrition levels and that of their children. The women asylum seekers I interviewed reported that the food is often past its expiry date and there is not enough to feed the family (AS22). Women respondents also complained of the toothbrushes being of poor quality, the shampoo and the lack of choice for basic food items and for baby formula.

The poor accommodation available to asylum seekers in Hong Kong makes life very difficult for asylum seekers and their families (see also Vecchio 2017, Chap. 10, in this volume). Vecchio's (2015) research has pieced together the political economy framing the accommodation of asylum seekers in Hong Kong, who receive an amount of rental assistance from the government that puts accommodation in legal structures beyond reach. Asylum seekers can only afford rent in illegal structures, creating new industries for landlords, some of whom are former farmers and accommodate asylum seekers in purpose-built illegal accommodation on their properties. In one example, former pig pens were transformed into accommodation for asylum seekers, out of which the landlords made a steady profit. I visited some of these slums that house asylum seekers and was deeply struck by the conditions—dirt floors, plywood walls occupying no more than 2 by 2 metres in which a mother and child would live or a family of two parents and three children whom I met. There was often an air-conditioner—essential in Hong Kong—but not always; although most did have a fan. Asylum seekers would cook, sleep and socialize out in the one small space. At other residences there was a common room. It was hot. At one point I had to climb a staircase made of plywood to get to a second floor in which the parents and a nine-month-old baby shared room no more than 3 by 2 metres. It was dangerous for the baby to move around with so many exposed items for cooking and electricity. The minimal assistance given to asylum seekers in Hong Kong necessitates their managing a liminal and precarious existence in substandard accommodation, with low-quality food and resources. Asylum seekers turn to illegal accommodation structures as one of the few mechanisms for promoting their own security.

NGOs and Precarious Livelihoods

The minimal assistance provided to asylum seekers is designed to deter other arrivals. To manage the impact of this situation, women asylum seekers spoke about various entrepreneurial strategies they adopted. One strategy was to engage the support of NGOs. There are at least five major NGOs in Hong Kong that cater to asylum seekers. Some provide additional food, clothing, legal services, psycho-social support services and advocacy. Some provide classes for asylum seekers such as English and Chinese language training, jewellery making, playgroups for children and drama classes. In this way, NGOs become enlisted in the entrapment of asylum seekers in Hong Kong.

Entrapment in Hong Kong means negotiating the long wait that follows applying for asylum. This represents one of the activities to which asylum seekers have become accustomed when seeking asylum in the Global North (Gerard 2014; see also Mathews 2014). Keeping busy was an important coping strategy for resisting entrapment and avoiding the dullness that can lead to thinking about the past, and livelihoods left behind in the country of origin. Two-thirds of the asylum seekers in my research observed that participating in activities hosted by NGOs was an important feature of their week. These activities also featured prominently in my research agenda as it was often at such classes that I met respondents, who talked about attending classes at different NGOs:

> I have many classes. I have English class on Monday, Tuesday and Wednesday at home. Thursday is playgroup with children, beauty class and English class. Friday is women's group. (AS39)

It was felt that going to classes was better than being idle, which tended to be a precursor to sadness.

> You cannot plan in Hong Kong. I cannot plan here. I have a short term only, what I will have for lunch, what I will wear. I would really like to wake up and plan my future. When they ask me where do I want to go, I say I want to go back to my children'. Why should I be hanging around in

places that don't help me? I would love to sink into something called a 'comfort zone' one day. (AS37)

Activities put on by NGOs assisted people to endure their entrapment. If they were also able to make items and sell them, this could be a form of income generation, albeit minor. The NGOs that offered these services provided a mechanism for spending time in Hong Kong that would not necessarily reduce economic precariousness but were perceived by asylum seekers as important for well-being.

In addition to the activities and classes described above, asylum seekers could also access other provisions and services. To illustrate, one NGO offered asylum seekers the opportunity to document some of the psychosocial aspects of their claim for refugee protection with the help of the organization's mental health team. This was a service that the Hong Kong government did not provide but which could enhance their asylum claim, for example, by documenting the persecution that formed part of their claim which could then strengthen their case. Certain baby supplies were also provided such as nappies, formula or prams. Some respondents spoke about selling these additional items for money as a way of supplementing the meagre food items available to them. Delit, from Indonesia, said that, because she breastfed her baby, she was able to sell the formula she received and use the money to purchase more nappies (AS 25). Another woman I interviewed, who was from Rwanda and had a seven-month-old baby, commented:

> Here in Hong Kong life is very hard. My baby cannot breastfeed, she doesn't like it. So she can drink milk. I ask for more milk and they say they can't give it to us. Sometimes we don't have any milk to give her and it's very difficult. She drinks only the formula. If she has another kind of formula she doesn't like it. ISS gives us some formula but it is not enough. I received the one from another [non-government organization] but she doesn't like it. She only likes the ISS one. She just vomits it back up. (AS 40)

Asylum seekers were able to mitigate some of the dehumanizing impacts of not being able to choose the right sustenance for their children by utilizing the resources of NGOs. They could then be strategic about what items they on-sold so as to get the right resources. This was seen as important in a context where respondents complained that the formula they received from official sources was not enough, as the baby food only lasted for six days yet the ISS only provided them with food every 10 days.

Not all asylum seekers were welcome to participate in these activities or receive provisions, however, and this enhanced the role of NGOs in entrapment. Asylum seekers were often required to register for services and it is via this process that the NGOs may valorize legal categories from above. In the interviews with NGO respondents, it was clear that only certain groups of asylum seekers were welcome to use their services. Even though the mechanism to apply for asylum exists in Hong Kong, a sharp distinction was drawn by some NGO respondents in this study as to who was deserving of asylum seeker and refugee status and who was illegitimate. One NGO participant said that their NGO automatically refuses Filipino or Indonesian foreign domestic workers:

> We had a Filipino asylum seeker come in here and try and register and I took her aside and said you are never going to get refugee status. You should just go home. You are not going to prolong your stay this way as you won't be successful and we are not going to help you. (NGO 6)

The strict legal categories governing the humanitarian protection process meant that certain asylum seekers had elevated status over others, prior to any determination of a claim for refugee protection. A common perception among the NGO workers I interviewed was that, in view of the finite resources they had, the only people who would satisfy the criteria for humanitarian protection were those from usual refugee-sending countries and that these were the only people deserving of assistance. This refusal of services and consequent humiliation for those refused was keenly felt by some of the ex–foreign domestic worker participants I interviewed. This situation was not universal, however, with some NGOs providing assistance to all asylum seekers and torture claimants, regardless of any adjudication of their claim.

My time in Hong Kong coincided with the peak of the Refugee Union movement, which provided an additional way for asylum seekers to resist their entrapment. A group of refugees had started a campaign, supported by resources from one NGO, to set up a Refugee Union and campaign against the minimal supports provided to asylum seekers (Vecchio and Beatson 2014). Vecchio and Beatson highlight how this was also a protest against the attempted social control enacted by NGOs. The campaign to increase the monthly allowance was ultimately successful. The asylum seekers I interviewed about their involvement in the Refugee Union found it to be a great way to relieve stress. For many, it became a safe space in which to connect and resist the precarious livelihoods that dominated their everyday experience. In addition, some issues were raised in relation to women's contribution to or empowerment through involvement in the Refugee Union process, both from NGO respondents. One respondent I interviewed felt that women's contribution to the union was not being valued. Another felt that the movement did not support women to be involved and that one woman was excluded from the union for being too vocal. I did not spend enough time in Hong Kong to explore this further. Three women asylum seekers I spoke to expressed their fulfilment in being involved with the Refugee Union in Hong Kong. Despite the above concerns raised by NGO respondents, overall advocacy campaigns such as this enable the precarious livelihoods of asylum seekers to be challenged and, in some cases, improved. The Refugee Union constituted a strategy utilized by asylum seekers to contest their entrapment.

Companionship and Entrapment

Companionship in the context of the asylum seeker community in Hong Kong provides an apt illustration of how migration shapes and reshapes gender roles and identities. As argued by Luibheid (2013), companionship can create unexpected possibilities yet also tensions and contradictions. In Hong Kong, intimate relationships between asylum seekers and between foreign domestic workers (who are largely female) and male asylum seekers have been the subject of much scholarly attention (Vecchio 2015; Constable 2014). Vecchio's (2015, p. 145) ethnographic research with over 75 male asylum seekers in Hong Kong found that 'the vast majority of male participants had one or more girlfriends in Hong Kong, most commonly Filipina or Indonesian nationals working as domestic helpers but also local Chinese or Western women'. Often, these companions supplemented the income of male asylum seekers and were seen as a survival strategy for the difficult conditions facing (male) asylum seekers in Hong Kong. One respondent from an NGO spoke of this phenomenon as recent:

> So, number one, there was a very available pool of men – they'd pulled the plug on working – I think that was only in 2008 too or maybe 2009. So we had this group of men who then had nothing to do and then, on the other side, we had a group of women who had really now in the 2000s they really started coming in in high numbers. By the time it got to 2011, I think, they were equal to the number of Filipinos, but only 10 years before that it had been dominated by the Filipinos market. And we had Indonesians. … They were less experienced in Hong Kong in general and they were less prepared in terms of their sexual empowerment or family planning. (NGO 5)

This characterization depicts these intimate relationships as leading to unexpected pregnancies. Respondents from NGOs criticized those male asylum seekers who were perceived as luring foreign domestic workers into relationships under false pretences (see also Vecchio 2015). It was felt by an NGO respondent I interviewed that foreign domestic workers are encouraged to overstay their visa by their male asylum seeker companions and then encouraged to apply for a torture claim, thereby also becoming an asylum seeker. Foreign domestic workers who cease their employment and do not secure additional employment within two weeks are deemed to have overstayed. According to one NGO respondent, this is when it is most likely for such women to fall pregnant, rather than pregnancy terminating their employment situation (NGO 5). In this regard, it was unclear from my interviews with respondents how the sequence of events played out for women in this situation. However, a fear of returning to one's home country was most often cited as the reason for applying for asylum.

During my research in Hong Kong, I spoke with six women asylum seekers who were former foreign domestic workers and who had children to asylum seekers. They were all still asylum seekers themselves and were awaiting determination of their claims. They were worried that if they went back to their home country, they would be rejected for having a child out of marriage. Thus, they were entrapped in Hong Kong and not able to move forward or return to their previous employment as a foreign domestic worker. They were therefore living a marginalized existence along with many thousands of other people awaiting humanitarian protection. These women were critical of the NGOs who refused them services, including basic provisions for their children. One respondent said that she was humiliated by staff at an NGO by having her request for nappies and baby formula rejected outrightly (AS 4).

Women asylum seekers in Hong Kong who become pregnant face unique financial challenges associated with pregnancy and birth. To some extent these can be mitigated by applying for asylum. Asylum seekers are entitled to some public healthcare services on a case-by-case basis (Wong et al. 2016). Women respondents complained about not having access to an ultrasound when pregnant (AS 34) so being very nervous about the health of their baby. Foreign domestic workers who overstay and have a baby face significant costs when they have their baby in hospital. Non-eligible persons, such as overstayers, are charged HK$100,000 to have the baby. During a visit to one of the houses in the slums, I met a woman, Giselle, who had a baby to an African asylum seeker. She and her baby lived in a room with a single mattress on the dirt floor, and the walls were made of plywood. The father of her child did not want to have contact with her or the child so she was a single parent. Giselle had submitted a torture claim (AS 4). She had then received papers requesting that she attend court about the debt of HK$100,000 she owed to the hospital for the birth of her baby. In Hong Kong, if a woman is unable to pay her hospital bill, the birth registry will not provide her with a birth certificate. Only when a foreign domestic worker applies for bankruptcy will the birth certificate be released. This chain of events sparks a maze of legal hurdles. Whereas hospitals used to wait until the birth of a child to check the mother's immigration status, they are now reportedly checking the mother's status throughout pregnancy—thus surveillance has become more systemic.

Couples who do want to stay together face protracted uncertainty and are entrapped by their unregulated migration status. If a couple want to join their torture/non-refoulement claims, so as to put forward one family application, they face policy confusion around whether or not the woman or child can unite with the primary applicant. If they want to get married, they face the challenge of having to prove the husband's status through documentation. Asylum seekers cannot easily acquire the Consular assistance necessary to obtain a passport. One respondent said that, if an asylum seeker already has a passport, it is then possible to apply to Immigration to get married; on this subject she commented, 'it is all very hard and difficult for these girlfriends and wives of asylum seekers' (NGO 5). I met one couple in this predicament, with one partner from Indonesia and the other from Bangladesh. They shared three children. The Indonesian government would not give her husband a visa to come to Indonesia, and they could not return to Bangladesh (AS 23). Staying in Hong Kong was the only way they could keep the family together. Thus, staying in Hong Kong and resisting onward migration was their strategy.

The forming of intimate relationships produces varied consequences for women asylum seekers in Hong Kong. Entrapment processes can diminish the transnational citizenship strategies that women seek for their children when they become pregnant (Luibheid 2013). Entrapment, however, may ultimately compound disadvantage and marginalization for asylum seeker women who are primary carers of young children in Hong Kong. Other studies with irregular migrant women who become pregnant show that women define responsible parenthood as creating a flexible future for your children (Luibheid 2013; Constable 2014). However, the attainment of a flexible future by choosing to stay in Hong Kong is made difficult by entrapment processes that aim to produce a liminal existence for asylum seekers. The endurance of these conditions thus evinces the strength and resilience of asylum seekers in managing the limited choices available to them.

Employment Strategies and Precarity

In this research, one strategy or coping mechanism adopted by asylum seekers to resist entrapment and the consequent poverty was to join the informal economy. This strategy, however, carried with it the risk of exploitation in the workplace, and prison if caught and punished by the government authorities. Thus, this strategy had the potential to compound already precarious livelihoods. Moreover, it served to entrench stereotypes of asylum seekers in Hong Kong as either 'bogus' refugees or 'genuine' asylum seekers. This section illustrates how this form of agency produced a mutually reinforcing cycle for the women in this research: precarity led to resistance by working illegally, which reinforced government policy aimed at deterring the arrival of asylum seekers, thereby increasing asylum seekers' reliance on informal economic activities.

Entrapment by legal categories meant adopting certain behaviours and rejecting others. Doing something meaningful, such as work, has been previously observed as critical to resisting the precarious living conditions engendered by 'doing time' in Hong Kong (Mathews 2014). Studies have also found that NGOs perceive that working illegally is a behaviour that 'genuine' refugees do not do for they will not take the risk (Constable 2014; Vecchio 2015). Constable (2014) argues that, for asylum seekers in Hong Kong, there are ways of acting that enhance the appearance of vulnerability and need, which are adopted in order to secure resources. The NGO respondents in my research held the same views about 'genuine asylum seekers' not risking work (NGO5, NGO2). Yet, many asylum seekers in Hong Kong do work (Mathews 2014; Mathews et al. 2014; Mathews and Yang 2012; Vecchio 2015). I also found that over half of the asylum seekers I spoke to wanted to work but only if it was legal, and they were aware of the punishments that met work—two years in jail.

In my research, the reasons advanced to explain why asylum seekers would risk working were associated with mitigating precarious livelihoods. Three asylum seekers said that the poor-quality food and accommodation and lack of medical supplies available meant that some asylum seekers had to turn to illegal forms of labour to access basic services. Yet there were several risks involved. One respondent from the Philippines described how she could earn up to HK$8000 per month working as a dishwasher in a restaurant but that she had to work 9 or 10 hours per day, seven days a week (AS 9). Thus, the risk of working could extend to exploitation. The risks could also extend to incarceration. One respondent told me that:

> My husband's friend, he worked as they have a baby and they cannot pay rent and they didn't have enough food and there was some medical emergency for the baby. So they go to work and police catch him and he went to prison for working. (AS20)

Working could therefore alleviate some risks and vulnerability borne of poverty, but could present further risks. Those respondents who did work adopted strategies to mitigate risk. Patricia, from Sri Lanka, worked in a restaurant but was very careful about whom she disclosed this fact to so as not to attract attention. She stated that if she were to have conflict with people they could report her and she could be arrested; so it was very important for Patricia to be discrete and avoid conflict. This strategy illustrates the meticulous care needed to negotiate participation in the informal economy in Hong Kong. Patricia took these risks because she could not subsist on the allowance given to her in Hong Kong as an asylum seeker. At the time of my interview with Patricia, she had just been released from 15 months' imprisonment for working illegally. A friend of another asylum seeker with whom Patricia worked had tipped off the immigration police and they had both been arrested. Working had thus compounded her vulnerability and effectively added justification to government policies that promote the securitization of migration.

Conclusion

The gendered consequences of entrapment for women seeking asylum in Hong Kong are clustered around four main dimensions: the politico-legal factors that shape asylum seeking, the role of NGOs as actors in entrapment processes, companionship and employment. Women asylum seekers and irregular migrants adopt coping strategies that are entrepreneurial, out of which emerge varied contradictions. Some strategies to resist entrapment carry the risk of punishment and produce illegality. Others involve less risk in terms of exposure to jail but may be more likely to limit access to resources and the ability to meet basic subsistence needs in Hong Kong. From the discussion of these issues in this chapter two main conclusions emerge. On the one hand, access to the refugee protection legal framework does not guarantee safety for women seeking asylum in Hong Kong. Rather, their daily lives are impacted by their experiences of and resistance to entrapment. On the other, non-government agencies operating in Hong Kong emerge as significant non-state actors in the entrapment process.

The Hong Kong government strives to sort asylum seekers into palatable legal categories on a spectrum that includes, on one end, a grant of refugee protection and, on the other, the status of rejected asylum seeker and/or rejected torture claimant. These categories imposed by the government are reinforced and supported by third-sector NGOs. In fact, some organizations use these definitions to allocate funding to groups readily identifiable as refugees, while those perceived as disingenuous refugees are refused service prior to any determination or assessment of their refugee claim. Entrapment in these legal categories can and does affect access to accommodation, medical services, education and psychosocial supports.

The policing of the border in Hong Kong and the imposition of these legal categories 'from above' produce preferences for specific types of asylum seekers while rejecting others. As Madokoro (2011, p. 408) writes, 'conceptualisations of migrants and refugees … depend not only on their physical, social, cultural and economic attributes but also on the frontiers they traverse'. Liminal existence in Hong Kong subjects asylum seekers to poverty and immiseration. Even those who enjoy a status as 'preferred asylum seekers' live a precarious daily life. It is important to make the connections between these groups and develop alliances across differences (Hyndman 2000). Otherwise, we foster the processes of inclusion and exclusion to which asylum seekers are already subject.

Notes

1. *Convention Relating to the Status of Refugees*, 28 July 1951.
2. In an attempt to address the grossly disproportionate numbers of women excluded from refugee protection, the United Nations and a number of states such as Canada and Australia have formulated guidelines targeting decision-makers and encouraging an understanding of gender-related persecution.
3. The International Social Services (ISS) is the organization contracted by the Hong Kong Government to provide support to asylum seekers and torture claimants in Hong Kong.

References

AMC. (2004). *Economic contributions of FDWs in Hong Kong*. Hong Kong: Asian Migrant Centre.

Brown, M., & Schept, J. (2016). New abolition, criminology and critical carceral studies. *Punishment & Society, 00*, 1462474516666281.

Chiu, J. (2012). Marchers call for fairer treatment of refugees in Hong Kong. *South China Morning Post*, Viewed 13 Jan 2015. http://www.scmp.com/news/hong-kong/article/1073434/marchers-call-fairer-treatment-refugees-hong-kong?page=all

Constable, N. (2014). *Born out of place*. Berkeley: University of California Press.

Constable, N. (2015). Temporary shelter in the shadows: Migrant mothers and torture claims in Hong Kong. In S. Friedman & P. Mahdavi (Eds.), *Migrant encounters: Intimate labour, the state, and mobility across Asia*. Philadelphia: University of Pennsylvania Press.

Gerard, A. (2014). *The securitisation of migration and refugee women*. Abingdon: Routledge.

Hage, G. (2009). Waiting out the crises: On stuckedness and governmentality. In G. Hage (Ed.), *Waiting*. Melbourne: Melbourne University Press.

HKJC. (2016). *Coming clean: The prevalence of forced labour and human trafficking for the purpose of forced labour amongst migrant domestic workers in Hong Kong*. Hong Kong: Hong Kong Justice Centre.

HKSAR. (2016). *Statistics on non-refoulement claims*. Immigration Department, Hong Kong Special Administrative Region: Hong Kong.

Labman, S., & Dauvergne, C. (2014). Evaluating Canada's approach to gender-related persecution: Revisiting and re-embracing "refugee women and the imperative of categories". In E. Arbel, C. Dauvergne, & J. Millbank (Eds.), *Gender in refugee law: From the margins to the centre*. Abingdon: Routledge.

LegCo. (2016). *Fact sheet: Handling of non-refoulement claims in selected places*. Hong Kong: Research Office, Legislative Council Secretariat.

Luibheid, E. (2013). *Pregnant on arrival: Making the illegal immigrant*. Minneapolis: University of Minnesota Press.

Macklin, A. (1995). Refugee women and the imperative of categories. *Human Rights Quarterly, 172*, 213–277.

Madokoro, L. (2012). Borders transformed: Sovereign concerns, population movements and the making of territorial frontiers in Hong Kong, 1949–1967. *Journal of Refugee Studies, 253*, 407–427.

Malkki, L. (1995). Refugees and exile: From "refugee studies" to the national order of things. *Annual Review of Anthropology, 24*, 495–523.

Massey, D. S., Durand, J., & Malone, N. (2002). *Beyond smoke and mirrors: Mexican immigration in an era of economic integration*. New York: Russell Sage Foundation.

Mathews, G. (2014). Asylum seekers in Hong Kong: The paradoxes of lives lived on hold. In J. Zhang & H. Duncan (Eds.), *Migration in China and Asia*. New York: Springer.

Mathews, G., & Yang, Y. (2012). How Africans pursue low-end globalization in Hong Kong and mainland China. *Journal of Current Chinese Affairs, 412*, 95–120.

Mathews, G., Lin, D. A. N., & Yang, Y. (2014). How to evade states and slip past borders: Lessons from traders, overstayers, and asylum seekers in Hong Kong and China. *City & Society, 262*, 217–238.

Mohanty, C. T. (2003). *Feminism without borders*. Durham: Duke University Press.

Núñez, G. G., & Heyman, J. M. (2007). Entrapment processes and immigrant communities in a time of heightened border vigilance. *Human Organization, 664*, 354–365.

Pickering, S., & Cochrane, B. (2012). Irregular border-crossing deaths and gender: Where, how and why women die crossing borders. *Theoretical Criminology, 17*(1), 27–48.

Ramsden, M., & Marsh, L. (2014). Refugees in Hong Kong: Developing the legal framework for socio-economic rights protection. *Human Rights Law Review, 142*, 267–299.

Robinson, W. C. (2004). The comprehensive plan of action for Indochinese refugees, 1989–1997: Sharing the burden and passing the buck. *Journal of Refugee Studies, 17*(3), 319–333.

Troeung, Y. D. (2015). Buried history and transpacific pedagogy: Teaching the Vietnamese boat people's Hong Kong passage. *ARIEL, 46*(1), 239–255.

Vecchio, F. (2013). The economy of seeking asylum in the global city. *International Migration, 54*, 19–31.

Vecchio, F. (2015). *Asylum seeking and the global city*. Abingdon: Routledge.

Vecchio, F., & Beatson, C. (2014). Asylum seekers' occupy movement in Hong Kong. *Race & Class, 562*, 96–104.

Weber, L., & Pickering, S. (2011). *Globalization and borders: Death at the global frontier*. London: Palgrave.

Wong, W. C. W., Cheng, S., Holroyd, E., Chen, J., Loper, K. A., Tran, L., & Miu, H. Y. H. (2016). A lost tribe in the city: Health status and needs of African asylum seekers and refugees in Hong Kong. *International Journal for Equity in Health, 15*(1), 158.

6

'This Time I Am Going to Cross!': Fighting Entrapment Processes Through the Provision of Human Smuggling Services on the US–Mexico Border

Gabriella E. Sanchez

Introduction: 'My Gordo[1] Is on His Way!'

The call came in early on a Saturday morning, and Nora's excitement and happiness made it hard for me to initially understand what she was saying. 'My *Gordo* is on his way! He crossed on Thursday night, *they* got him all the way in really quick, just one try and he was on this side!' The day Nora had been longing for had finally arrived. After two years of failed attempts, Ramón, her youngest brother, had managed to cross the border in record time with the assistance of a *coyote*—the colloquial name given to smuggling facilitators along the US–Mexico border. After having invested an estimated US$5000 into Ramón's unsuccessful crossings (which included his arrest and subsequent deportation by US Customs and Border Protection [CBP] on at least one occasion), Nora connected, through a last-minute tip from an acquaintance, with a woman who was reportedly having success at facilitating crossings along a segment of the

G.E. Sanchez (✉)
Migration Policy Centre, European University Institute,
Florence, Italy

F. Vecchio, A. Gerard (eds.), *Entrapping Asylum Seekers*, Transnational Crime, Crime Control and Security, DOI 10.1057/978-1-137-58739-8_6

US–Mexico border. Less than 48 hours later, Ramón had re-entered the United States extra-legally and was on track to reunite with his sister in a city in the US Southwest. 'I can't believe my Gordo is back. I am so, so excited!'

Nora's excitement was justified. Amid increased border enforcement, dangerous environments, tensions surrounding drug trafficking–related violence in Mexico and the widespread criminalization of migration in the USA, successfully completing an extra-legal border crossing across the US–Mexico divide is a feat worthy of celebration. US immigration enforcement efforts, alongside the socioeconomic and political conditions in both the USA and Mexico, have led to significant decreases in the levels of irregular migration from Mexico (Pew Research Center 2012), and fluctuations in the smuggling market (Izcara-Palacios 2012a, b; Andreas 2001), while the US–Mexico border continues to be one of the riskiest borders for those seeking extra-legal crossings—in 2016, 267 people lost their lives, according to numbers from the International Organization for Migration (2017). As in other parts of the world, the lethality and risks inherent to irregular border crossings from Mexico to the USA have translated into the widespread reliance among migrants (which over the last few years has included a growing number of asylum seekers) on smuggling facilitators who provide guidance and support. By virtue of being articulated by migrants and asylum seekers in transit as unofficial mechanisms for migration, yet also in response to the attempts to deter their mobility, the facilitation of human smuggling constitutes—to follow Scott—a weapon of the weak (Scott 1985; Spener 2009). Furthermore, despite its growing criminalization, to most migrants and asylum seekers smuggling does not constitute a crime. Rather, it is often described as a legitimate set of collectively devised strategies aimed at reducing the risks posed by state initiatives to prevent mobility—a form of human security from below.

Smugglers have often been vilified in the migration literature by law enforcement, policy makers and academics alike, described as taking advantage of the vulnerability of migrants, and portrayed as abusive, even exploitative *men* from the Global South, organized into sophisticated transnational criminal networks of vast reach. These characterizations, however, fail to explain the continued reliance of people in transit on smugglers, or to reflect migrants' perspectives of their dealings with smugglers—aside from the most graphic, violent and tragic of cases.

The present chapter seeks to address that gap in the literature. It draws from ethnographic work conducted in February 2015 with a family of Mexican migrants in the USA who were successful in their efforts to cross the US–Mexico border with the assistance of smuggling facilitators or *coyotes*. It explores the role of the family (as a social unit related by consanguinity or social obligations) in identifying and monitoring the safety of its members as they travel with smugglers. Simultaneously, by mapping the work of smugglers it makes visible the ways in which the structures deployed by the state to counter migrants' mobility are avoided through mechanisms often grounded upon solidarity and mutual support. The chapter relies on qualitative data to describe the ways in which smuggling services are located, evaluated, negotiated and eventually deemed successful by those seeking to enter the USA extra-legally and/or their families. Focusing primarily on the experiences of Nora Hernandez (a pseudonym) in securing transits for her two young daughters and brother, the chapter lays out how undocumented migrants and their families covertly defy the movement controls (Nuñez and Heyman 2007) of the immigration authorities along the US–Mexico border.

Rather than defining it solely along the lines of risk, danger, violence and crime as mainstream academic, law enforcement and policy discourses do, the hiring of human smugglers is in this paper framed as it is perceived by those who rely on it: as a legitimate and necessary element that increases the likelihood of successful—if precarious—transborder, extra-legal journeys; and as an illicit, yet not criminal practice aimed at reuniting families separated by migration regimes. While acknowledging 'the efforts in which police and other state agencies impose significant risk on the movement of undocumented people,' the chapter also outlines the ways in which 'people exercise various forms of agency by both forgoing [specific forms of] travel and covertly defying movement controls' (Nuñez and Heyman 2007, p. 354) as part of their bottom-up efforts to exercise transnational mobility. Securing effective human smuggling services—amid the increased enforcement and criminalization at borders—constitutes one of the ways in which those excluded from the protection of legal migration regimes exercise their mobility as safely and swiftly as possible. I argue that human smuggling services constitute a solidarity-based mechanism whereby families, alongside people in transit and facilitators—all targets of migration controls—collaborate through the mobility processes of those unable to secure state protections amid mechanisms that work to entrap, criminalize and discipline them and their communities.

Human Smuggling and the Family

Human smuggling is the legal term used to designate the facilitation, in exchange for a fee or in-kind payment, of a transit or series of transits that allow an individual to travel into a country/countries other than his or her own, while avoiding state controls. These transits are often facilitated by community-based brokers of varied expertise and resource—known colloquially among the migrant community of the Americas as *coyotes* or *polleros*. Coyotes generate business on the basis of referrals from former customers who attest to their reputation.

Human smuggling is depicted within contemporary, official narratives of irregular migration as an inherently violent and exploitative activity. Its tragic nature is almost always highlighted in the aftermath of extraordinary tragedies involving mass casualties of vulnerable migrants (e.g., the deaths of thousands of migrants in transit in the Mediterranean in the context of the so-called "Migration Crisis" in Europe have been largely attributed to smugglers). The effectiveness of the smuggling-as-heinous narrative is dependent upon the simultaneous mobilization of three fundamental notions: that migrants and asylum seekers are naïve, ignorant and susceptible to manipulation; that human smugglers take advantage of this vulnerability; and that the flows facilitated by the latter pose grave risks to the security of the nation-state (see Agustin 2014; Weber and Grewcock 2011). All three notions combined obscure the role of the state in creating the very conditions in which these journeys take place, as well as the enforcement mechanisms that compel those on the move into situations of high risk, furthering and justifying immigration criminalization processes (Pickering 2001, 2004).

The levels of vulnerability and risk endured by migrants and asylum seekers in the context of extra-legal journeys cannot be denied—thousands of people die or go missing during their transits, many in fact as a result of their interactions with smuggling facilitators. Yet it is important to emphasize how the rhetoric characterizing the hyper-visible field[2] of human smuggling–related tragedies often obscures the fact that those who rely on extra-legal mobility mechanisms do so in an attempt to reduce the occurrence of risk and injury in their journeys. The focus on narratives of catastrophe reduces the likelihood not only that the efforts of those hurt while trying to reach safety will be acknowledged, but also that the lives of those who perish in transit will be accounted for (Weber and Pickering 2011). It also renders invisible the collective efforts involving extended groups of families and friends to provide, despite the structural limitations that surround them, layers of protection from afar—a form of multi-site, transnational care.[3]

The families of migrants and asylum seekers in transit play a key role in securing extra-legal border crossings—which include smuggling services. Most often it is family members who provide the finance and contacts that allow these journeys to occur (Ayalew 2016). Yet families have most often been ignored by a migration scholarship largely concerned with the transnational experiences of the individual migrant (evidenced by the abundant academic output on migrant labour, remittances, transnational parenting and political involvement).[4] This chapter reflects, therefore, on the role of the family in securing successful smuggling services for its members amid the precarity of the latter's extra-legal status. It shows how families, far from being absent or uninvolved, are active participants in the identification of smuggling facilitators as a means to protect family members at a time of increased vulnerability and uncertainty.

The Organization of Human Smuggling

Contrary to state and media representations of it as a highly elaborate process, reliant on complex transnational networks operating with surgical precision across continents and yielding multibillion dollar profits (Aronowitz 2001; UNODC 2010; Shelley 2010), human smuggling is a jumbled, imprecise and rudimentary, if often successful, activity. It is dependent upon the flexibility and availability of its facilitators, who are loosely organized in groups of friends, families and acquaintances spanning across vast distances and who rely on their immediately accessible social capital and other available resources to facilitate extra-legal transits.

Smuggling relies on a labour force often available within communities along the migrant trail who take advantage of opportunities to generate supplemental income through their participation in activities that, while criminalized by the state, are not perceived by their actors as criminal in nature (Coutin 2005; Galemba 2012; Venkatesh 2006). Smugglers are both men and women, and often migrants, refugees and asylum seekers in transit themselves (Sanchez 2015; Achilli 2015). Some become involved in smuggling while trying to finance segments of their own journeys (Van Hear 2004). Others are employed or underemployed in the local mainstream economy and use their participation in smuggling as a means to supplement their income (Sanchez 2015; Zhang 2008). Smuggling is highly gendered. The tasks most often associated with the practice (the actual transportation of migrants and asylum seekers) are typically facilitated by men (van Liempt 2007; Sanchez 2015). Women are often in charge of meal preparation, childcare, and janitorial or cleaning duties (Zhang et al. 2007), although they also coordinate journeys, recruit clients and often troubleshoot transits (Sanchez 2016).

Smuggling facilitators tend to perform one task at a time (Zhang 2008; Sanchez 2015). Some facilitators only provide driving services, while others focus on financial transactions like cashing money wires or withdrawing deposits, and recruiters identify likely travellers. Most facilitators work independently, and so hierarchies or vertical structures conducive of leadership are unnecessary (Zhang 2008; Sanchez 2015). Interactions with other illicit or underground markets like drug trafficking or prostitution vary in nature and scope from accidental to quasi-symbiotic (Zhang 2008; Lopez-Castro 1998; Sanchez and Zhang forthcoming)

The ability to work in an illicit activity such as smuggling (devoid of the stigma of drug trafficking or sex work) often redeems and dignifies its facilitators. Participation in human smuggling grants significant social recognition, often restoring the confidence and self-respect of its actors—most often members of highly marginalized communities. Smuggling collaborations strengthen community ties and create reputations that translate not only into additional business, but also long-lasting ties of friendship and trust.

From an organizational stance, the success of smuggling activities depends primarily on an individual's immediate access to social connections and resources (Zhang 2008) that, when combined with those of other friends and families, can enable the facilitation of a successful transit for a traveller. In other words, it is the personal ties of local individuals along the migrant trail—rather than hierarchical networks of dark repute—which are best positioned to place a migrant or asylum seeker on a path to safety (Khoser 2008; Zhang 2008; Khosravi 2010).

The resources mobilized by smugglers are often rather simple and include access to a vehicle; the ability to drive; possession of a valid driver's licence, border-crossing permit or birth certificate; being the renter or owner of a dwelling; knowing other family members or friends in nearby or distant cities; and owning a bank account. It is easier to mobilize resources and relationships among friends and relatives than among strangers when it comes to facilitating the transits of those seeking to travel extra-legally (Khosravi 2010).

Most often the process leading to a journey is initiated by an aspiring traveller who approaches a specific individual known to facilitate transits or connections to such travel, and expresses a willingness (or need) to travel (Khosravi 2010). As previously mentioned, human smuggling is, first and foremost, a referral-based business. Smugglers are most often recommended by trusted clients who have successfully completed a journey under their guidance or support, or whose transits were, if not ultimately successful, at least safe (Spener 2009; Zhang 2008; Khoser 2008). Contrary to depictions of migrants and asylum seekers hiring unknown smugglers, aspiring travellers and their friends and family members may often travel with known facilitators, having conducted extensive research on their reputation, and having agreed on the price and services to be provided for the smuggling fee (Spener 2009).

Smuggling and Entrapment on the Border

In the case of US-bound irregular migration from Mexico, those seeking to cross the border irregularly often travel on their own to a crossing point on the US–Mexico border following instructions from a coordinator.

Once the traveller is on the border, another contact provides them with room and board up until the time of the crossing. With the assistance of a guide, and depending on the amount paid (there is a wide range of smuggling services dependent on price), the traveller embarks on a journey through sections of the US–Mexico border (which include deserts, mountainous regions, swamps, rivers and urban clusters), usually on foot or by vehicle, or a combination of the two[5], to a specific meeting or drop-off point. Here, the traveller can be picked up by friends, family members or secure transportation, often upon the payment of additional fees, to journey to other locations in the USA. Fees are typically due once the traveller's arrival at a prearranged destination is verified through a call or in person, thus reducing the likelihood of scams. Payments are usually made via wire transfer services like Western Union and Money Gram.

It would be amiss to depict interactions between smuggling facilitators and their clients as merely transactional or uneventful collaborations. Some smuggling facilitators do take advantage of the vulnerability of their clients (de Haas 2015), and reports of practices ranging from fraud to threats of physical abuse, extortion, kidnapping, sexual violence and murder have been well documented globally. On the US–Mexico border, multiple researchers and activists have also collected testimonies involving cases of migrants abandoned by smugglers when unable to keep up due to illness or injury (O'Leary 2009); robbed at gunpoint by gangs, the military or members of other criminal organizations like drug trafficking groups (Martinez et al. 2013); or kidnapped (Slack 2015). While violence is often present in smuggling, it does not occur in a vacuum. Yet the focus on smuggler-initiated violence obscures the continuum of victimization and entrapment present in migration control regimes along the US–Mexico border—which compel migrants to rely on smuggling facilitators.

In the 2000s, having become the main point of entry for undocumented migrants into the country, the US Southwest became the ground zero of US immigration control. Anecdotal claims of an exponential increase in the number of migrants robbed and kidnapped by smugglers and robbers led to the passage of the Coyote Law—a piece of state legislation crafted by the state of Arizona legislators to prosecute smugglers found to engage in the victimization of migrants. However, the law was used instead to prosecute undocumented migrants with conspiring to commit their own human smuggling. While the law was eventually found to be unconstitutional, it led to the convictions of at least 1000 irregular migrants (Billeaud and Kitell 2014). Alongside the criminalization of smuggling, throughout the USA the signing of agreements between US Immigration and Customs Enforcement and local law enforcement agencies allowed the latter to enforce immigration law (ICE 2014). Employment verification raids and checkpoints in predominantly migrant neighbourhoods and businesses further generated widespread fear and anxiety throughout the region (Provine and Sanchez 2011).

Despite the level and intensity of immigration enforcement, irregular border crossings did not diminish, as evidenced by the number of arrests reported by US CBP. In fact, during this time the local smuggling market became stronger as facilitators rushed to provide their services to help migrants avoid the intensive level of policing and surveillance along the border (Sanchez 2014). Smugglers' services allowed migrants and their families to avoid forms of state entrapment, as well as risks that, in the course of their journeys, could compromise their physical well-being. While smugglers have often been blamed for placing their clients in situations of immense risk, demand for their services along the US–Mexico border has remained constant despite the risks posed by the desert landscape environs and the potential consequences of detection and arrest at the hands of immigration authorities (Hagan 2008; Izcara-Palacios 2012b). And so amid the criminalization of irregular migration by the state, the heightened risks posed by the environment and the potential for interactions with criminal groups, smuggling is often described by migrants as a much sought-after form of security for those travelling irregularly.

Nora, Olga and Teresa

I first met Nora in the parking lot of a shopping centre about 300 kilometres from the US border with Mexico, as she waited for Olga and Teresa, her two young daughters. The girls—at the time 8 and 10 years old, respectively—were about to be delivered by a coyote who had crossed them from

Mexico into the USA a couple of hours earlier with the use of two authentic birth certificates. The girls were on their way to reunite with their mother, whom they had not seen in over three years. When I asked Nora if the persons in charge of crossing her daughters were trustworthy, she explained the process she went through in deciding whom to hire and trust:

> [My husband and I] wanted to bring the girls for a long time. But when I crossed the border [I did it] on foot. We walked for almost an entire month and I knew I did not want for my girls to come that way. So I started to ask around, but nobody would cross children. I was told it was too risky. Finally, a lady from work told me she knew of a guy who did, and I contacted him. I told him I was concerned about my girls' safety, that I did not want for them to walk through the desert or to suffer. And he said, 'No ma'am, we don't cross children through the desert, we would never do that.' Instead, the man said, his contacts would get the girls through the checkpoint and would then drive them all the way to my home.

But Nora's concerns did not end there. The crossing was taking place in a period of heightened surveillance along the US–Mexico border. Her daughters were to be dropped in a location known for the systematic execution of immigration raids and inspections targeting people suspected of being in the country undocumented. Local sheriffs were also known to patrol local highways, often stopping drivers suspected of being undocumented on the basis of their attire, music tastes, or car model or make (Provine and Sanchez 2011; Romero 2006). Even under those circumstances, Nora opted to drive into the city in the company of her father's girlfriend, a black woman from Puerto Rico, considering that, by virtue of her appearance, the latter would not be questioned:

> But I decided to come get [the girls], despite all the rumours that the sheriffs here are mean and arrest Mexicans. I asked my dad's girlfriend to come with me. We drove for 11 hours, taking turns, and here we are.

I asked Nora whether she was aware that, in addition to local law enforcement assuming de facto immigration roles, attacks against migrants in transit by robbers were allegedly on the rise. Her response was a testimony of the steps she had taken to ensure that her children would be safe, despite the conditions they faced:

> My mother accompanied the girls all the way from our hometown in Mexico to the border. Once she got there she went at the hotel [where she was to be contacted by the guides], and two men came at different times asking for the girls. My mother called to let me know and I called the first coyote, who gave me a code word the men who were supposed to cross the girls would use so that I knew they were the real thing. We did not want for the girls to end up in the wrong group or in the wrong hands. The men crossed the girls one at a time through the border checkpoint as my mother watched nearby. My babies made it through the checkpoint in less than 15 minutes, got in a car with a couple who drove them, and they are now on their way here. I have been checking up on them by cell phone; they have been saying that they are OK and the coyote driving them said they will be here soon.

Olga and Teresa's journey was far from Nora's first experience of border crossings. Three years earlier, Nora herself had crossed the border with the help of a coyote whose contacts had transported her sister Josefina and her father from their hometown in Mexico into the USA.

To call Nora's border-crossing experience chaotic would be an understatement. She laughed as she recalled the 23 days of her journey, describing the multiple mishaps she encountered simply as 'unfortunate': 'I just had bad luck. Can you imagine? My girls got to the border and crossed the following morning. A few more days and it would have taken me a month.'

While Josefina had done everything possible to ensure the safety of her sister (such as arranging contacts, securing money for the journey and additional expenses, and providing cell phones), a series of miscommunications resulted in Nora and her husband being abandoned repeatedly at isolated locations. On one occasion, they were found by immigration officers and placed into custody—fortunately, they were released shortly after without being fingerprinted. On another occasion, they were robbed by a group of young gang members. And once, having run out of food after waiting for four days in the desert to be picked up, Nora and the other women in her group (a total of six) retraced their steps to Mexico to demand to be reassigned to a reliable smuggling guide. Led by a new team of coyotes (which included a young child), Nora, her husband and four other people (including a pregnant woman) finally made it across the border and to their destination.

The entire experience—followed by her husband's three-month hospitalization as a result of a parasitic infection acquired from drinking contaminated water in the desert—led Nora to become extremely cautious in planning to bring her daughters from Mexico with the help of smugglers. Finding a smuggler who transported children proved difficult. As she discovered, smugglers take additional precautions when transporting individuals whose health or well-being may be compromised, some asking travellers to postpone their journeys until their conditions have improved, or even refusing to transport specific kinds of migrants (Hagan 2008; Sanchez 2015, 2016). Nora was able to locate a group who specialized in the transportation of children, yet their prices were not low.

Specialized journeys—often providing for the comfort of migrants who are particularly vulnerable or in need of special care, like children, the elderly and pregnant women—involve the use of special routes, vehicles, legitimate documents or personal connections, and therefore command higher fees. Yet such costs are translated into greatly improved travel conditions, like shorter travel times and limited environmental exposure, significantly reducing physical risks (Hagan 2008; Sanchez 2015). Once she checked the smuggler's references and met with him herself, Nora decided to hire him to transport her daughters. At that time, the fee per child was twice that for an adult. Yet the price and the terms of the agreement gave her peace of mind and fortunately led to her safe reunification with her children. Nora paid for her children's fees through savings, pawning jewellery and her salary as a janitor. Working alongside her husband an average of 100 hours per week combined, it was only a matter of months before they paid off the debt they had incurred to cover their children's transit fees.

Ramón, 'La Lady' and David

In early 2015, Nora came home from work on a Wednesday night and found Lupe—her tenant—and his friend Mario in the kitchen. Mario had been smuggled two days ago and was sharing the details of his journey. Nora laughed. 'There's no way you could have crossed that fast,' she said. 'Seriously, *Doña*,' Mario said. 'This woman, *La Lady*, she is crossing people very fast.'

Nora immediately called her brother Ramón in Mexico: '*Gordo*, would you like to try again? There is a woman who is crossing people real fast.' Having already attempted to cross the border twice, unsuccessfully, Ramón replied: 'It takes a lot of money, sister.' Nora replied: 'That is not a problem. I have David's [her husband's] truck's title and I will go pawn it and get the money to bring you if you want to come.' Ramón said yes and Nora immediately began planning the journey. She recalled:

> I called my sister and asked her to get Ramón a plane ticket to the border. She asked, 'For when?' And I said: 'For tonight.' My mom barely had time to go give Ramón her blessing, and he was on his way to the border a couple of hours later. He arrived to the Mexican side of the border on Thursday, and on Friday morning Ramón texted: 'The smuggler got us through right next to the river.'

But then the following message Nora received did not contain very good news. Ramón reported: 'I think *La Migra*[6] saw us.' *La Lady*—who had guided the men with a cell phone—had managed to get Ramón and four other young men across, but the group was now stuck and in sight of a US CBP vehicle. Ramón and his companions waited for about three hours for the vehicle to move, with no luck.

For several hours Nora was unaware of Ramón's whereabouts. Drawing from her own experiences, she feared Ramón had been arrested or even robbed. Nora finally decided to call *La Lady*: 'I called her to find out what was going on. She said my brother had already crossed and then she asked for a portion of the fee.'

Nora hesitated. She had already lost a considerable amount of money financing Ramón's prior journeys. The first time he had been able to cross but became separated from his girlfriend during transit by accident. The young woman, who like Ramón was also a minor at the time, was held by US CBP and later released to Mexican authorities, who placed her in foster care until a family member claimed her. Broken hearted, Ramón decided not to stay in the USA. More recently, he had attempted to cross with a woman who worked as a smuggler but who cashed his smuggling fee without providing the service. 'That old bitch kept my money,' Nora said. 'She said the fee was good for 90 days and that Ramón could continue trying his luck with her but why would he want to wait that long? He just decided to go back home.'

That was all in the past. That night, Ramón *could* already be on US territory, and *La Lady* would not allow him to continue without payment. 'And so I figured that if I didn't pay she would not let him through, so I sent in the money—US$1500. I took that chance.'

The reference to 'chance' depicts how risk is managed and understood by the families of irregular migrants in transit. Lack of payment could result in a migrant being abandoned in a remote location where help would be hard to come by (O'Leary 2009); simultaneously, being abandoned could also increase the risk of being detained by the immigration authorities and fingerprinted—an outcome that migrants attempt to avoid at all costs, since having a record of immigration detentions can lead to incarceration terms for illegal entry (Nuñez and Heyman 2007).

Success!

The final text message from Ramón came a few hours later. It only said 'I made it.' Despite them being in close proximity to a vehicle from CBP, *La Lady* had managed to pick up Ramón's group, and drove them to her home on the American side of the border. Here, a driver from an American parcel company picked up the group of four men and transported them to a location 250 kilometres north-east of the border, where they were greeted by their families. 'We even went through a checkpoint, but I guess nobody suspected the driver,' said Ramón. '*La Lady* said I could wait and stay at her home for the next driver going north if I wanted, but that would have taken another 10 days, so I just left with the rest of the guys.' David, Nora's husband, was commissioned to drive to pick up Ramón, and asked Nora to wire Ramón some money so that he could spend the night at a hotel while he waited for David to arrive. Yet one of the young men in the group was travelling in the same direction of Nora's city, and offered Ramón a ride: 'He told me, you can come with me and my family. You can stay with us while your brother-in-law comes to get you.' Less than a day after his crossing, Ramón was already 716 kilometres north of the border, waiting to be picked up by David.

Nora explained: 'As I understood the people who offered my brother a ride were not *really* the guy's family … I guess the guy just helped him because they were from the same town. Later on we heard that the man sells mobile homes and that he let Ramón stay in one while he waited for David.' Nora told Ramón that she would wire him US$100 to compensate the man 'for the inconveniences of keeping [him] there.' Ramón laughed and replied dismissively: 'Forget that, he was the one who gave me US$100 for my expenses.'

Ramón's journey was not devoid of moments of vulnerability and risk. Nora had to pawn the only valuable property her family owned in order to secure the services of a smuggler. Yet the transit, the result of impromptu referrals and negotiations, had been successful and Ramón was on his way home to his sister. Despite concerns over the potential for the smuggler to keep the fee without delivering the service, in the end she provided a safe transit, relying on her local connections. Furthermore, the sense of solidarity and camaraderie that emerged among the people in the group allowed Ramón to join his family at a location distant from the border, where they would have been likely to encounter checkpoints or face inquiries into their immigration status (Nora and David are, to this date, as are their two daughters and Ramón, irregular migrants). But the sharing of contacts and resources among friends and family members, past border-crossing experiences, the market obligations that led the smuggler to provide her services effectively, and the solidarity that emerged among those travelling, all created the mechanisms that allowed Ramón to safely travel and join his family 2200 kilometres away from the point on the border where he initially crossed—his journey exemplifying how migrants rely on one another to bear the uncertainty of their journeys (Hagan 2008, p. 131).

Conclusion

David calls from the road. He is halfway through the journey to pick up Ramón. He rented a brand-new vehicle to avoid being profiled and had to take a longer route to avoid a checkpoint where he would have been questioned by police. While he has a valid driving permit he is always careful to avoid encounters with law enforcement where questions pertaining to his immigration status could arise. Nora asks him to stop and take a break, to which he replies: 'No, I want to get there and back fast. I do not want to take long. I've heard cops in that state are real sons of bitches. My coworkers said to stay below the speed limit. I will get there and Ramón can drive on the way back. I will be on my way back tomorrow.'

David's fears are warranted. While he was not stopped by police, he was aware—just like his wife a few years earlier when she picked up her children—of the tactics law enforcement relies upon in predominantly migrant communities in the USA to justify traffic stops. A cracked windshield. Failing to signal a turn. Even not making eye contact with an officer could render a driver suspicious. David, as many undocumented migrants, is careful of what he wears to avoid being read as undocumented. When preparing to pick up Ramón, he chose to wear a dressy shirt, nice jeans and dark glasses that made him, in the words of the neighbours and friends who have gathered to send him way, like a hipster. David's appearance generates friendly mockery, yet those around him know that 'passing' for someone who cannot be read as undocumented is key to avoid an encounter with law enforcement that could lead to an arrest or even deportation, which would have devastating consequences for David and his family.

Nora and David, through her low wages, have financed the crossings of three of their family members. Despite the mechanisms deployed by the state to restrict irregular migratory flows, the incessant patrolling of migrant communities, the checkpoints, and the cutting off of access to highways and public places, undocumented migrants continue to find ways to circumvent and overcome controls to their mobility through their reliance on smuggling services. But the common depiction of smuggling journeys as inherently criminal by law enforcement, policy makers and scholars—often centred on the most tragic of migrant journeys—masks the efforts of people like Nora, David, and the friends and families who supported the journeys of Olga, Teresa and Ramón. It would be naïve to claim that all irregular journeys are as successful and uneventful as those described here—every year thousands of people die while crossing deserts and oceans, in immigration detention facilities, in unreported accidents and as a result of violent crimes, while many more go missing, unable to escape the traps of the state. Yet risk-taking acts like smuggling journeys which are effective at overcoming efforts to control mobility often strengthen social ties and infuse them with 'a particularly compelling moral character' (Nuñez and Heyman 2007, p. 360).

Nora considered Ramón's crossings a success. In her view, the service was fast, safe and, in a sense, reasonably priced at US$5000. Nora and Ramón's relatives were thrilled by the speediness of the crossing, and urged Nora to quickly get Ramón a job so that he could start paying off the fee she had paid. 'There is in fact a lot of work cleaning offices right now,' Nora stated. 'But Valentine's Day is around the corner and I need him to help us first with our rose stand. We are driving to Los Angeles next weekend, and we already have the permits from the city to sell at the corner by the house. After Valentine's he can start working. I need him to help me with the stand until then.' When asked about the money invested and lost in Ramón's crossings, Nora stated: 'This time was as if we had recovered the losses from the first two times. [The journey] was fast, and he did not get arrested.' Ramón, using less calculating terms when asked what went through his mind as he crossed, laughs and says: 'Well, this time I thought … if [immigration] sees me and starts to chase me, I will tell them, with all due respect Mr. Officers, fuck you! This time I'm going to cross!'

Notes

1. 'Fat Boy.'
2. Fonow and Cook (2005) warn researchers of the perils of conducting work in fields of study that are hyper-represented, as is the case for smuggling. By focusing on the roles played by family members in securing smuggling services, my goal is to open the discursive field of smuggling dominated by the monolithic, simplistic narratives that focus on exploitation and violence as inherent elements of irregular migration journeys, to describe instead its community roots and connections.
3. Here I echo Parrenas' definition of care as 'the labor and resources needed to ensure the mental, emotional and physical well-being of the individual,' coordinating care and protection 'from great geographical distances' (12–13).

4. As Ahmad expresses with disappointment, discussions on smuggling often rely upon one-dimensional portraits of migrant and refugee journeys as solely dictated by economic need (2011, pp. 6–7).
5. A commonly purchased crossing service along the US–Mexico border involves a trek lasting from a few hours to several days, followed by consecutive segments traversed by car to a prearranged location.
6. US CBP.

References

Achilli, L. (2015). *The smuggler: Hero or felon?* (Migration Policy Centre Policy Brief). Florence: European University Institute.

Agustin, L. (2014). Somaly Mam, Nick Kristof, and the cult of personality. *Jacobin*. New York, June Edition.

Ahmad, A. N. (2011). *Masculinity, sexuality, and illegal migration: Human smuggling from Pakistan to Europe*. Routledge: Ashgate Publishing.

Andreas, P. (2001). Migrant smuggling across the US–Mexican border. In D. Kyle & R. Koslowski (Eds.), *Global human smuggling: Comparative perspectives*. Baltimore: Johns Hopkins University Press.

Aronowitz, A. (2001). Smuggling and trafficking in human beings: The phenomenon, the markets that drive it and the organizations that promote it. *European Journal on Criminal Policy and Research, 9*, 163–195.

Ayalew, T. (2016). The struggle of mobility: Organizing high risk migration from the Horn of Africa. *Beyond Trafficking and Slavery*, 8 April 2016, viewed 16 December 2016. https://www.opendemocracy.net/beyondslavery/hsr/tekalign-ayalew-mengiste/struggle-of-mobility-organising-high-risk-migration-from-horn

Billeaud, J., & Kitell, L. (2014). Arizona county to drop appeal in illegal immigrant smuggling case. *Associated Press*, 31 July 2014, KGUN9.

Coutin, S. (2005). Contesting criminality: Illegal immigration and the spatialization of illegality. *Theoretical Criminology, 9*(1), 5–33.

De Haas, H. (2015). *Don't blame the smugglers: The real migration industry*, 23 September. Available at: http://heindehaas.blogspot.com/2015/09/dont-blame-smugglers-real-migration.html

Fonow, M., & Cook, J. (2005). Feminist methodology: New applications in the academy and public policy. *Signs, 30*(4), 2211–2236.

Galemba, R. (2012). Taking contraband seriously: Practicing "legitimate work" at the Mexico–Guatemala border. *Anthropology of Work Review, 33*, 3–14.

Hagan, J. M. (2008). *Migration miracle: Faith, hope and meaning of the undocumented journey*. Connecticut: Harvard University Press.

Immigration and Customs Enforcement (ICE). (2014). *ICE287(g) program removal statistics for FY2012. Request under freedom of information act 2014FOIA2760.* https://muckrock.s3.amazonaws.com/foia_files/2-25-14_MR8942_RES_ID2014FOIA2760.pdf. Accessed 2 Jan 2016.

International Organization for Migration (IOM). (2016). *Missing migrants project: Latest global figures of migrant fatalities worldwide*, viewed 16 December 2016. https://missingmigrants.iom.int/latest-global-figures

Izcara-Palacios, S. P. (2012a). Coyotaje y grupos delictivos en Tamaulipas. *Latin American Research Review, 47*, 41–61.

Izcara-Palacios, S. P. (2012b). Opinión de los polleros tamaulipecos sobre la política migratoria estadounidense. *Migraciones Internacionales, 6*, 173–204.

Khoser, K. (2008). Why migrant smuggling pays. *Journal of International Migration, 46*(2), 3–26.

Khosravi, S. (2010). *'Illegal' traveller: An autoethnography of borders*. London: Palgrave Macmillan.

Lopez-Castro, G. (1998). Coyotes and alien smuggling. In *Migration between Mexico and the United States: Binational study, research reports and background materials* (Vol. 3). Washington, DC: Mexican Ministry of Foreign Affairs and the US Commission on Immigration Reform.

Martinez, D., Reineke, R., Rubio-Goldsmith, R., Anderson, B., Hess, G., & Parks, B. (2013). *A continued humanitarian crisis on the border: Undocumented border crosser deaths recorded by the Pima county office of the medical examiner, 1990–2012*. Tucson: The Binational Migration Institute, University of Arizona.

Nuñez, G., & Heyman, J. (2007). Entrapment processes and immigrant communities in a time of heightened border vigilance. *Human Organization, 66*(4), 354–365.

O'Leary, A. (2009). The ABCs of migration costs: Assembling, bajadores and coyotes. *Migration Letters, 6*(1), 27–35.

Parrenas, R. (2005). *Children of global migration: Transnational families and gendered woes*. Stanford: Stanford University Press.

Pew Research Center. (2012). In J. Passel, J. D'Vera Cohn, & A. Gonzalez Barrera (Eds.), *Net migration from Mexico falls to zero – And perhaps less*. Washington, DC: Pew Research Center.

Pickering, S. (2001). Common sense and original deviancy: News discourses and asylum seekers in Australia. *Journal of Refugee Studies, 14*(2), 169–186.

Pickering, S. (2004). The production of sovereignty and the rise of transversal policing: People-smuggling and federal policing. *ANZ Journal of Criminology, 37*(3), 362–379.

Provine, M., & Sanchez, G. (2011). Suspecting immigrants: Exploring links between racialized anxieties and expanded police powers in Arizona. *Policing and Society, 21*(4), 468–479.

Romero, M. (2006). Racial profiling and immigration law enforcement: Rounding up of usual suspects in the Latino community. *Critical Sociology, 32*(2–3), 449–475.

Sanchez, G. (2015). *Human smuggling and border crossings*. London: Routledge.

Sanchez, G. (2016). 'Women as human smugglers in the US Southwest', Manwaring, C. and Bridgen, N. (eds), Special Issue: Beyond the Border: Clandestine Migration Journeys, *Geopolitics, 21*(2), 387–406.

Sanchez, G., & Zhang, S. (forthcoming). Casual encounters? Changing market conditions and organizational responses among smugglers of migrants and drugs, Special issue on human smuggling. *Annals of the American Academy of Political and Social Sciences*.

Scott, J. (1985). *Weapons of the weak: Everyday forms of peasant resistance*. New Haven: Yale University Press.

Shelley, L. (2010). *Human trafficking: A global perspective*. New York: Cambridge University Press.

Slack, J. (2015). *Captive bodies: Migrant kidnapping and deportation in Mexico*. London: AREA Magazine.

Spener, D. (2009). *Clandestine crossings: Migrants and coyotes on the Texas/Mexico border*. New York: Cornell University Press.

UNODC. (2010). *Issue paper: Organized crime involvement in trafficking of persons and smuggling of migrants*. Geneva: United Nations.

Van Hear, N. (2004). *I went as far as my money would take me: Conflict, forced migration and class* (Centre on Migration, Policy and Society Working Paper No. 6). Oxford: University of Oxford.

Van Liempt, I. (2007) *Navigating borders: Inside perspectives on the process of human smuggling into the Netherlands*. Amsterdam: University of Amsterdam Press.

Venkatesh, S. (2006). *Off the books: The underground economy of the urban poor*. Cambridge: Harvard University Press.

Weber, L., & Grewcock, M. (2011). Criminalising people smuggling: Preventing or globalizing harm? In F. Allum & S. Gilmour (Eds.), *The Routledge handbook of transnational organized crime* (pp. 379–390). London: Routledge.

Weber, L., & Pickering, S. (2011). *Globalization and borders: Death at the global frontier*. Hampshire: Palgrave Macmillan.

Zhang, S. X. (2008). *Chinese human smuggling organizations: Families, social networks, and cultural imperatives*. Stanford: Stanford University Press.

Zhang, S. X., Chin, K.-L., & Miller, J. (2007). Women's participation in Chinese transnational human smuggling: A gendered market perspective. *Criminology, 45*(3), 699–733.

7

Asylum Seekers and Strategic Litigation

Frances Webber

On 2 July 2015, then British Immigration Minister James Brokenshire announced the suspension of the 'detained fast track' for asylum seekers, a system of accelerated decision-making in which asylum seekers whose claims were deemed 'straightforward' (i.e., likely to be refused) were detained from the time they claimed asylum, through refusal (over 99 per cent of cases were refused) (Immigration Law Practitioners' Association 2008) and the appeal process, to removal. The detained fast track, in which speedy disposal was the main aim, had been a target for political and legal campaigning for a decade and a half because of its grotesque unfairness. Its suspension followed a series of test cases brought by campaigning and support group Detention Action[1] on behalf of vulnerable detained asylum seekers, which challenged the impossibly tight timeframes for the preparation of claims and appeals and the failure of safeguards designed to prevent the detention of torture and trafficking survivors. At the time, it represented a victory—albeit provisional and partial—for the asylum seekers, detainee support groups and lawyers whose coordinated efforts

F. Webber (✉)
Institute of Race Relations, London, UK

F. Vecchio, A. Gerard (eds.), *Entrapping Asylum Seekers*, Transnational Crime, Crime Control and Security, DOI 10.1057/978-1-137-58739-8_7

brought it about. But a year on, similar numbers of asylum seekers are detained throughout the asylum process, and much of what was won through the litigation has evaporated.

The process of bringing these test cases illustrates both the growing significance of strategic litigation brought by or involving asylum seekers and migrants in securing and defending their rights, and the often temporary and fleeting nature of gains in the absence of a strong popular movement. In this chapter, after a brief survey of migrant organizing and the way legal challenges are brought, I describe migrants' struggles in the UK which have involved test case litigation in the fields of asylum support, detention, the treatment of women asylum seekers, removal and the use of force, before turning to consider the ways in which the government has fought back against this use of test case litigation with policy changes that emphasize executive discretion, and legislation that makes access to the courts more difficult and more expensive.

Self-Organizing, Getting Involved in Campaigns

There is a long history of organization among migrants in the UK. The celebrated strike at Grunwicks film processing laboratory in 1976, which attracted the support of the mighty National Union of Miners, was organized by South Asian women and, like the strikes of Asian workers at Imperial Typewriters in Leicester in 1974, and at Woolfs in Southall in 1965–6, received strong community support (see 'From resistance to rebellion: Asian and Afro-Caribbean struggles in Britain', in Sivanandan 2008). In these early days of mass migration to the UK, those involved in organizing, whether at the workplace or against police harassment, educational exclusion or discrimination in housing, were British or Commonwealth citizens with settlement rights in the UK and an entitlement to work. This settled status, together with the lingua franca of English and the fact that migration tended to involve large numbers from the same areas of (for example) the Punjab or the Caribbean settling in the same neighbourhoods, gave those organizing against exploitation or injustice advantages denied to the disparate, multilingual and precarious groups of asylum seekers and undocumented migrants who came from all over the world from the 1980s onward (for examples of these early struggles, see Campaign Against Racism and Fascism/Southall Rights 1981; Sivanandan 1990; Newham Monitoring Project/CARF 1991).

The nature of the struggles of these later groups has of necessity been different. For asylum seekers and undocumented migrants, work is necessarily illegal and clandestine. Undocumented workers are, by definition, disposable. The precarious immigration status of asylum seekers and undocumented migrants has generally dictated the struggles they have fought: around the enforced destitution of asylum seekers, immigration detention and forcible, sometimes brutal, removal. Workplace rights cannot be fought for without the security of legal status.

Ironically, it is thanks in part to New Labour's draconian and hugely unpopular policy of compulsory dispersal of asylum seekers from 1998 onwards, enforced by the withdrawal of asylum support for those who do not stay where they are placed, that significant communities of asylum seekers and refugees now exist throughout the UK. New communities organize for mutual support and solidarity, practical help for new arrivals and around particular issues. The Regional Refugee Forum North East, for example, covering the Tyneside and Teeside region of England, has 45 refugee-led member groups, and previously had another 50 such groups which are no longer active, as new communities have settled or returned home as it has become safe to do so. Refugee Voice Wales brings together another 39 refugee-led community organizations. Groups cohere around members' continent or country of origin (African Refugee Association, Latin American Community Association, Ethiopian Community Association, Zimbabwe Association), around ethnicity or minority status (Tamil Refugee Action Group, Kurdish Community, Roma Rights), around gender (African Women's Group, Sisters Together, Mamas Rise Up), age (Young People's Sports Group, Youth Ahead), language (Notre Voix, Communidad Hispano-Americana de Pennywell en Sunderland), geography (Gloucester Association for Refugees and Asylum Seekers) or a mixture of these (Roma North East, Tees Valley Women's Voice).

Local women's refugee and asylum seeker groups based on nationality come together through organizations such as Women Asylum Seekers

Together (WAST) in London and Manchester, and the London Refugee Women's Forum, which campaigns on issues such as the destitution facing refused asylum seekers. The latter group started as a project of the Movement for Change, which works on a variety of issues including housing and living conditions for the UK's poor communities, and this means that links of solidarity are formed with local communities, undermining government attempts to keep asylum seekers and refugees separate, segregated and apart—the classic strategy of divide and rule. WAST is linked with the solidarity group Women for Refugee Women.

There are also local support, activist and campaigning groups all over the country with which asylum seekers get involved. Solidarity and campaign groups exist wherever there are immigration or asylum detainees: the volunteers of Oxford's Asylum Welcome visit detainees in the local Campsfield Immigration Removal Centre (IRC), and Yarl's Wood Befrienders do the same in Bedfordshire's Yarl's Wood IRC. The Campaign to Close Campsfield has held monthly pickets of the centre since it opened over 20 years ago. The Movement for Justice also regularly pickets IRCs. Detainee support groups form a network under the umbrella organization Detention Forum, an advocacy and campaigning coalition with over 35 member organizations. Networks like this ensure that information about a death in immigration detention, a hunger strike or a new report is quickly disseminated. The national campaigning group Still Human Still Here brings together over 60 organizations and local councils campaigning against and seeking to counter the destitution of refused asylum seekers.

Solidarity links are particularly important in anti-deportation campaigns. As then Labour Home Secretary David Blunkett explained in 2002, the rationale of his plan to segregate 3000 asylum seekers in four huge accommodation centres in remote areas, with onsite health and education provision, was that it was necessary to facilitate the removal of asylum seekers once refused—a process that was 'almost impossible' once children were integrated in local schools.[2] Local 'no borders' and anti-deportation groups, like the Sheffield Campaign to Defend Asylum Seekers, campaign to prevent the deportation of refused asylum seekers in the area and to have their cases reopened. A National Coalition of Anti-Deportation Campaigns (NCADC) existed for decades, recently changing its name to Right to Remain, which performs a similar function. Refugee and Migrant Forum of Essex and London (RAMFEL) runs campaigns against immigration policing of local communities, and supported two members in a legal challenge against the Home Office's Operation Valken, involving a billboard van which in the summer of 2013 toured streets carrying the message 'Go Home, or face arrest!' targeted at undocumented migrants. RAMFEL argued that the operation had been launched without consultation and without regard to the impact on equality and community cohesion. Public anger ensured the premature end of the operation before the case came to court.

Migrants and asylum seekers frequently become involved with organizations that have helped them to secure status in the UK, working as volunteers to support newer arrivals. Once they are settled in the UK and can work, they may continue as paid staff members as well. Medical Justice, a charity and campaigning organization with many volunteer doctors and lawyers working on issues such as health care in detention, has an ex-detainees' committee which helps formulate policy and has formal input into reports, briefings and public speaking and outreach work. Detention Action (formerly the London Detainee Support Group), which helps detainees in Harmondsworth and Colnbrook IRCs and campaigns against immigration detention, has an associated group of ex-detainees, Freed Voices, ready to speak and write about their experiences to inform public debate.

Such groups work with a network of sympathetic lawyers, in private practice or law centres. Lawyers who take up immigration and asylum law tend to fall into two polarized camps: those who do it for the money, and those who do it from political or personal commitment. The second group spends a lot of time clearing up the messes left by the first—as I know from personal experience.[3] But support groups frequently have regular, tried-and-tested lawyers to whom they refer cases, often on a pro bono basis. Southall Black Sisters (SBS), an advice, campaigning and resource centre for black and minority women experiencing domestic or gender violence, works with specialist lawyers, as well as doctors or medical experts for documentation of injuries. Kalayaan does the same for migrant domestic workers who leave abusive employers.

Asylum seekers and migrants become involved in strategic litigation in a number of ways. Their own case might become a test case because it raises important legal issues. Their testimony might feature in a test case brought by their own organization or, more often (because of the costs involved in litigation by organizations), in a challenge brought by a national support or campaigning organization such as the Joint Council for the Welfare of Immigrants, Detention Action or Medical Justice. Or one of these organizations might intervene in an individual's case, relying on the testimony of their clients.

Judicial Review

Judicial review is a relatively quick and inexpensive way of challenging administrative decisions and checking executive abuse of power. So, for example, a detained asylum seeker would apply to the First Tier Tribunal (Immigration and Asylum Chamber) for bail, but would challenge the lawfulness of his or her detention by judicial review, in the High Court. Judicial review is used to challenge the lawfulness of ministerial decisions, regulations and policy, in accordance with tests of relevance, fairness, reasonableness, proportionality, compatibility with human rights obligations and compliance with ministerial powers.

Two aspects of judicial review have made it a useful tool for refugee, asylum seeker and detainee support and campaigning groups.[4] First, the rules on standing have been generous. It has not been necessary to be a 'victim' of an administrative decision, or to be directly and negatively affected by it, in order to bring a legal challenge against it; it has been enough to have 'a sufficient interest' (Senior Courts Act 1981, s 31[3]). The phrase 'sufficient interest' has been interpreted broadly, so as to enable pressure groups campaigning in the area to which the decision relates—such as immigration detention—to bring challenges. Additionally, interest groups have been able to intervene in cases brought by others. In addition to refugee support organizations, human rights group Liberty, housing charity Shelter and mental health charity Mind have intervened in cases involving asylum support, immigration detention and removal.

A second feature of the judicial review system that enables challenges by campaigning groups is the protective costs order. Higher court judges have had complete discretion in deciding how costs should be awarded, but the normal or default rule is that the loser pays the winner's legal costs as well as his or her own. If this rule were applied strictly in 'public interest' litigation, it would bankrupt activist or support groups, and prevent them from intervening to correct executive abuses of power in difficult areas. Protective costs orders are a judicial invention, first used in a case brought by the Child Poverty Action Group (*R v Lord Chancellor's Department ex parte Child Poverty Action Group* [1998] EWHC 151 (Admin); see also Havers, P. QC) against the Lord Chancellor, who was refusing to provide public funding in social security cases raising difficult issues of European law. They allow a judge to order, before the hearing of a case, that a losing party only pays his or her own costs, or at most, a capped contribution towards the winner's costs, provided that the issues raised by the case are of general public importance, it is in the public interest for the issues to be resolved, the applicant has no private interest in the outcome, the parties' respective financial resources make such an order fair and just, and without the order the applicant would not proceed with the challenge. Protective costs orders mean that support and activist groups can be confident at an early stage of litigation that, even if their challenge fails, the group will not be wiped out. Traditionally, lawyers taking cases on behalf of campaigning groups act pro bono, so the costs of litigation are kept to a minimum.

In 2011, immigration and asylum cases accounted for three-quarters of all judicial reviews brought—up from around half at the turn of the century (*Guardian* 2012). Most are individuals' cases brought to challenge imminent removal, and jurisdictional changes mean that most of these must now be heard in the Upper Tribunal rather than in the High Court.[5] The number of test cases brought by or with the involvement of support organizations is small, but they are hugely disproportionate in their effect. One of the early cases took on the enforced destitution of asylum seekers.

Challenges to Enforced Destitution

When asylum seekers began to arrive in Britain in large numbers, in the mid- to late 1980s, there were few rules governing their reception or support. Immigration control had always been exercised at the borders and, once you had arrived in the UK, as Lord Hoffmann observed, 'the welfare state did not look at your passport or ask why you were here … immigration status was a matter between you and the Home Office, not the concern of the social security system' (*Westminster City Council v National Asylum Support Service* [2002] UKHL 38 at para 19). By the early 1990s, things had changed somewhat, with those 'subject to immigration control' eligible only for 'urgent cases' payments,[6] 90 per cent of means-tested basic welfare benefits for the unemployed—but this basic benefit acted as a passport to other benefits such as housing benefit, which paid the rent. By the mid-1990s, the tabloid press, which plays the same role in the UK that a far right party might play in continental Europe, was regularly stirring up righteous anger at the 'hordes' of 'bogus refugees' and 'scroungers' allegedly pouring in to Britain to access welfare benefits (see, e.g., 'It cost £400 millions to keep 30,000 immigrants on social security' 1991; see also 'Racism and the press in Blair's Britain' 1999).

So in 1996, the (Conservative) government brought in regulations excluding from welfare benefits two groups of asylum seekers seen as particularly unworthy: those who failed to claim asylum on arrival in the UK, and those waiting to appeal against refusal of asylum. Before the regulations were brought in, the Social Security Advisory Committee took evidence from 250 organizations, including refugee organizations who explained that many genuine refugees did not claim at the airport for fear of immediate detention or deportation, and that, banned from working and with no other means of livelihood or support, they faced the bleak choice of starving, begging, stealing or abandoning their asylum claim or appeal. The Committee advised the minister not to proceed (Social Security Advisory Committee, *Report on Social Security (Persons from Abroad) (Miscellaneous Amendments) Regulations 1996*)—but he took no notice and the regulations came into force. Destitution was being used as a weapon against asylum seekers, to discourage them from coming and to force them to leave. But refugee communities, churches, temples and mosques took on the burden of support, opening night shelters and soup kitchens for the newly destitute.

The Joint Council for the Welfare of Immigrants (JCWI) decided to launch a test case against the regulations. The JCWI had been set up in 1967 by immigrants from the 'New Commonwealth' countries of the Caribbean and the Indian subcontinent, growing out of informal mutual help initiatives. Over the decades, in addition to campaigning for migrants' rights, it had become a major provider of legal help and advice for new migrants and refugees. Its challenge argued that the parent Act, the Social Security Act 1992, did not empower the minister to make the regulations. A Zairean asylum seeker, Ms B, refused access to any support because she claimed asylum at the Home Office on the day of her arrival rather than at the airport, participated in the test case, for which refugee organizations and support groups also provided evidence. The High Court rejected the challenge, but the Court of Appeal allowed the appeal by a 2:1 majority, with Lord Justice Simon Brown saying:

> A significant number of genuine asylum seekers now find themselves faced with a bleak choice: whether to remain here destitute and homeless until their claims are finally determined or whether instead to abandon their claims and return to face the very persecution they have fled. … Parliament cannot have intended a significant number of genuine asylum seekers to be impaled on the horns of so intolerable a dilemma. (*R v Minister for Social Security ex parte B, ex parte JCWI* [1997] 1 WLR 275)

This was a great victory for asylum seekers—although of short duration, since weeks later, the government pushed through primary legislation to achieve the same effect.[7] However, the networks and relationships between refugee organizations, asylum and migration support groups and lawyers were to endure beyond the case that forged them, to foster further significant legal challenges.

In 1999, the new Labour government removed rights to welfare benefits and social housing from non–European Union migrants, and instituted a new system of support for asylum seekers. Administered centrally by a new Home Office agency, the National Asylum Support Service, it provided destitute asylum seekers with no-choice housing, mainly away from London and the south-east, and assistance in the form of vouchers exchangeable for food in nominated supermarkets. The system combined strict control (support would be suspended or terminated for misconduct or absence without leave from the asylum hostel), enforced dependency, penury (the level of support was about two-thirds of the minimum needed to live on) and the degradation of having no cash and being publicly rebuked by supermarket cashiers for attempting to use vouchers for 'luxury items' like yogurt or shampoo. Trade unions joined refugee groups' political campaign to replace vouchers with cash, and the campaign succeeded. Cash replaced vouchers—but cashless support re-emerged for refused asylum seekers, and no campaign has abolished them.

In the harsh winter of 2003, new provisions once again removed all support from asylum seekers who failed to claim 'as soon as reasonably practicable' (defined by the Home Office as 'at the port', and by the courts as 'taking into account the practical opportunity and personal circumstances of the claimant, the earliest possible opportunity') (*R (Q) v SSHD* [2003] EWCA Civ 364, in which JCWI and Liberty intervened). By now, though, human rights were incorporated into UK law, requiring support to be provided to late claimants if denial would cause a breach of fundamental rights.[8] As asylum seekers queued round the block in the snow outside the Home Office, the mosques, temples and churches opened their doors once again, while lawyers formed rotas to deal with the flood of applications for injunctions ordering the Home Office to provide emergency accommodation. Battle was joined over the issue of the level of destitution a 'late-claiming' asylum seeker had to suffer to become eligible for support on human rights grounds. Support groups working with homeless, destitute and sick asylum seekers provided stark evidence of the effects of the new law. Three large national organizations—civil rights groups Liberty and Justice, and homelessness charity Shelter—joined in on the asylum seekers' side, intervening in a test case (*R (Adam, Limbuela and Tesema) v Secretary of State for the Home Department* [2005] UKHL 66) which, after a long battle ending in the House of Lords (the precursor of the Supreme Court) established that late-claiming asylum seekers had to be housed before they reached the level of utter destitution and street-homelessness, to avoid breaching the absolute ban on inhuman treatment. This was a vitally important ruling which not only secured material support for thousands in the UK at the time, but later helped to prevent the removal under the Dublin regulation[9] of asylum seekers to EU countries where they were likely to endure street-homelessness (see, e.g., *R (EM Eritrea) v Secretary of State for the Home Department* [2014] UKSC 12, Supreme Court).

Almost a decade after *Adam and Limbuela*, another important test case on asylum support was brought, this time by a large, Home Office–funded refugee charity, Refugee Action, which became involved in the campaign for decent levels of support through its work with destitute asylum seekers. The case was brought after the rate of support for asylum seekers was frozen for the third consecutive year in 2013, so that the support for a single adult was in real terms 26 per cent lower than that provided in 2007, and in some cases only half the basic subsistence-level benefit to which British citizens were entitled. The evidence from Refugee Action's own survey, and from two organizations working with survivors of torture, Freedom from Torture (FfT) and the Helen Bamber Foundation, demonstrated how food, warm clothes, sanitary products, cleaning materials, phone calls and travel had to be foregone by those seeking to live on the amounts provided. The judge concluded that the Home Secretary's decision to freeze support was irrational—specifically, the information on which it was based was insufficient for a rational decision—and so unlawful (*R (Refugee Action) v SSHD* [2014] EWHC 1033 [Admin]).

As with the *JCWI* case, however, the legal victory was temporary and insubstantial, and threw into sharp relief the limitations of judicial review, which cannot reverse decisions on their merits but can only demand that the decision-maker re-take the decision lawfully. The Home Secretary subverted the judgment by reaching the same conclusion on fuller information (see Gillett 2014). Since then, the amount provided for children has been slashed by a third, while the categories of refused asylum seekers that are eligible for continuing support have been severely restricted through legislation.

Once an asylum seeker's claim was refused and appeals exhausted, unless there were dependent children, all support was removed in most cases, causing enormous hardship for many: those wrongly refused asylum; others who could not return home, including (in the early 2000s) most Zimbabweans, Somalis and Iraqi Kurds; others still whose claims and appeals had not told the full story and wanted to present further evidence. A statutory provision for support for refused asylum seekers was extremely narrow in its terms, and a Home Office policy extending this support to a wider range of refused asylum seekers was unknown and unpublicized. It was only through litigation by a community law firm that the existence of the more generous policy became widely known, and the Home Office was rebuked for its failure to inform those who might be eligible for support.[10]

Legal challenges are most successful when they go hand in hand with political campaigning, and there is more scope for direct involvement by asylum seekers, refugees and their community organizations. A mock shanty town was erected outside the London headquarters of the United Nations High Commissioner for Refugees during a 2004 protest at the treatment of asylum seekers ('Asylum policy sparks protests', *BBC News*), and parliamentary committees have taken evidence from asylum seekers and their organizations on the impact of deterrent policies.[11] The Still Human Still Here coalition campaigns on the issue and right-to-work campaigns have been organized by refugee groups.

Challenging Detention

The routine and increasing use of detention—the UK detains around 30,000 migrants and asylum seekers annually, with around 3500 held at any one time (Migration Observatory 2015)—affects not only asylum seekers but also undocumented migrants and migrant offenders, who can remain in immigration detention for years after their sentence ends.[12] The detention of these groups in the same places (named 'immigration removal centres' to remind residents of the purpose of their detention) creates opportunities for joint action, with detainee support groups in solidarity with hunger strikes and other protests by detainees, and for more sustained campaigning. Thus, a large coalition against immigration detention has been created, encompassing both asylum seekers and migrants, with current and former detainees frequently playing a leading role, and with test cases an integral part of the battle.

The infamous 13-month detention of the Ay family, a Kurdish mother and her four children aged from 7 to 13, who were held from July 2002 to August 2003 in Dungavel in Scotland, galvanized the campaign against the immigration detention of children in the UK (see, e.g., 'Rowling slams treatment of child refugees'). The family received the support of celebrities including JK Rowling and Colin Firth, and eventually won a six-figure settlement in compensation for unlawful detention (see 'Child asylum seekers win compensation for 13-month detention', *Guardian*). But it was the political campaign rather than strategic litigation which was hugely significant in—if not ending, then rendering unacceptable—the immigration detention of children.[13] The campaign brought together 'mainstream' children's charities such as Save the Children and the Children's Society with the UN High Commissioner for Refugees, the Refugee Councils of England, Wales and Scotland, Bail for Immigration Detainees (BID) and other detainee support groups, under the slogan 'No place for a child'. Reports by Medical Justice, BID, HM Inspector of Prisons and the Children's Commissioner provided powerful ammunition, and the coalition government announced that it would end children's immigration detention in 2010.[14]

The political campaign against the indefinite immigration detention of adults, fought for years by groups such as Detention Action (through reports like *Detained Lives* and *The State of Detention*) and the Detention Forum (which brings together campaigning, and visitors' and welfare groups), has come up against the stubborn resistance of successive governments, who have refused to set a time limit. But history was made on 17 July 2014, when members of the All Party Parliamentary Group Inquiry into Immigration Detention heard directly by mobile phone from current detainees in Colnbrook IRC, and from former detainees in person. The panel's chair, Sarah Teather MP, recorded in the foreword to the ensuing report the collective gasp greeting one man's revelation that he had been detained for three years (see *The Report of the Inquiry into the Use of Immigration Detention in the United Kingdom* 2015). The oral and written testimony of current and former detainees gave a reality and an urgency to the inquiry, and played no small part in shaping the key recommendations of the report: that immigration detention should be used as seldom as possible and limited to 28 days. In September 2015, in a House of Commons debate on the report, MPs voted in favour of a radical reform of immigration detention, including a time limit (see 'MPs back call to end indefinite immigration detention' 2015). The unprecedented vote is not binding on the government, but helps create a climate in which change is possible.

Legal challenges to the indefinite nature of detention have consistently failed, with the courts ruling that detention is limited at common law to the period 'reasonably necessary' to fulfil its purpose, whether identification or removal, and giving the Home Office huge latitude in deciding what is reasonable. But there has been some progress in challenging the detention of vulnerable adults. Awards of damages for unlawful detention are now commonplace, following a series of cases in which the High Court has ruled that the detention of particularly vulnerable people violated their right to freedom from inhuman or degrading treatment (see Detention Action, *A crisis of harm*; 'Immigration detention: signs of spring or false dawn?' 2015). The issue has become one of public concern. In 2014, Medical Justice, a small independent charity that sends volunteer doctors into detention centres to document injuries and challenge medical mistreatment, joined Mind, a large mental health charity, to intervene in an appeal involving the immigration detention of sufferers from mental illness (*R (Das) v SSHD* [2014] EWCA Civ 45). The evidence it produced, like its reports on the impact of detention on torture survivors, pregnant women and HIV sufferers, was informed partly by the experiences of its committee of ex-detainees. The Court of Appeal ruled that the Home Office policy should be applied so as to prevent detention and protect health so far as was possible. In February 2015, the Home Secretary announced a review of the welfare of vulnerable people in detention—and although the terms of reference explicitly excluded the decision to detain,[15] the report called for a dramatic reduction in both the numbers detained and the length of detention, and recommended a presumption against the detention of mentally ill and other vulnerable people and a total ban on pregnant women's detention.[16] Campaigners also produced their own report, *Rethinking vulnerability in detention: a crisis of harm* (Report by the Detention Forum's Vulnerable People Working Group 2015).

The majority of immigration detainees are current or refused asylum seekers, and the 'detained fast track' has been an important target for campaigners against immigration detention ever since its inception in March 2000, when a former military barracks was used to detain asylum seekers so their claims could be speedily processed. At that time, asylum seekers whose claims were deemed 'straightforward' following screening were held for seven to ten days, but were released once a decision—positive or negative—was reached. But once the UK courts accepted the principle of detention purely for administrative convenience, this gave way to what was known as 'end to end detention'—detention from screening of the claim, through refusal and dismissal of any appeal, until removal some months later. Asylum seekers in the fast track had only days to prepare their claim and obtain corroborative evidence, and, when refused (as 99 per cent were), only two days to lodge an appeal (although, once the appeal was dismissed, as 99 per cent were, they remained locked up for months pending removal). This sausage-factory processing gave asylum seekers no time to prepare claims or appeals, but a legal challenge by the Refugee Legal Centre resulted in a 2004 Court of Appeal ruling that the detained fast track was not inherently unfair or unlawful, as unacceptable risks of unfairness could be avoided so long as the system was flexible (*R (Refugee Legal Centre) v SSHD* [2004] EWCA Civ 1481). The judgment encouraged the Home Office in its ambition to process one-third of asylum claims in this way.

For some years, the battle against the detained fast track was carried out mainly on the political front. Amnesty International produced *Seeking asylum is not a crime* in June 2005. BID produced *Working against the clock: inadequacy and injustice in the fast track system* in March 2006, and the following year, *Refusal factory: women's experiences of the DFT asylum process at Yarl's Wood IRC.* Human Rights Watch produced *Fast tracked unfairness: detention and denial of women asylum seekers in the UK* in 2010. Detention Action produced *Fast track to despair* in 2011.

The first important legal success came in 2006 (*D and K* [2006] EWHC 980), when the fast-track detention of two torture survivors was ruled unlawful because of the failure to perform medical screening within 24 hours, as the detention centre rules demanded. But in 2013, Detention Action, which until then had campaigned solely on the political front,[17] decided that the unfairness its members saw in the fast-track system was systemic and had to be challenged in law. In July 2014, the High Court accepted that the tight timetable between detainees seeing a lawyer and their asylum interview rendered the process so unfair as to be unlawful (*R (Detention Action) v SSHD* [2014] EWHC 2245 (Admin)). The Home Office responded by ensuring that asylum seekers had four working days between being allocated lawyers and the asylum interview, but in December 2014, in a further challenge, the Court of Appeal ruled that the criteria for continued fast-track detention after refusal of a claim were unclear and unlawful (*R (Detention Action) v SSHD* [2014] EWCA Civ 1634). The judgment meant that detainees awaiting an appeal had to be released unless there were other good reasons for their detention (such as a risk of absconding). And in June 2015, the High Court ruled that the fast-track appeal system was structurally unfair and unjust, as the Secretary of State, by detaining appellants, put them at a serious procedural disadvantage as a result of the impossibly short time limits and the restrictions on judges' case management powers. The Court of Appeal upheld the decision in July, and in November the Supreme Court refused the Home Office permission to appeal.

In parallel with the Detention Action cases, a group of torture and trafficking survivors brought a legal challenge to their detention under the fast track, arguing that none of the safeguards that should have prevented their detention worked (*R (JM, RE, KW, MY)* v *SSHD* [2015] EWHC 2331 (Admin)).The Helen Bamber Foundation, which provides holistic treatment for survivors of torture and cruelty, provided evidence that over 90 per cent of fast-track detainees referred to them in the previous five months should not have been there. This was conclusive evidence that the system was failing to identify vulnerable claimants unsuitable for detention, which caused the Home Office to concede the cases, and was the final blow to the detained fast track as then constituted. The ministerial suspension of the detained fast track system followed.

But celebration turned to concern and anger as the detention of vulnerable asylum seekers continued. It appeared that a majority of those in the fast track were overstayers or illegal entrants, rather than port claimants, and could be detained for immigration control reasons anyway. And so, in practice, all that changed was the timescale for making asylum claims and for appeals. The detained fast track became simply the detained track, or 'detention asylum casework' in official parlance, and those identified as vulnerable were still detained under a new Home Office policy which allowed immigration control factors to outweigh vulnerability in the detention decision. In June 2016, the High Court ruled that the new policy was not unfair and that those detained under it were not unlawfully detained (*Hossain and others v SSHD* [2016] EWHC 1331 (Admin)). In August, the Court of Appeal refused permission to appeal (*R (TH) (Bangladesh) & Ors, v SSHD* EWCA Civ 815). For now, the challenge to the detention of vulnerable asylum seekers has been lost—at least for those who are 'immigration offenders'.

Women in the System

For women, the asylum system—whether it involves detention or a destitute existence on asylum support—brings added difficulties. Quite apart from the inhumanities of reception or detention, there is the ever-present threat of sexual harassment, or of violence from a traumatized partner; and there are further difficulties, including the shame suffered by victims of sexual violence which inhibits disclosure, the failure of Home Office officials and judges to understand sexual violence, to take it seriously enough or to realize fully what it means in traditional communities. It is in this context that groups like WAST, Women for Refugee Women (WRW), SBS and Women Against Rape (WAR) provide support, friendship and a route to medical, financial or legal help, as well as campaigning, supporting strategic litigation and securing evidence. SBS has lobbied and used strategic litigation to secure access to welfare benefits, social housing and legal aid for migrant survivors of domestic violence. WRW has helped develop a network of local women's refugee groups and produced reports on women in detention and the experiences of women refused asylum. Refugee support groups also link up with 'mainstream' women's groups such as Maternity Action, which has worked on access to primary care for migrant and refugee women, and the effects of compulsory dispersal on pregnant asylum seekers.

WAR became involved in a 1997 case involving a Ugandan multiple-rape victim who had been unable for years to disclose what she had been through. Her asylum claim made no mention of it. It was rejected, and the appeal dismissed. Only after receiving therapeutic help through WAR was she able to talk about her experiences of regular sexual violence. She made a fresh claim. Under the rules, such a claim could be accepted only if the new evidence relied on by the claimant was previously unavailable. WAR obtained a medical report from the Medical Foundation for the Care of Victims of Torture (now Freedom from Torture), which supported her claims and described the psychological impossibility of disclosure without therapeutic intervention. On the basis of this evidence, the judge accepted that the new evidence had not been previously available, and ordered the Home Office to treat it as a new claim (*R v SSHD ex p Ejon* [1998] INLR 195, 9 October 1997). Although the case has not always been followed, it was the first to give judicial recognition to the psychological effects of sexual violence.

Challenging Forcible Removal

The forcible removal of refused asylum seekers has been a site of bitter contest between refugee campaigners and the Home Office for decades, with direct action to stop removals going hand in hand with legal challenges. Direct action in this field has a long history, since Viraj Mendes took sanctuary in a Manchester church for over two years in the 1980s, putting the sanctuary movement on the map (see Weller 1987). UN condemnation failed to stop forced removals to conflict zones such as Somalia, Iraq, Afghanistan, Sri Lanka and Sudan in the early 2000s ('UN condemns British policy on deportees' 2015), but the UK branch of the Federation of Iraqi Refugees worked with the Coalition to Stop Deportations to Iraq (a coalition of activist and support groups and lawyers), lodging hundreds of applications at the European Court of Human Rights for orders preventing removal of Iraqis, until the Court ruled in November 2010 that all deportations there should be stopped because of the deteriorating security situation ('European Court demands halt to forcible return of Iraqi asylum seekers'). In 2012, it was the Tamils' turn, as refugee activists joined with anti-deportation campaigners in a series of direct actions, preventing coaches carrying Tamil deportees from leaving the removal centre for the airport, for long enough to allow lawyers to get injunctions to prevent their removal to Sri Lanka. These actions, together with TV documentaries and human rights reports,[18] led to an unprecedented ruling in February 2013 by the High Court—a blanket injunction preventing the removal of all passengers on a deportation flight to Sri Lanka because of the high risk of torture ('Tamil deportations from UK checked by London High Court'). Charter flight deportations—less visible than the use of commercial airlines, and enabling mass removal of up to 80 deportees at a time—continue to be resisted, with detainees using blogs and sites like Detained Voices to mobilize outside support for protests and direct actions aimed at blocking deportations while lawyers go to court. Right to Remain (formerly the National Coalition of Anti-Deportation Campaigns) has published a toolkit for would-be anti-deportation campaigners.

Following outrage at and judicial disapproval of pre-dawn swoops for immediate removal, in 2007 the Home Office agreed to give 72 hours' notice of proposed removal, or five days (including two working days) for charter flight removals, to provide adequate time for detainees to obtain legal advice and issue a legal challenge if necessary. But then, it began creating exemptions, whereby less or even no notice was given—where there was a risk of suicide, or harm to someone else, such as their child; where the proposed deportee was a child who might abscond; or where someone was detained and an organized protest was feared.[19] Medical Justice brought a legal challenge to the no-notice removals, which was upheld in July 2010, with the High Court ruling that the lack of notice failed to ensure access to justice for those affected (*R (Medical Justice) v SSHD* [2010] EWHC 1925 [Admin]).

The Use of Force

The death of Jimmy Mubenga in October 2010, under restraint by three G4S guards on the floor of a British Airways plane about to take off from Heathrow to Angola, drew public attention to the dangerous restraint techniques and levels of force used in detention and during removal—an aspect of the culture of racism and brutality within immigration enforcement against which activists had campaigned for years. An explosive 2008 report by Medical Justice and others, *Outsourcing abuse: the use of state-sponsored force during detention and deportation*,[20] had already forced a government inquiry.[21] It is frequently the use of force on detainees that leads to protests and riots in detention centres, and certain centres, such as Yarl's Wood and Harmondsworth, are notorious for excessive force. The campaign launched after Mubenga's death united anti-racist campaigners, the charity for those bereaved by a death in custody, INQUEST, campaigners against G4S and members of Mubenga's family and the Angolan community in the UK. Through events such as pickets of the Crown Prosecution Service, which decides whether to prosecute and has a very poor record with regard to prosecuting police or other officials responsible for deaths in custody (see Athwal and Bourne 2015), the campaign ensured that the guards faced criminal charges, although they were acquitted after the judge controversially decided to suppress evidence of racism (see 'The Jimmy Mubenga case exposed a system in denial over racism').

The Government Fights Back

It is apparent from this brief survey that migrant and refugee voices have increasingly been heard in the courts, through individuals' cases and the strategic litigation brought by campaigning and support groups. In the areas of detention and removal, in particular, due process rights have been extended. But the government uses a number of parallel strategies to co-opt or silence voluntary and community organizations.

The process of co-option started with the New Labour treatment of voluntary groups as stakeholders, 'turning a community of protest into a community of supplicants'.[22] Large refugee support organizations were increasingly treated as service providers, losing grant aid and being expected to bid for contracts instead, in areas ranging from asylum support to voluntary departures. Sometimes they were subcontractors delivering specialist services to large corporations; voluntary sector organizations can be used as 'bid candy' by corporate 'partners', which then marginalize them and ignore their specialist skills and local knowledge. But as the Panel on the Independence of the Voluntary Sector warned in its 2014 report, independence of voice, of action and of purpose are all threatened by these partnerships, and by a government that increasingly treats the private and voluntary sectors as interchangeable delivery arms of the state and actively discourages speaking out.[23]

The children's charity Barnardo's is a paradigmatic example of this co-option. Barnardo's joined the campaign against the detention of children. But then, it took a Home Office contract to work in 'family pre-departure accommodation' run by G4S, where children in families were detained pending their removal. Barnardo's involvement, while leading to improvements in the process and the experience of detention for children and families, both masked the reality of detention and, by cooperating with that detention, removed the possibility of the organization campaigning against it.[24]

Some contracts have gagging clauses, but even without them, organizations fearful of losing contracts (because of their sense of obligation to the client group) may keep quiet about abuses. Barnardo's Chief Executive Officer admitted in 2012 that the charity did not proceed with a complaint against G4S because of this fear. And it is a real one. Refugee Action, which in 2014 won a case against the government on asylum support rates, was told in June 2015 that its funding for assisted voluntary removals was ending in November.

The Home Office said at the time that it was taking voluntary removals in-house. But it turns out that it has been seeking to co-opt community organizations in carrying out 'voluntary' returns—for free. In 2014, it ran a six-month pilot scheme, Operation Skybreaker, over five of the most racially diverse London boroughs, seeking 'community engagement' with local voluntary and faith groups to get them to persuade undocumented migrants to return home voluntarily. RAMFEL reported that the Home Office wanted to do local 'surgeries' at their offices. So groups that exist to further the interests of refugees and migrants and to expose and challenge official racism in enforcement strategies—like the 'Go Home' message on vans touring east London in the summer of 2013—are being actively encouraged to participate in these strategies.

In a parallel strategy, the government has attempted to make litigation more difficult for migrants and campaigning groups. As part of a broad attack on legal aid, it stopped all those not legally resident in the UK for over 12 months from having access to legal aid for almost any purpose. In July 2014, a three-judge Divisional Court declared unlawful the new residence test, in a challenge brought by the Public Law Project using a compelling body of evidence from a large number of migrant and refugee organizations (*R (Public Law Project) v Lord Chancellor* [2014] EWHC 2365 (Admin)). The judges accepted that the test would, by definition, exclude from legal aid meritorious cases including human rights violations by officials, making access to the courts virtually impossible. This made the regulations ultra vires the Act, in which need and the importance of the issue were the criteria for public funding. 'He who is subject to English law is entitled to its protection,' they said.[25] The judgment was reversed in November 2015. In a shockingly reactionary judgment, the Court of Appeal ruled that legal aid was a welfare benefit rather than an important aspect of the right to access to justice, and that the government was at liberty to impose tests that cut across need and merit. In April 2016, the Supreme Court allowed the Public Law Project's appeal, ruling that the regulations were ultra vires by denying legal aid services to a group of people in a way not permitted by the Act (*R (Public Law Project) v Lord Chancellor* [2016] UKSC 39).

Meanwhile, in September 2013, the government proposed narrowing the standing test for judicial review, so that a 'direct and tangible interest' in the proceedings would be a prerequisite for litigation (Ministry of Justice 2013). There were widespread objections that public interest groups would no longer be able to fulfil their function, vital to the rule of law, of bringing test cases that individuals might not have the time, resources or expert evidence to bring, and enabling voices to be heard which would otherwise go unheard. The proposal was withdrawn, but the government enacted other restrictions on judicial review, massively hiking the fees in 2014, and, in 2015, curtailing judicial discretion, limiting protective costs orders (renamed costs capping orders) and exposing interveners to liability for the costs of all parties in various situations. These provisions are likely to act as a serious deterrent to public interest litigation (Criminal Justice and Courts Act 2015, s 88, in force August

2016). All these measures are part of a direct and explicit attack by the government against strategic litigation by campaigning groups.

Conclusion

As this chapter demonstrates, strategic litigation undertaken by or with the participation of refugee and asylum support groups has had mixed success. In the field of asylum support, it has thwarted the government policy of starving asylum seekers out to force them to leave the country, but has been unable to improve the destitution-level amount of support provided, or prevent the removal of support from most categories of refused asylum seekers once their appeals are exhausted. It has forced decision-makers to recognize the psychological impact of severe human rights violations on the ability of asylum seekers to tell their story. It has recognized the systemic unfairness of accelerated processes in asylum decision-making and appeals, an unfairness exacerbated by detention, but has not stopped the detention of the vulnerable. Neither litigation nor political action has succeeded in imposing a time limit on immigration detention, but political action has succeeded in making the detention of children politically unacceptable.

Perhaps one of the important benefits of strategic litigation is the process itself. For one of the least powerful groups in society, with no political voice and at the mercy of a crushing bureaucracy, turning the tables and forcing the government to justify its actions in court can be profoundly empowering, even if ultimately unsuccessful. The sense of active engagement it can engender does not end with the litigation, but continues in forms of political and community organizing towards the same ends.

Notes

1. *R (on the application of Detention Action) v Secretary of State for the Home Department* [2014], *Detention Action v First Tier Tribunal (Immigration and Asylum Chamber) and others* [2015].
2. Hansard HC 24.4.2002 col. 353.

3. Many times, I and my colleagues have had to repair and re-present good claims lost on appeal by shockingly poor practice by solicitors, including failure to take witness statements or to obtain easily accessible evidence in support of the claim. Generally, it is migrant support groups who take up the cases and look for fresh representatives.
4. The Public Law Project has produced a guide to strategic litigation for community groups (PLP 2015).
5. The Lord Chief Justice's Direction of 21 August 2013 sets out which judicial review cases must now be issued in the Upper Tribunal. See Law Society Practice Notes: immigration judicial review, section 5.
6. Under regs 70–72, Income Support (General) Regulations 1987, SI No. 1967. See Cracknell (1996).
7. The Asylum and Immigration Act 1996. The doctrine of parliamentary sovereignty allows the government to enact legislation that breaches fundamental rights. Although the courts cannot quash primary legislation, since October 2000 (when the Human Rights Act 1998 came into force) the higher courts may issue declarations of incompatibility (telling the government that the law violates fundamental rights). For the full story of what happened next, see my *Borderline justice: the fight for refugee and migrant rights* (2012).
8. The Human Rights Act 1998 brought the provisions of the 1950 European Convention on Human Rights and Fundamental Freedoms, ratified by the UK in 1951, within UK law. Section 55 of the Nationality, Immigration and Asylum Act 2002 removed support from late claimants but restored it 'to the extent necessary for the purpose of avoiding a breach of the person's Convention rights'.
9. An EU regulation stipulating that asylum claims should generally be dealt with by the first EU country entered by the asylum seeker.
10. *Salih and others v Secretary of State for the Home Department* [2003].
11. Organizations including the All African Women's Group and the Zimbabwe Association, along with many support groups, gave evidence to the House of Lords House of Commons Parliamentary Joint Committee on Human Rights' inquiry on the treatment of asylum seekers: see its 10th report (2007).
12. There is no statutory time limit on immigration detention, and although most detainees are held for under two months, some have been held for over a year, and a small number for three, four and even five years, awaiting deportation. See Migration Observatory (2015).

13. First came the long campaign against the UK's immigration reservation to the UN Convention on the Rights of the Child, which subsumed children's welfare to immigration control. The reservation was withdrawn in 2009 and the 'best interests of the child' became central to officials' decisions through the Borders, Citizenship and Immigration Act 2009 s 55.
14. See *Borderline justice* (2012), Chapter 9, for a fuller account of the campaign to end child detention. Children are still detained—on arrival, at airports and ports, and for removal, in families; see 'The business of child detention', 2014. Cedars, the UK's only 'child-friendly' detention building, was closed in August 2016.
15. The Shaw review, announced on 9 February 2015, https://www.gov.uk/government/news/home-secretary-announces-independent-review-of-welfare-in-detention.
16. The review can be accessed through the EIN website, 'Home Office releases Shaw review into the welfare of vulnerable persons in immigration detention' 2016.
17. With reports such as *Fast track to despair: the unnecessary detention of asylum seekers* (2011).
18. Freedom from Torture and Human Rights Watch all published reports in 2011 and 2012 documenting the torture of returnees to Sri Lanka. FfT produced a follow-up report in September 2014.
19. This last exception was in force, although unpublished and unknown, since 2007, when disturbances at Campsfield IRC had followed receipt of removal notices. In 2009, when the unpublished policy came to light, the Home Office was ordered to return a deportee removed under it: *R (N) v SSHD* [2009].
20. A report on nearly 300 alleged assaults on detainees by guards, co-authored by solicitors Birnberg Peirce & Partners, Medical Justice and the NCADC (now Right to Remain), July 2008.
21. The O'Loan inquiry, which reported in March 2010 and made 22 recommendations for change.
22. Alison Harvey, Legal Director of the Immigration Law Practitioners' Association (ILPA), in her obituary of Helen Bamber OBE.
23. Panel on the Independence of the Voluntary Sector.
24. See 'The fading red line: Barnardo's role in the detention and removal of children'. The government announced the closure of Cedars in July 2016 and the return of families to ordinary detention facilities.
25. A quotation from Lord Scarman in *ex p Khawaja* at 111–2.

References

Asylum policy sparks protests. *BBC News*, 30 January 2004. http://news.bbc.co.uk/1/hi/uk_politics/3445121.stm

Athwal, H., & Bourne, J. (2015). *Dying for justice*. London: IRR.

Birnberg Peirce & Partners, Medical Justice and the National Coalition of Anti-Deportation Campaigns. (2008). *Outsourcing abuse: The use of state-sponsored force during detention and deportation.*

Blunkett, D. Debate on the Nationality, Immigration and Asylum Bill, Hansard HC 24.4.2002 col. 353.

Campaign Against Racism and Fascism/Southall Rights. (1981). *Southall: The birth of a black community*. London: Institute of Race Relations and Southall Rights.

Child asylum seekers win compensation for 13-month detention. *Guardian*, 6 January 2012. https://www.theguardian.com/uk/2012/jan/06/child-asylum-seekers-win-compensation

Cracknell, R. (1996, January 19). *Social security changes for asylum seekers and other claimants from abroad* (Parliamentary Research Paper 96/9).

Detention Action. (2011). *Fast track to despair: The unnecessary detention of asylum seekers*. London: Detention Action.

Detention Action. (2014). *A crisis of harm*, 16 September 2014. http://detentionaction.org.uk/a-crisis-of-harm

Detention Forum, Vulnerable People Working Group (2015). *Rethinking vulnerability in detention: A crisis of harm.*

European Court demands halt to forcible return of Iraqi asylum seekers. *Guardian*, 5 November 2010, viewed 17 November 2015. http://www.theguardian.com/uk/2010/nov/05/strasbourg-forcible-returns-iraqi-asylum

Gillett, G. (2014, August 7). The UK must reform its treatment of asylum seekers. *New Statesman.*

Greater Manchester Immigration Aid Unit. (1993). *Immigration controls are out of control: The new asylum and immigration bill.* Manchester: Greater Manchester Immigration Aid Unit.

Guardian, 19 November 2012, Datablog. http://www.theguardian.com/news/datablog/2012/nov/19/judicial-review-statistics

Havers, P. Q. C. *Protective costs orders: Fair play or a complainants' charter?* Viewed 4 November 2015. http://www.1cor.com/1155/records/1212/PH%20public%20law%20handout.pdf

Home Office releases Shaw review into the welfare of vulnerable persons in immigration detention. Electronic Immigration Network, 14 January 2016. https://www.ein.org.uk/news/home-office-releases-shaw-review-welfare-vulnerable-persons-immigration-detention

House of Commons. (2015). *The report of the inquiry into the use of immigration detention in the United Kingdom*. A Joint Inquiry by the All Party Parliamentary Group on Refugees & the All Party Parliamentary Group on Migration, March 2015. https://detentioninquiry.com/report/

House of Lords House of Commons Joint Committee on Human Rights. (2007). *The treatment of asylum seekers tenth report of session 2006–07*. Available at: http://www.publications.parliament.uk/pa/jt200607/jtselect/jtrights/81/81i.pdf

Immigration detention: Signs of spring or false dawn? *IRR News*, 9 April 2015. http://www.irr.org.uk/news/immigration-detention-signs-of-spring-or-false-dawn/

Immigration Law Practitioners' Association. (2008). *The detained fast track process*. www.ilpa.org.uk/data/resources/13264/ilpa_bpg_detained_fasttrack.pdf

Law Society Practice Notes: Immigration judicial review. https://www.lawsociety.org.uk/support-services/advice/practice-notes/immigration-judicial-review/

Migration Observatory. (2015). *Briefing on immigration detention*, February 2015. http://migrationobservatory.ox.ac.uk/briefings/immigration-detention-uk

Ministry of Justice. (2013). *Judicial review: Proposals for further reform*, September 2013. https://consult.justice.gov.uk/digital-communications/judicial-review/supporting_documents/Judicialreviewproposalsforfurtherreform.pdf, para 80.

MPs back call to end indefinite immigration detention, 10 September 2015, website of Inquiry into the use of Immigration Detention. https://detentioninquiry.com/2015/09/10/mps-back-calls-to-end-indefinite-immigration-detention/

Newham Monitoring Project/CARF. (1991). *Newham: The forging of a black community*. London: NMP/CARF.

Public Law Project. (2015). *Guide to strategic litigation for community groups*. http://www.publiclawproject.org.uk/data/resources/153/Guide-to-Strategic-Litigation.pdf. Accessed 4 Nov 2015.

Racism and the press in Blair's Britain. CARF 48, 1999. http://www.irr.org.uk/carf/feat22.html

Rowling slams treatment of child refugees. *Guardian*, 11 April 2004. https://www.theguardian.com/society/2004/apr/11/asylum.books?INTCMP=ILCNETTXT3487

Sivanandan, A. (1990). *Communities of resistance*. Verso, New York.

Sivanandan, A. (2008). *Catching history on the wing: Race, culture and globalisation*. London: Pluto.

Social Security Advisory Committee. *Report on social security (Persons from Abroad) (Miscellaneous Amendments) Regulations 1996*, Cm. 3062.

Tamil deportations from UK checked by London High Court. *BBC News*, 28 February 2013, viewed 17 November 2015. http://www.bbc.co.uk/news/world-asia-21610953

The business of child detention. *IRR News*, 24 July 2014. http://www.irr.org.uk/news/the-business-of-child-detention-2/

The fading red line: Barnardo's role in the detention and removal of children. *IRR News*, 15 May 2014. http://www.irr.org.uk/news/the-fading-red-line-barnardos-role-in-the-detention-and-removal-of-children/

The Jimmy Mubenga case exposed a system in denial over racism. *Guardian,* 19 December 2014. http://www.theguardian.com/commentisfree/2014/dec/19/jimmy-mubeng-case-racism

UN condemns British policy on deportees. *Observer*, 12 June 2005, viewed 17 November 2015. http://www.theguardian.com/politics/2005/jun/12/immigration.immigrationandpublicservices

Webber, F. (2012). *Borderline justice: The fight for refugee and migrant rights*. London: Pluto.

Weller, P. (1987). *Sanctuary: The beginning of a movement*. London: Runnymede Trust.

Cases

D and K [2006] EWHC 980.

Hossain and others v SSHD [2016] EWHC 1331 (Admin).

R (Das) v SSHD [2014] EWCA Civ 45.

R (Detention Action) v SSHD [2014] EWCA Civ 1634.

R (Detention Action) v SSHD [2014] EWHC 2245 (Admin).

R (EM Eritrea) v Secretary of State for the Home Department [2014] UKSC 12, Supreme Court.

R (JM, RE, KW, MY) v *SSHD* [2015] EWHC 2331 (Admin).

R (Medical Justice) v SSHD [2010] EWHC 1925 (Admin).
R (N) v SSHD [2009] EWHC 873 (Admin).
R (Public Law Project) v Lord Chancellor [2014] EWHC 2365 (Admin).
R (Public Law Project) v Lord Chancellor [2016] UKSC 39.
R (Q) v SSHD [2003] EWCA Civ 364.
R (Refugee Action) v SSHD [2014] EWHC 1033 (Admin).
R (Refugee Legal Centre) v SSHD [2004] EWCA Civ 1481.
R (TH) (Bangladesh) & Ors, v SSHD EWCA Civ 815].
R v Lord Chancellor's Department ex parte Child Poverty Action Group [1998] EWHC 151 (Admin)
R v SSHD ex p Ejon [1998] INLR 195, 9 October 1997.
Salih and others v Secretary of State for the Home Department [2003] EWHC 2273 (Admin), http://www.bailii.org/ew/cases/EWHC/Admin/2003/2273.html
ex p Khawaja [1984] AC 74 at 111-2.
R (on the application of Detention Action) v Secretary of State for the Home Department [2014] EWHC 2245 Admin, 9 July 2014, [2014] EWHC 2525 (Admin), [2014] EWCA Civ 1634.
Detention Action v First-Tier Tribunal (Immigration and Asylum Chamber) and others [2015] EWHC 1689 (Admin), upheld [2015] EWCA Civ 840, 29 July 2015.
R v Minister for Social Security ex parte B, ex parte JCWI [1997] 1 WLR 275.
R (Adam, Limbuela and Tesema) v Secretary of State for the Home Department [2005] UKHL 66.

Legislation

Asylum and Immigration Act 1996
Borders, Citizenship and Immigration Act 2009
Criminal Justice and Courts Act 2015
European Convention on Human Rights and Fundamental Freedoms
Human Rights Act 1998
Nationality, Immigration and Asylum Act 2002
Senior Courts Act 1981
Social Security Act 1992

8

'Hostile' UK Immigration Policy and Asylum Seekers' Susceptibility to Forced Labour

Hannah Lewis, Louise Waite, and Stuart Hodkinson

Introduction

This chapter considers the development of new *restrictions* intended to target the daily lives of refused asylum seekers and irregular migrants in the UK, with a focus on the intersection of employment and immigration status. It explores recent policy changes in the UK that restrict access to housing, healthcare services, banking and legal representation, and increasing penalties for unauthorized working. Drawing on our research

We would like to thank the editors of this collection for their helpful comments which strengthened the chapter.

H. Lewis (✉)
Department of Sociological Studies, University of Sheffield,
Sheffield, UK

L. Waite • S. Hodkinson
School of Geography, University of Leeds,
Leeds, UK

F. Vecchio, A. Gerard (eds.), *Entrapping Asylum Seekers*, Transnational Crime, Crime Control and Security, DOI 10.1057/978-1-137-58739-8_8

on experiences of forced labour among refugees and asylum seekers, we highlight how the policy areas under attack in the Coalition government's *Immigration Act 2014* and Conservative government's *Immigration Act 2016* could operate to increase labour exploitation among people seeking asylum and other irregular migrants. The specific restrictions introduced or proposed in this recent legislation target areas we have found to contribute to entry into, or preclude exit from, forced labour. Indeed, these changes are explicitly intended to generate an environment of hostility towards migrants in general, including people seeking asylum, and we argue that they facilitate an environment in which labour exploitation can flourish. This outcome is quite contradictory with government claims that it wishes to rid the UK of the 'scourge of modern slavery' (May 2014) through the *Modern Slavery Act 2015*. This new legislation on immigration is intended to filter into everyday life and is likely to have destructive effects on the lives of not only people seeking asylum, but also all migrants and people of colour, though its main aim is arguably to assuage perceived xenophobic anxieties of the electorate which have only been buoyed by the Brexit vote to leave the European Union (EU) in June 2016.

This chapter is also framed by the inter-relationship of irregular migration and asylum (see further discussion in the section on 'Immigration Policy and Susceptibility to Forced Labour'). Refused asylum seekers are part of the irregular migrant population; but, also, some people who are refugees in the broader sense may enter the UK through other migration channels and later become irregular, sometimes without knowing about or exercising their right to claim asylum, based on a well-founded fear of persecution. On this point, it is pertinent to note that immigration categories and socio-legal statuses are not fixed for any one individual—there is a slipperiness and complexity to people's immigration trajectories through time as they move between statuses, either agentically or as a consequence of structural barriers (Düvell and Jordan 2002; Koser 2010; Bloch et al. 2011).

The chapter considers how the production of deterrence, discomfort and hostility, long part of UK immigration policies (Schuster and Solomos 1999; Flynn 2005; Somerville 2007; Lewis et al. 2014b), has become more strident in the current regime insofar as they have become an explicit goal. The next section outlines the focus of this chapter, which is not only the macro-scale politics underpinning the considerable attacks on the core rights of migrants to seek asylum, work, reside and access welfare, but also the growth of 'in-sourced' (Back and Sinha 2013) 'everyday bordering' practices that drive immigration controls into micro-settings of everyday practices and quotidian spaces. The links between immigration policy and susceptibility to forced labour, the definition of forced labour and the kinds of labour activities available for people in the asylum system are then summarized in a section outlining the 'Precarious Lives Research' study on which this chapter draws. The main part of the chapter then highlights five areas targeted in the current legislation (housing, banking, healthcare services, legal aid and appeals, and 'illegal' working) and argues that these restrictions could serve to increase susceptibility to labour exploitation for migrants journeying in and around the asylum system in the UK. We conclude by summarizing the everyday consequences of these restrictive immigration policies.

Deterrence, Discomfort and Hostility as Policy Goals

Looking at the issue of irregular migration through an understanding of intersecting policy arenas is no longer an idea proposed only by scholars or encouraged as good practice for service providers. It is increasingly an organizing device of policy, legislation and governmental controls in response to irregular migration. Indeed, we suggest that the pushing of border controls into various areas of public life has been a central goal of successive governments seeking to generate 'discomfort' for all migrants through policies that have hitherto primarily targeted those who apply for asylum.

The principle of producing discomfort and hostility within the Immigration Acts 2014 and 2016 was not dreamt up by the then UK Home Secretary, Theresa May, but is a central feature of successively restrictive immigration acts—certainly over the past two decades, and arguably since the 1905 *Aliens Act* (Schuster and Solomos 1999). 'Managed migration' was initially promoted under the auspices of shaping immigration to serve UK employers; latterly, the focus on restricting immigration has reflected the goal of asserting state control (Flynn 2005; Somerville 2007).

This shift must be seen against a backdrop of enhanced 'migration securitization', amid a more general post-9/11 securitization landscape, coupled with New Labour's (1997–2010) retreat from the multiculturalist idiom and its embracing of an increasingly neo-assimilationist policy approach to immigration, citizenship and belonging (Joppke 2004; Tyler 2010; Waite 2012). This means that the context of immigration policy has become more strongly linked to the goal of enhanced national security; restrictionism as an end in itself has therefore been wholeheartedly pursued by at least the past three administrations. With the 2015 Conservative general election victory and that party's confidence buoyed by being a parliamentary majority once again, we have seen a renewed zeal for, and zenith of achievement in, immigration restrictionism that revolves around the creation of discomfort and hostility through mechanisms such as making access to healthcare services, privately rented housing and banking more difficult for those with insecure immigration status.

The idea that discomfort and hostility can dissuade potential new arrivals from travelling to the UK or encourage those already in the country to leave is particularly prevalent in deterrence policies aimed at people seeking asylum. These policies have included the 'four Ds of deterrence' (Webber 2004)—dispersal, detention, deportation and destitution—together with the removal of the right to work and effective denial of access to public funds for refused asylum seekers. While the detail of the approach to the management of these policies has shifted over the past decade and a half, the rationale has survived through changing administrations: to deter new arrivals claiming asylum in the UK, and to encourage those in the UK to leave. The *Immigration Act 2014* seeks to extend these principles to broader groups of migrants—primarily irregular migrants. While the current Conservative government claims ownership of hostility as a policy goal, the environment has already been considerably hostile for some time—for people seeking asylum, irregular migrants and indeed, to a lesser extent, regular migrants. The internalization of border controls that requires immigration checks to be conducted by citizens and service providers was already a central feature of immigration policy. This process of 'in-sourcing' (Menjivar 2014) is part of what has become known as everyday bordering (Yuval-Davis et al. 2016) which encompasses immigration controls that extend beyond the border and seep into quotidian life.

Two prominent examples of in-sourcing in the immigration regime that predate the 2014 legislation relate to healthcare charges and international student checks. Charges for overseas patients for secondary care in the National Health Service (NHS) already served to deter many migrants, and particularly people refused asylum, from accessing any public health service. For those refused asylum, the fear of either being charged for healthcare, or of health professionals checking their immigration status with the Home Office and potentially sparking removal proceedings, discourages them from accessing healthcare. A second mechanism that already affects those in higher education is the requirement since 2009 for universities and colleges to check the immigration status of international students regularly (introduced in the light of the government's concern that some higher education institutions were misusing their 'highly trusted sponsor status' to admit non-genuine international students). In 2013, a move by the universities of Sunderland and Ulster to fingerprint students in lectures was sharply criticized by the National Union of Students, with the Home Office saying that the move represented an interpretation that went beyond requirements (Finnis 2013). Such developments are just one indication of how the proliferation of restrictions can take on a life of their own in street-level bureaucracy (Lipsky 1980), when institutions and individuals who are not border control staff are engaged as actors of immigration control regimes, and fear of breaching requirements can manifest in a general anxiety surrounding migrants. Increasing levels of restrictionism are often generated, which encroach even further into everyday life than the legislation intended.

The move to implement processes of everyday bordering and the desire to make certain migrants *uncomfortable* are made clear in the *Immigration Act 2014* and *Immigration Act 2016*. The creation of a 'hostile environment'—was stated as an explicit goal by then Home Secretary Theresa May in 2013 (Travis 2013). So, although these principles are not new to immigration policy, what is distinctive is that the recent Conservative and Coalition governments have been strident in emphasizing *hostility* as an intentional outcome of their immigration policies. These governments have also been outspoken within Europe on restricting immigration and have resisted burden-sharing agreements or cooperation with other European states in dealing with the refugee flows that sparked a humanitarian crisis at the borders of the EU from the spring of 2015 onwards.

In terms of the specific details, the *Immigration Act 2014* contains provisions to change the removals and appeals system, making it easier and quicker to remove those the government says have no right to be in the UK; end what the government calls 'the abuse' of Article 8 of the *European Convention on Human Rights*—the right to respect for family and private life; and prevent illegal immigrants from accessing and abusing public services or the labour market. The *Immigration Act 2016* extends some of these provisions and seeks to implement a number of measures that were outlined in the Conservative Party's 2015 General Election manifesto, and in the then Prime Minister's key speech on immigration, delivered on 21 May 2015 (Cameron 2015). The 2016 Act is intended to contribute to the government's broader objective of reducing net migration and creating a 'hostile environment' for people living in the UK without a valid immigration status. The Act has three main areas of focus: (i) dealing with the exploitation of low-skilled workers by increasing the negative consequences of employing 'illegal workers' and strengthening the penalties for working illegally; (ii) preventing irregular migrants from accessing services such as privately rented accommodation, bank accounts and driver's licences; and (iii) making it easier to remove people from the UK if they do not have a valid immigration status, including by extending the use of electronic tagging of 'immigration offenders' outside detention, restricting appeal rights and increasing immigration officers' powers. Other measures in the Act include reducing financial and accommodation entitlements for refused asylum seekers and certain other categories of immigrant, and introducing an English language fluency requirement for public sector workers which will further decrease decent work opportunities, particularly for asylum seekers, who are not entitled to free English classes.

As such, the proposed changes are sweeping and extensive in terms of the implications for vulnerable migrants in the realms of housing, financial resources (banking), healthcare and legal assistance. We argue that, while the erosion of core rights to welfare, work and residency has fundamentally weakened the position of asylum seekers, refused asylum seekers and refugees in the labour market, current policy is targeting quotidian practices and spaces as places of enforcement. These changes will collectively increase the susceptibility of certain migrants to workplace exploitation and forced labour—acting as they will to intensify and exacerbate situations we have previously described as 'hyper-precarious' (Lewis et al. 2014a).

Precarious Lives Research

Our research into 'precarious lives' of refugees and asylum seekers involved a period of participant observation outreach that put us in touch with over 400 contacts, which led to in-depth interviews in 2011–12 with 30 people who had made a claim for asylum and had experiences of labour that met one or more of the indicators of forced labour set by the International Labour Organization (ILO) (involving practices such as the withholding of wages, the threat of denunciation to authorities, debt bondage, excessive working hours or confinement to the workplace). The interviewees were 12 women and 18 men from 17 countries in Africa, the Middle East, Central Europe, and South and Central Asia. Many of these individuals were referred to us by welfare organizations that offered them holistic support, which had allowed the gatekeeping organizations to learn of their labour exploitation. If issues requiring further support emerged during the interview process, individuals were referred to appropriate support organizations (see Lewis 2016 for further discussion of the ethical considerations of the research). We also conducted interviews with 23 practitioners working in frontline, policy-making, support and advocacy organizations focused on migrants' rights and/or employment issues, and undertook a sustained period of outreach and participant observation to access the interviewees.

As many have argued (Cohen 2002; Schuster 2003; Lynn and Lea 2003), successive UK governments have systematically undermined the basic rights of asylum seekers. Asylum seekers have no permission to work (government policy since 2002, except in exceptional circumstances) and are supported under a highly conditional system of basic welfare. Some asylum seekers, therefore, feel compelled to seek alternative means of income, often in informal and unregulated sectors of the economy that shield unscrupulous employers. Refused asylum seekers also have no right to work, and have little or no recourse to public funds. Under section 4 of the *Immigration and Asylum Act 1999*, the Home Office may grant destitute asylum seekers who agree to take reasonable steps to leave the UK minimal 'hardcase' support. This has taken the form of a cashless voucher system designed to be deliberately punitive to deter continuing residence in the UK. Most refused asylum seekers do not access section 4 support, however, because they are unwilling to take the stipulated 'reasonable steps' to leave the UK. In common with other irregular migrants, refused asylum seekers are therefore likely to turn to clandestine work in highly insecure jobs in both the formal and informal labour markets in the face of policies that officially sanction their enforced destitution (Joint Committee on Human Rights 2007). While the 30 people we spoke to were selected because they had engaged in work in the UK that met at least one indicator of forced labour, it is reasonable to assume that many of the tens of thousands of destitute refused asylum seekers in the UK have faced at some point the prospect of engaging in labour under such conditions in order to survive. Furthermore, during our period of participant observation outreach, it became clear that payment below the National Minimum Wage was a normalized reality not only for refused asylum seekers, but also for refugees with rights to work, claim welfare and reside in the UK.

Refugees and others who receive leave to remain in the UK (including via refugee status, humanitarian protection and discretionary leave, or other discretionary grants) have permission to work and are theoretically able to find employment or receive benefits. However, they experience some of the highest unemployment rates of any group in the UK (Bloch 2002) and face barriers when accessing social security benefits due to a combination of delays or mistakes in Home Office documentation, limited English language skills, a lack of prior work experience in the UK and/or non-recognition of qualifications attained prior to arrival. Further, highly coercive working arrangements previously entered into out of necessity may continue long after refugee status has been secured. Sustained periods of precarious work and immigration status can be difficult to break out of, creating a lasting precarity track for refugees (Goldring and Landolt 2011). Engagement in severely exploitative labour may therefore be the only viable means of supporting themselves.

The exploitative labour experiences we encountered ranged across a spectrum of exploitation and involved either single, protracted labour situations that typically featured high levels of confinement and multiple ILO indicators of forced labour or consisted of individuals with three or more different work experiences—moving between several different jobs in various sectors and with varying degrees of middling to poor labour conditions (the latter was the experience of the majority—22 of 30—of our interviewees).

The 107 labour situations that our 30 interviewees told us they had participated in during their time in the UK ranged across a spectrum from decent work to forced labour.[1] Of these 107 labour situations, 78 featured one or more indicators, 59 featured two or more, and a striking 26 featured four or more indicators of forced labour. These labour exploitation experiences ranged across a number of sectors—a finding replicated in other forced labour research (Anderson and Rogaly 2005; Craig et al. 2007; Equality and Human Rights Commission 2010; Skřivánková 2010; Kagan et al. 2011; Dwyer et al. 2011; Scott et al. 2012; Geddes et al. 2013). Table 8.1 shows that most of our participants performed a

Table 8.1 Work breakdown

Work breakdown	Frequency
Takeaway restaurant worker	**16**
Domestic worker	**14**
Packing and distribution operatives	**14**
Care worker	**10**
Cleaner in commercial premises	**9**
Food processing worker	**8**
Construction worker	6
Shop assistant	6
Various agency jobs	6
Odd jobs	5
Security staff	4
Car wash attendant	3
Hair braiding	3
Agricultural worker	2
Manufacturing machine operative	2
Volunteer	2
Administrator	1
Hotel assistant	1
Underground criminal activities	1

relatively small range of work-based roles during their time in the UK. Three-quarters of the labouring situations were in just six types of employment: making or serving fast food, domestic work, factory packing, care work, cleaning and food processing.

We now explore further some of the reasons why our interviewees became susceptible to these conditions, and how recent legislative changes and proposals will exacerbate vulnerabilities to poverty and labour exploitation.

Immigration Policy and Susceptibility to Forced Labour

Many (although not all) of our interviewees were in various ways irregular when they experienced the most severe forms of labour exploitation. In order to understand the relationship between asylum seeking and irregularity, it is instructive to look at modes of entry into the UK. For our respondents, there were three distinct modes of entry: asylum seekers on entry, irregular migrants or trafficked migrants. Seventeen interviewees were *asylum seekers on entry* who lodged an initial asylum claim soon after entering the UK. Seven interviewees were *irregular migrants*, sometimes referred to as undocumented or 'illegal' migrants, who entered or remained without legal permission from the state (Valentine 2010). Lacking any rights to legal residence, work or welfare, all of these irregular migrants claimed asylum at varying points to attempt to regularize their status and due to fear of persecution if returned to their country of origin. Finally, six interviewees entered the UK as *trafficked migrants*, meaning that they had been brought to the UK by means of threat or deception specifically for the purpose of sexual, criminal or forced labour exploitation as defined by Article 3 of the United Nations Trafficking Protocol (UN General Assembly 2000). Five females claimed asylum weeks, months or years after escaping sustained periods of work in domestic settings including domestic work, care work and sexual exploitation. The single male was trafficked 'through' the asylum system and subsequently forced into criminal activity (he was directed by the person overseeing his entry to the UK to claim asylum and later routed by this person into exploitation).

These individuals' experiences of exploitative labour variously occurred *before* an asylum claim was made, *while* awaiting a claim to be processed or *after* a claim had been refused or granted. For the majority of asylum seekers on entry and irregular migrants, their experiences of exploitative labour came after their immigration status changed—either because their asylum claim was refused or their visa expired—and they became destitute (so they were either refused asylum seekers or irregular migrants who worked before claiming asylum). This situation then contributed to the lack of alternatives available to them, leaving them with little choice but to engage in exploitative work. We also found severe labour exploitation among refugees with rights to remain and the ability to legally access work and welfare, which is an important reminder that regularization alone does not resolve labour exploitation among migrants when not coupled with improvements to universal labour rights (Lewis et al. 2014b). This chapter concentrates on the more precarious position of those in the asylum system, awaiting a decision or who have been refused asylum, and irregular and trafficked migrants who enter the asylum system after a period of exploitative work to seek protection and regularization.

It is important to emphasize that these jobs involved both informal and formal employment relationships, and included other forms of labour relations which we identify as transactional or servitude connected to trafficking (see Table 8.2). Forty-one labouring situations were traditional and, in theory, the employee received a formal wage and National Insurance (NI) contributions. Informal waged work accounted for around 46 experiences, where employees worked for 'cash in hand', with little if any verbal agreement or assurances of conditions. Twelve were of a wageless, transactional nature where the worker undertook work or service in

Table 8.2 Labouring situations

	Total
Formal waged employment	41
Informal waged employment	46
Transactional unwaged	12
Trafficked into unwaged servitude	8
Total	**107**

the belief they were engaging in an exchange for a good or service, such as food, accommodation or clothes. The exchange may be cashless but may also involve some element of cash payment, but any element of payment is typically below a deemed acceptable market rate. A further eight experiences involved forms of involuntary and unpaid servitude connected to trafficking in which the worker entered the UK either already in or destined to be trapped in a forced labour situation.

It is important to understand forced labour not as a static situation, but as both a process and part of a continuum of 'unfreedom'. The experiences of our 30 interviewees point to widespread workplace abuses as part of a broader environment of precarious labour that makes movement along a continuum of exploitation (Skřivánková 2010) towards forced labour more likely. An important backdrop to migrant labour exploitation in general is the historical transformations wrought by neoliberal globalization since the 1970s, both in the flexibilization of labour markets and the dismantling of post-war welfare systems. Such factors are further compounded by ever-more restrictive migration regimes and the heightened economic insecurities created by the recent recession. The emerging reality for most Global South migrants is that stratified entry and emergent socio-legal status delimit welfare and employment entitlements and therefore exacerbate vulnerabilities in unregulated and low-paid labour markets (discussed further in Lewis et al. 2014b). But we also found that the areas of everyday bordering highlighted in this chapter and the creation of 'discomfort' targeted particularly at irregular migrants in recent legislative restrictions played, and we expect will continue to play, an important role as *facilitators* of forced labour, alongside the major infringements on rights to work, welfare and residency. It is further sobering to note the juxtaposition of recent immigration legislation with the *Modern Slavery Act* that passed into law in March 2015. The latter was trumpeted by the government as being a world-leading piece of legislation with echoes of the fine traditions of British transatlantic slavery abolitionists. However, many commentators have noted with dismay that a presumably unintended consequence of the *Immigration Act 2016* will be to create the conditions in which slavery will *flourish* in the UK, which will undo much of the government's intention to tackle modern slavery.

In the rest of this section, we concentrate on the aspects of people's narratives of entry into, continuation in, or preclusion of exit from forced labour situations and how they relate to key areas of restriction emphasized in the recent *Immigration Act 2014* and *Immigration Act 2016*: housing, banking, healthcare, legal representation and 'illegal working' sanctions.

Housing

One component of the *Immigration Act 2016* is the 'Right to Rent' scheme. This is seen as a central part of the government's immigration crackdown agenda and consists of obliging landlords to see evidence of a person's right to remain in the UK by examining their passport or biometric residence permit. The legislation is intended to create a blacklist of landlords and letting agents persistently letting to irregular migrants to allow councils to know where to concentrate their enforcement action. Although rogue landlords are the intended targets, as with many similar hostile policy proposals, it will be the migrant population who suffer. An independent evaluation of a pilot scheme of this policy in the West Midlands conducted by JCWI (2015) shows clear evidence of discrimination by landlords towards non-British passport holders, and even those with foreign accents or names.

We fear that this tightening of opportunities to obtain accommodation in the private rental sector will contribute to irregular migrants entering perilous straits as a result of obtaining lodgings in more informal spheres. Residing in others' homes informally, rather than formally renting or living on the street, has the advantage for irregular migrants and refused asylum seekers of being less visible and therefore potentially less liable to detection by the authorities.[2] In our research, we found that many irregular migrants were forced to accept the relatively short-term and fractured nature of housing assistance; Mohamed described a rapidly changing patchwork of support when he observed, 'so many people, so many friends, one night here, two nights here'. Such precarity inscribes the lives of irregular migrants, but also reflects the stretched livelihoods of those typically offering support. Frank even described getting assistance from a friend in a homeless shelter:

> Later on, he got destitute as well, but he was lucky, he got a place at [the homeless shelter], one room, just one room. He told me, no worries, you can come and stay with me in this little room, but make sure you come late. And make sure you leave early. So I was getting there, around midnight. 4 or 5 o'clock I have to move out.

For those individuals housed in friends/acquaintances' homes, the need to pay or contribute to rent was a major factor pushing people into exploitative working arrangements to avoid the dangers of street homelessness. If such work was unobtainable, some individuals in our research entered into situations of 'transactional work' in the household in which they were residing. Transactional work is understood here as an individual undertaking work—such as domestic labour, garden chores or sexual favours—in the belief that they are engaging in an exchange for a good or service, like food, accommodation or clothing. The exchange may be cashless, yet may also involve some element of cash payment—but any element of payment is most typically below a deemed acceptable market rate. The outcomes of transactional exchanges for irregular migrants are contingent and changeable; in these contexts, there is no clear line between hospitality and exploitation, on the one hand, and unfreedom, on the other (see further discussion in Waite and Lewis 2017). In the excerpt below, John explains his desire to engage in transactional labour in the form of domestic work in exchange for his hosts' support, together with feelings of being a burden in an ultimately undesirable situation:

> I do feel if somebody is doing good to me, if I am able to return something nice to them I will do it. … I help around, you know like these guys were going to colleges, working, you know I had to make sure the house is tidy, cookings, shopping, you know? … Not that they forced me to do the shopping, but me myself I say, I do the shopping and I'll put the money on the table, so that people could see you are also feeling the pains they are going through, because I was a little bit of a burden there. (John)

Under the proposed 'Right to Rent' scheme, irregular migrants will find it increasingly hard to secure rented accommodation. Facing genuine fears of persecution on return to their country of origin, they may feel that they have 'no real or acceptable alternative' but to turn to less-detectable informal lodgings. This may in turn lead to transactional labouring experiences that act as a driver for entry into exploitative and forced labour conditions.

Banking

The *Immigration Act 2014* disqualified irregular migrants from opening a bank account in the UK. The new *Immigration Act 2016* builds on these measures, through a requirement for banks and building societies to check the immigration status of all account holders and report on customers who are potentially breaching immigration controls. Nevertheless, it was already very difficult for someone without permanent residence ('leave to remain') to open a bank account in the UK, and the use of constructed or borrowed documents to do so was already covered by fraud legislation. One of our participants, Dedem, did manage to save up a sum of £8000 for a flat deposit over years spent working irregularly in the UK. He wanted to make an investment for his son, born in the UK, and managed to take out a loan using a false passport and associated documents he had applied for using that identity. However, he was later arrested, charged and served a prison sentence for using a false instrument. As it was already very difficult for someone without the full range of identity papers to open a bank account, it is not clear what the changes to banking requirements in the *Immigration Act 2016* will lead to, apart from the likelihood of widespread discrimination as bank personnel are now required to identify anyone who they think could be a foreign national, as in the case of landlord checks.

Our findings indicate that not having a bank account is a risk factor that can contribute to susceptibility to exploitation as workers do not have control over their own money, especially if their wages are paid directly into a bank. This can facilitate a type of third-party exploitation—not of the kind featuring organized labour intermediaries or gangmasters frequently invoked in these labourscapes, but of a very informal and personal kind. Frank, for example, was desperate to seek work after his family, from whom he had been separated as a result of conflict, was located after fleeing from home to another African state. Although he was receiving limited support for himself (as offered under section 4, *Immigration Act 1999*) at the time, he needed money for his family's basic and medical needs. A friend who had recently been granted leave to remain offered to lend him his NI number to find work, and to use his bank account for wage payments. But the friend began to take money, and then agreed to split his wages by half; and their agreement was routinely broken as the friend arbitrarily emptied the account, and Frank could do nothing but plead with him.

> The money goes straight to him. And he was living in [another city], so if he decide to say I'm not going to give you money today, that's it I cannot go and accuse to someone he has taken my money. So what I have to do is to play, sort of diplomacy with him in order to get something from him.

Frank's precarious situation and inability to hold a bank account led to him commenting that he had become 'the instrument for him [third-party exploiter] to generate income'. His acquaintances' knowledge of Frank's urgent need to remit money to support his family in his country of origin was used as leverage over him and led to a deterioration of the relationship over time. Among the participants in our research, the occasional use of someone else's bank account was seen as a largely positive 'sharing' activity that enables access to earned money. However, in many instances, the co-use of a bank account is a risky activity for irregular migrants as it can make them vulnerable to losing control over their wages to a third-party bank account holder who can readily withhold their wages (Burnett and Whyte 2010). This facilitates being sucked further into a 'tunnel of entrapment' within highly exploitative labour relations (Morgan and Olsen 2009).

Health

In terms of health, the most important thing to note is that all of our interviewees talked about how their working lives had resulted in psychological and physical damage. As discussed by Burnett and Whyte (2010), the risks of irregular work relate to both a heightened incidence of injury through questionable health and safety protection in informal sector work and a reluctance to access healthcare services due to a fear of being detected by the authorities. Several participants in our research mentioned how they considered suicide as the only way out of their situation.

> And the stress actually was rising, you leave the house, from this time I say, oh my god where am I going? I went to the train station, I sleep there, I found some homeless people, they sleep from the cartons outside and it is my first time actually. I feel very cold and snowing, it was November, very, very cold. I wanted to commit suicide, yes, I wanted to kill myself because I didn't know what to do. To return back, I think, war is the worst it will kill me anyway, even be tortured badly. Better to drink something to die. (Pascual)

Indeed, in a couple of cases, a suicide attempt is what led to the intervention of health professionals who had been fundamental to an effective response to their clients' complex needs. Nanda, who had also been exploited by someone who let her use their bank account and had an abusive partner who controlled her movements and took her wages, was too scared to go to the police. But she was eventually referred to appropriate support agencies following her suicide attempt.

> I did suicide attempt. I was in … hospital. I got liver failure and everything; they give me blood and everything, my blood level gone down. They said it's like domestic violence, they said if you want you can call police. I said, I was scared, I was scared I didn't do nothing.

For those participants who did interact with healthcare services, this was often at a critical moment for those in the worst situations. Health workers—more so than workers from any other type of public agency—gain insights into people's personal situations that can allow them to detect abuse. In a number of cases, such intervention contributed to durable exit from abusive and violent relationships or forced labour. The referral routes resulting from these interactions were vital to people in enabling them to gain access to solicitors, regularize their stay or claim asylum, or get psycho-social support.

Yet the idea that the intervention of health professionals can facilitate exit from an exploitative labour situation is not always borne out by irregular migrants' experiences. First, the more common story for many of those we spoke to was that exit from one labouring situation amounted to movement away from severe exploitation, but often into other exploitative or precarious survival situations still within the unfreedom continuum—a situation we conceive as a hyper-precarity trap (Lewis et al. 2014a). Second, the reluctance among irregular migrants to seek healthcare will not have improved following the *Immigration Act 2014* and subsequent secondary legislation. These further changes saw the introduction of an annual Immigration Health Surcharge of £150–200 for nationals outside the European Economic Area who intend to stay in the UK for longer than six months. There is great concern about the extent to which data on chargeable patients is shared with the Home Office; for example, in 2014, the Home Office launched a series of communication measures to target irregular migrants, including the introduction of posters in all NHS services reminding patients that they may need to prove their right to reside in order to receive treatment (Jones et al. 2015). Commenting on these measures, Bowsher et al. (2015) concluded that, 'by requiring general practitioners to take on the burden of assessing immigration status, this legislation has the potential to erode the foundations of modern medical practice based on confidentiality, compassion, and care for the patient and public as a whole' (p. 853).

Further, in late 2015, the Department of Health announced a consultation on its new proposals to extend charging in primary care, ambulance services and Accident and Emergency. The department has stated that people seeking asylum and refugees will be exempt from charging procedures but that all refused asylum seekers, and other irregular migrants, *will* be chargeable. As stated by Hargreaves et al. (2016), these new proposals 'make the NHS the most restrictive healthcare system in Europe for undocumented migrants', with potentially serious consequences for those 'who are already marginalised, vulnerable to abuse and exploitation, and have poor health outcomes' (p. 685). It is highly likely, therefore, that the new health deterrence measures will deter, actively exclude or wrongly refuse (due to the complex categories of migrant among those subject to the surcharge) the most vulnerable groups from accessing healthcare services. Apart from the obvious negative health outcomes of this, the policy will also act as a deterrent to individuals exiting damaging work situations, as opportunities for exit will be missed by non-presentation before health professionals. Additionally, avoiding public healthcare services can add another pressure to enter the paid labour market at the lowest point to get cash pay to cover alternative healthcare or medicine obtained privately.

Legal Aid and Appeals

All of the legislative changes outlined so far in the *Immigration Act 2014* and *Immigration Act 2016* have taken place against a general backdrop of severe cuts in legal aid, and in the sphere of immigration and asylum in particular, since 2004. Access to legal advice for migrants and families is vital, enabling many to avoid becoming undocumented if they can access good immigration advice to regularize their situation, or ensuring eligibility for some kind of support. Because of the complexity of their legal cases and needs, this may have been the case for some of the people in our research had their situation been better understood by skilled practitioners. Far from burdening public resources, many had never sought help for the abuses they had experienced. Yet the 'residence test' for legal aid now limits access for persons who do not have a lawful right of residence in the UK. This inevitably reduces opportunities for undocumented migrants to gain legal advice and assistance in their efforts to legally regularize their status in the UK.

Although not at first glance seeming to directly affect undocumented migrants, there is a sting in the tail in the part of the *Immigration Act 2016* that has brutally scythed appeal rights for 'legitimate' migrants (those who have been lawfully resident up until the Home Office has rightly or wrongly refused their immigration application). If the Home Office now wrongly denies someone leave to be in the UK, there are no appeal rights to the First-tier Tribunal (Immigration and Asylum Chamber—except in a human rights and/or asylum case, as these are exempt). An individual can request an 'internal administrative review' by the Home Office, and, if this does not alter the outcome, their only route of challenge is via Judicial Review. However, access to Judicial Review has recently been limited, which, combined with the above-mentioned 'residency test', significantly restricts access to legal aid. The result is that fewer people will be able to access this remedy. The stark outcome of this is that, by taking away full rights of appeal from migrants,[3] and pushing the cost of independent legal remedy to the more expensive process of Judicial Review, more people are going to be unable to secure their status and thus will be more likely to become undocumented.

Some of the people in our study had arrived under a range of visa categories and overstayed as irregular migrants, entering exploitative labour as destitute irregular migrants without recourse to public funds or the right to work. They made a claim for asylum usually only years later when they accidentally came into contact with support services. All of this group were refugees in the broader sense. Some left their countries of origin, escaping violence or political persecution, using the migration route available to them at the time to enter the UK for their protection. In a couple of cases, the situation they left behind worsened or changed while they were in the UK in such a way that return was no longer safe. For this group, the creation of greater barriers to securing leave to remain by the removal of any chance for appeal will be devastating.

Another important proposed change in the *Immigration Act 2016* in this realm is to give the Secretary of State power to remove the right of an in-country appeal for a person being deported from the UK following a court recommendation for deportation or the decision of the Secretary of State that the person's presence in the UK is not conducive to the public good. Deportation cases were taken out of scope for legal aid in 2012; so now, not only will deportees have to represent themselves, but they will also have to attempt to do so from outside the UK. Thus, we see the doctrine of 'deport now, appeal later' emerging. This will amount to a dramatic reduction of judicial oversight of detention, despite the strong recommendations of the recent Parliamentary Inquiry on Detention that powers of detention be limited and judicial scrutiny increased in this area (APPG 2015).

The proposals will also limit access to asylum support for migrants in detention, meaning that many will be unable to apply for bail (due to the proposed Home Office removal of its current provision of an address for bail application—this is necessary for the application to proceed but many destitute migrants cannot provide an address). This will likely lead to an increase in long-term detention for some, causing great harm to individuals' mental health (Detention Forum 2015). Others who are released from detention as a result of barriers to their removal will likely feel compelled to provide an address where they cannot actually live in the long term, in order to avoid indefinite detention. Without support, many may become homeless, have little incentive to comply with Home Office reporting restrictions and thus further swell the ranks of undocumented migrants who have no right to work and are forced to eke out a living in risky exploitative labour markets.[4]

The continuing cuts to legal aid in immigration and asylum are resulting in the formation of legal deserts and uneven geographies of access to advice and legal representation (Burridge and Gill 2017). Asylum seekers are particularly affected by these cuts through being subjected to compulsory dispersal to available accommodation around the UK. The outcome of this is that asylum seekers often find themselves unable to access sources of legal advice and representation, which can result in self-representation at appeal without legal counsel (as Dedem in our research recounted, '*I did it on my own*'). Indeed, recent data shows that *un*represented asylum claimants are appearing more often in the Asylum Chamber of the Upper Tribunal (Tribunals Judiciary 2013). Yet, legal representation can make a crucial difference to the outcome of a case. Compared to the 23 per cent success rate of all appellants (represented and unrepresented) before the Asylum and Immigration Tribunal, appellants with legal representation have a 51 per cent success rate (Louveaux 2015). It is therefore clear that those who are unable to source legal representation are disproportionately more likely to receive a negative outcome to their appeal, and thus face the risk of deportation, or being forced to take their chances absconding and entering the twilight world of undocumented work, with all its risks of severe exploitation.

'Illegal Working'

In announcing the Immigration Bill 2015 as a 'radical' crackdown on immigration, former Prime Minister David Cameron (BBC 2015) emphasized proposed measures to create a stand-alone illegal working criminal offence, with a maximum penalty of a 51-week prison sentence and an unlimited fine. Other measures in this battery will allow immigration officials wide-ranging powers to seize property and earnings, to enter and search properties, and to close down businesses. As noted by Bloch and McKay (2015), such measures have, until now, been reserved for terrorist cases. Although some of the measures are directed at employers (such as increased sanctions), they are also likely to materially affect workers through greater exploitation as a result of employers seeking to manage risks by lowering wages and/or increasing working hours. As identified by the MRN (2008), we found instances of employers displacing the risk of penalties onto workers. In our research, Alex told us that he 'did the maths', working out that the gain to his employer of paying him half of the wage given to his documented colleagues meant that his employer made back over a year more than the £10,000[5] he would be charged if subjected to an immigration raid. Both Alex, and another interviewee Mohamed, told us of being at work during immigration raids but not being arrested. Both were 'told off' and warned not to work; thus, it is not always the case that employers face charges for every 'illegal' worker.

Unauthorized workers themselves who face having their wages seized and becoming criminalized for the new offence of 'illegal working' will also face deportation without appeal if they do not have leave to remain in the UK (see section on 'Legal Aid and Appeals'). The principle of 'deport now, appeal later' could have profound implications for those facing a genuine fear of persecution in their country of origin. In our research, three people had been criminalized for using a false instrument, yet two of them went on to be granted refugee status through the appeals procedure as their need for protection was recognized. Such routes will be highly unlikely in the future.

The proposal to seize the wages of 'illegal workers' is likely to direct irregular migrants into even riskier parts of the labour market (such as a reliance on transactional and wageless labour), where the chances of detection are deemed less but severe exploitation is likely to deepen. As such, this area of the Bill was received with great alarm by many migrant advocacy groups. Don Flynn of the MRN said that removing earned wages would force some people into 'systems of modern slavery without hope of protection from the law' (see BBC 2015). He also noted that 'Mr Cameron seems to want British police officers to go rifling through the purses and wallets of people suspected in breach of the rules to seize whatever cash they have on them as the "proceeds of crime". This is not money earned by robbery or fraud: it is all too often the meagre earnings from long hours of work in exploitative workplaces'.[6] In terms of the *consequences* of wage seizing, it is hard to see how the removal of the wages of irregular migrants can be understood as anything other than theft and state-sanctioned facilitation of exploitation.

Conclusion: Creating a Really Hostile Environment

It is quite clear that the government wishes to create an ever-more 'hostile environment' for irregular migrants in the UK. The general goal of producing hostility and discomfort and the specific provisions in the *Immigration Act 2014* and *Immigration Act 2016* will further contribute to the overarching egregious experience of 'illegality' in irregular migrants' everyday lives. Our research indicates that creating an increasingly hostile environment by in-sourcing immigration controls through exclusion from formal banking and housing, and measures to prevent access to public services, will generate further exploitation—particularly for those in the asylum system. Moreover, this hostile environment plays into the hands of exploitative employers and traffickers. Discomfort primarily targets migrants, not those profiting from their labour, which, coupled with a reduction in labour regulation, produces an ever-more *comfortable* environment for exploitative employers.

The insidiousness of the *Immigration Act 2014* and *Immigration Act 2016* has resulted in a clamour of voices predicting direct and indirect deleterious effects such as growing workplace exploitation, the facilitation of discrimination, the damaging of race relations and the deepening of societal intolerance (see, e.g., Robinson 2015; Mayblin 2015; Blomfield 2015; Bloch and McKay 2015). While the intended outcome of the rise of in-sourcing immigration controls is to increase government statistics on removals, it is our contention that recent and proposed policies, as outlined in this chapter, will enhance entry into, encourage continuation within and/or preclude exit from exploitative labour relations for vulnerable migrants. In the case of refused asylum seekers who do not have the right to work and who cannot return to their country of origin, their destitution is an intentional outcome of immigration policy, an outcome of which is to trap them in the UK as a super-exploitable workforce. Furnishing an environment conducive to the exploitation of people seeking asylum in forced labour is perhaps an unintended outcome of such policies.

Our chapter has provided an empirical demonstration of this in its story of restrictive and draconian policies being a driver of the production of labour exploitation among migrant workers in the UK, especially those with irregular immigration status such as refused asylum seekers. That is not to say, however, that the Immigration Acts of 2014 and 2016 are only intended as attacks on irregular migrants. On the contrary, it seems the hostile measures are unlikely to be effective in reducing migrant numbers by acting as a deterrence to new arrivals or encouraging existing irregular migrants to leave to fulfil the government's desire to cap immigration. Rather, the legislation is aimed at assuaging the populist reactions of the electorate, which the Conservative government perceives to be predominantly anti-immigration in tone. Electoral results in time will tell if this yields ballot box results for the government. Yet, what a pyrrhic victory it is indeed for those driving forward the *Immigration Act 2016*—as any 'success' of the policies in terms of enhancing public feelings of migration security will be built on the blood, sweat and tears of exploited workers.

Notes

1. Forced labour as a term and concept is predominantly shaped by the ILO. ILO Convention No. 29 defines forced labour as all work or service that is exacted from any person under the threat of a penalty and for which the person has not offered himself or herself voluntarily. This definition is now accompanied by associated 'indicator' instruments. In 2005,

the ILO detailed six indicators of forced labour: threats of actual physical or sexual violence, restriction of movement of the worker, bondage where the worker works to pay off debt, withholding wages or refusing to pay the worker, retention of identity documents and threat of denunciation to the authorities. More recently (ILO 2012), this framework has been expanded to 11 indicators by adding isolation, abuse of vulnerability, abusive working and living conditions, excessive overtime and deception.

2. There has been a growth in the detention and deportation regime in the UK (Bloch and Schuster 2005); the term *deportability* has come to mean not only the actual risk of deportation, but also its constitution as a lived experience of state enforcement of border controls (De Genova 2002).
3. Such a regressive step is brought into sharp focus when considering the high rate of success in appeals—nearly 50 per cent of managed migration and entry clearance appeals were successful in 2012–13 and 30 per cent of appeals against deportation from the UK were successful (MRN 2013), indicating that the initial decision-making of the Home Office is often poor.
4. Paradoxically, in introducing these recent legislative proposals, the government may also be placing a greater burden on the asylum system justification for their state has sought to restrict for many years now. This is because, although a significant proportion of migrants in detention have never claimed asylum, this may become the only potential regularization route for third-country nationals already in the UK.
5. Alex was talking in 2011. The civil penalty for employing an 'illegal worker' is now up to £20,000, with the threat of a prison sentence of up to two years.
6. See https://community.lebara.com/thread/1296#.VV284JbSNeU.twitter.

References

Anderson, B., & Rogaly, B. (2005). *Forced labour and migration to the UK.* London: Trades Union Congress.

APPG. (2015). *The report of the inquiry into the use of immigration detention in the United Kingdom.* All Party Parliamentary Group on Refugees and the All Party Parliamentary Group on Migration, London.

Back, L., & Sinha, S. (2013). You've got a text from UKBA: Technologies of control and connection. *Discover Society,* viewed 19 February 2016.

http://discoversociety.org/2013/10/13/stop-press-youve-got-a-text-from-ukba-technologies-of-control-and-connection-2/

BBC. (2015). David Cameron won't "cave in" on migration target despite new figures, viewed 18 February 2016. http://www.bbc.co.uk/news/uk-politics-32816454

Bloch, A. (2002). *Refugees' opportunities and barriers in employment and training* (DWP research report No 179). Leeds: Department for Work and Pensions.

Bloch, A., & McKay, S. (2015). *Sanctioning employers does not prevent exploitation and unfree labour.* Available at: https://www.opendemocracy.net/beyondslavery/alice-bloch-sonia-mckay/sanctioning-employers-does-not-prevent-exploitation-and-unfree

Bloch, A., Sigona, N., & Zetter, R. (2011). Migration routes and strategies of young undocumented migrants in England: A qualitative perspective. *Ethnic and Racial Studies, 34*, 1286–1302.

Blomfied, P. (2015). The Immigration Bill 2015: Creating the conditions for exploitation? *Open Democracy*, viewed 18 February 2016. https://www.opendemocracy.net/beyondslavery/paul-blomfield/immigration-bill-2015-creating-conditions-for-exploitation

Bowsher, G. M., Krishnan, R. A., Shanahan, T. A., & Williams, S. K. (2015). Immigration Act 2014 challenges health of migrants in the UK. *The Lancet, 385*, 829–914.

Burnett, J., & Whyte, D. (2010). *The wages of fear: Risk, safety and undocumented work*. Leeds: PAFRAS and the University of Liverpool.

Burridge, A., & Gill, N. (2017). Conveyor-belt justice: Precarity, access to justice, and uneven geographies of legal aid in UK asylum appeals. *Antipode, 49*, 23–42.

Cameron, D. (2015, May 21). *PM speech on immigration*. London: The Home Office.

Cohen, S. (2002). Dining with the devil: The 1999 Immigration and Asylum Act and the voluntary sector. In S. Cohen, B. Humphries, & E. Mynott (Eds.), *From immigration controls to welfare controls*. London: Routledge.

Craig, G., Gaus, A., Wilkinson, M., Skrivankova, K., & McQuade, A. (2007). *Contemporary slavery in the UK: Overview and key issues*. York: Joseph Rowntree Foundation.

Detention Forum. (2015). *The Immigration Bill 2015 and immigration detention: Briefing – Second reading*.

Düvell, F., & Jordan, B. (2002). Immigration, asylum and welfare: The European context. *Critical Social Policy, 22*, 498–517.

Dwyer, P., Lewis, H., Scullion, L., & Waite, L. (2011). *Forced labour and UK immigration policy: Status matters?* York: Joseph Rowntree Foundation.

Equality and Human Rights Commission. (2010). *Inquiry into recruitment and employment in the meat and poultry processing sector*. Manchester: Equality and Human Rights Commission.

Finnis, A. (2013). Is this really necessary? Universities introduce fingerprinting for international students. *Independent*, 21 October.

Flynn, D. (2005). New borders, new management: The dilemmas of modern immigration policies. *Journal of Ethnic and Racial Studies, 28*, 463–490.

Geddes, A., Craig, G., Scott, S., Ackers, L., Robinson, O., & Scullion, D. (2013). *Forced labour in the UK*. York: Joseph Rowntree Foundation.

Goldring, L., & Landolt, P. (2011). Caught in the work–citizenship matrix: The lasting effects of precarious legal status on work for Toronto immigrants. *Globalizations, 8*, 325–341.

Hargreaves, S., Nellums, L., Friedland, J. S., Goldberg, J., Murwill, P., & Jones, L. (2016). Extending migrant charging into emergency services. *British Medical Journal, 352*, 685.

JCWI (Joint Council on the Welfare of Immigrants). (2015). *'No passport equals no home': An independent evaluation of the 'Right to Rent' Scheme*. London: Joint Council for the Welfare of Immigrants.

Joint Committee on Human Rights (2007), The treatment of asylum seekers: Tenth report of the session 2006–07, Vo 1 House of Commons, London.

Jones, H., Bhattacharyya, G., Davies, W., Dhaliwal, S., Forkert, K., Gunaratnam, Y., Jackson, E., & Saltus, R. (2015). *Go home: Mapping the unfolding controversy of Home Office immigration campaigns*. Warwick: University of Warwick.

Joppke, C. (2004). The retreat of multiculturalism in the liberal state: Theory and policy. *The British Journal of Sociology, 55*, 237–257.

Kagan, C., Lo, S., Mok, L., Lawthom, R., Sham, S., Greenwood, M., & Baines, S. (2011). *Experiences of forced labour among Chinese migrant workers*. York: Joseph Rowntree Foundation.

Koser, K. (2010). Dimensions and dynamics of irregular migration. *Population, Space and Place, 16*, 181–193.

Lewis, H. (2016). Negotiating anonymity, informed consent and "illegality": Researching forced labour experiences among refugees and asylum seekers in the UK. In D. Siegel & R. de Wildt (Eds.), *Ethical concerns in research on human trafficking*. Cham: Springer International Publishing.

Lewis, H., Dwyer, P., Hodkinson, S., & Waite, L. (2014a). Hyper-precarious lives? Migrants, work and forced labour in the Global North. *Progress in Human Geography, 39*, 580–600.

Lewis, H., Dwyer, P., Hodkinson, S., & Waite, L. (2014b). *Precarious lives: Forced labour, exploitation and asylum*. Bristol: The Policy Press.

Lipsky, M. (1980). *Street-level bureaucracy: Dilemmas of the individual in public services*. New York: Russell Sage Foundation.

Louveaux, J.-B. (2015). *Asylum appellate project. 2nd year report*. Plymouth: Devon Law Centre.

Lynn, N., & Lea, S. (2003). "A phantom menace and the new apartheid": The social construction of asylum-seekers in the United Kingdom. *Discourse & Society, 14*, 425–452.

May, T. (2014). Modern Slavery Bill, viewed 19 February 2016. https://www.gov.uk/government/news/modern-slavery-bill-published

Mayblin, L. (2015). Why the UK's 2015 Immigration Bill is bad for vulnerable migrant workers. *Open Democracy*, viewed 18 February 2016. https://www.opendemocracy.net/beyondslavery/lucy-mayblin/why-uk-s-2015-immigration-bill-is-bad-for-vulnerable-migrant-workers

Menjivar, C. (2014). Immigration law beyond borders: Externalizing and internalizing border controls in an era of securitization. *Annual Review of Law and Social Science, 10*, 353–369.

Morgan, J., & Olsen, W. (2009). Unfreedom as the shadow of freedom: An initial contribution to the meaning of unfree labour. *Manchester Papers in Political Economy* (Working paper).

MRN (Migrants' Rights Network). (2008). *Papers please': The impact of the civil penalty regime on the employment of rights of migrants in the UK*. London: MRN.

Robinson, C. (2015). Modern slavery and labour exploitation: The UK government's dilemma. *Open Democracy*, viewed 18 February 2016. https://www.opendemocracy.net/beyondslavery/caroline-robinson/modern-slavery-and-labour-exploitation-uk-s-government-s-dilemma

Schuster, L. (2003). *The use and abuse of political asylum in Britain and Germany*. London: Frank Cass.

Schuster, L., & Solomos, J. (1999). The politics of refugee and asylum policies in Britain: Historical patterns and contemporary realities. In A. Bloch & C. Levy (Eds.), *Refugees, citizenship and social policy in Europe*. Basingstoke: Macmillan.

Scott, S., Craig, G., & Geddes, A. (2012). *The experience of forced labour in the UK food industry*. York: Joseph Rowntree Foundation.

Skřivánková, K. (2010). *Between decent work and forced labour: Examining the continuum of exploitation*. York: Joseph Rowntree Foundation.

Somerville, W. (2007). *Immigration under new labour*. Bristol: The Policy Press.

Travis, A. (2013). Immigration bill: Theresa May defends plans to create "hostile environment". *The Guardian*.

Tribunals Judiciary. (2013). *Guide for unrepresented claimants in the upper tribunal immigration and asylum chamber*.

Tyler, I. (2010). Designed to fail: A biopolitics of British citizenship. *Citizenship Studies, 14*, 61–74.

United Nationals General Assembly. (2000). *Protocol to prevent, suppress and punish trafficking in persons, especially women and children, supplementing the United Nations convention against transnational organized crime*. Geneva: United Nations.

Valentine, R. (2010). *Hope costs nothing: The lives of undocumented migrants in the UK*. London: Migrants Resource Centre and Barrow Cadbury Trust.

Waite, L. (2012). Neo-assimilationist citizenship and belonging policies in Britain: Meanings for transnational migrants in northern England. *Geoforum, 43*, 353–361.

Waite, L., & Lewis, H. (2017). Transaction or exploitation? Sharing and coercion among precarious asylum seeking migrants. *Annals of the American Association of Geographers, 107*, 964–978.

Webber, F. (2004). Asylum: From deterrence to destitution. *Race and Class, 45*, 77–85.

Yuval-Davis, N., Wemyss, G., & Cassidy, K. (2016). Changing the racialized "common sense" of everyday bordering. *Open Democracy*, viewed 29 September 2016. https://www.opendemocracy.net/uk/nira-yuval-davis-georgie-wemyss-kathryn-cassidy/changing-racialized-common-sense-of-everyday-bord

9

Funding Precarity: Non-profit Organization and Refugee Negotiation of Italian and European Asylum Policies

Michele Manocchi

Introduction

One of the most common misrepresentations about asylum seekers and refugees—prevalent in public opinion but also among many government and third-sector service providers—is that they are offered preferential support and opportunities by the institutional reception system that a 'normal' economic migrant does not receive. With this chapter, I aim to make two main arguments in this regard. First, the concrete experiences that I have had the opportunity to observe challenge the assumption that asylum seekers and refugees are recipients of strong support from institutions. Second, the labelling processes engaged in by government authorities and organizations, in addition to the confusing organization and management of the reception system, trap refugees in limiting experiences that not only obstruct their social integration but also foster their exclusion and precariousness.

M. Manocchi (✉)
Western Centre for Research on Migration and Ethnic Relations, Western University, London, ON, Canada

F. Vecchio, A. Gerard (eds.), *Entrapping Asylum Seekers*, Transnational Crime, Crime Control and Security, DOI 10.1057/978-1-137-58739-8_9

In this chapter, I condense some of the results that were collected from a long ethnographic study I conducted in Piedmont (a Northern Italian region) between late 2007 and early 2011. During this period, Turin was facing a tremendous increase in the number of asylum seeker and refugee arrivals due to both the establishment of one of the Territorial Commissions[1] appointed for the asylum application hearing process and the chain of communications among refugees at the time that was identifying Turin as the new preferred big city destination (after Rome, Milan and Florence). This refugee increase was foreseen and announced by several local organizations that support refugees, but the local authorities and refugee reception system[2] did not adequately prepare to manage and serve these new beneficiaries. Consequently, a series of unauthorized occupations of abandoned buildings (squattings) occurred, some of those still active in Turin at the time of publication of this chapter (2017).

Methodologic Notes

My fieldwork started in Turin during this period, and I had the unique and fortunate opportunity to follow and observe the events outlined above. The ethnographic method was deemed most suitable (Atkinson and Flint 2001; Cardano et al. 2011) as I was trying to describe and analyse an on-going complex situation in which several different social actors were interacting: local authorities, organizations formally involved in the governmental reception system, non-profit organizations and community-based voluntary associations, refugees more or less self-organized, and the general population. During these three years of fieldwork, I met mostly male refugees from Sudan, the Horn of Africa and sub-Saharan countries, with few people from other African countries, as well as some men from Afghanistan, Iraq and South America. The majority of the interviews (around 40 in total) were conducted through repeated friendly conversations (Spradley 1979), sometimes held one on one, at other times in small groups, but almost always in a location where refugees were living, and only after I had spent several weeks with them, during which I frequently engaged in supportive actions to improve their daily situation. In doing so, I was moving back and forth along the four different types of participant involvement that Gold (1958) described as 'complete participant', 'participant as observer', 'observer as participant' and 'complete observer'.

Indeed, as a member of one of the voluntary associations involved in the supportive actions, I had access to many places, people and situations to which local authorities and formal institutions did not. Thanks to cultural mediators, I was then able to reach out to a few women. As a man, my presence was difficult for these women, in part because of cultural differences, but mostly due to the negative and violent experiences with men they had faced in their previous countries and during their perilous migratory journey to Italy. However, the support of female cultural mediators, and my focus on refugees' experiences in Italy instead of their previous experiences, facilitated my access to and interaction with these women. It should be noted that their number was small (fewer than 10), as I identified them almost solely through cultural mediators. Further, they originated almost exclusively from the Horn of Africa.

Finally, as is common to all ethnographic research, every time I started to frequent a specific place—a squat, a group, an association or a place where refugees were hanging out—I had to first become the object of observation and be subjected to the moral judgements of those I sought to observe, before I could begin my own investigation (Atkinson et al. 2001; Cardano 2011; cf. Adler 1990; cf. Rodgers 2004). Because my fieldwork was carried out in several settings and places, I spent a significant amount of time building my reputation, situation by situation, as a trustworthy and reliable person, before being able to ask any questions. Within these complex situations, I carried out also semi-structured interviews with ten other refugees who had been living in Italy for a longer period of time, as well as with ten representatives of local authorities and various non-profit organizations that were involved in the asylum system (consisting of around 20 interviews).

The Labelling Process

Asylum claimants' and refugees' experiences are to a large extent defined by the bureaucratic apparatus that is in charge of receiving and processing their applications, as well as supporting them afterwards (cf. Butler

2009). A multitude of social actors and organizations intervene in this process. This includes government authorities, at both the local and national level, and organizations with different types of goals (e.g., related to assistance, advocacy, emergency support or legal assistance) in the heterogeneous world of non-profit and volunteer organizations. It is through the relationships between these social actors that the bureaucratic labelling processes take form (Zetter 1991).

The literature has long demonstrated and criticized the negative consequences of the labels used to identify refugees, such as 'victims', 'without support', 'needy persons', 'bearers of suffering' and 'unable to act', as well as 'bogus refugees', 'queue jumpers' and 'ungrateful' (cf. Zetter 1991; Van Aken 2008; Manocchi 2012). I interpret the 'labelling process' as the production and reinforcement of conceptual frameworks through which we read our surrounding reality. However, instead of reasoning about the nature of these frameworks, I prefer to focus on who holds the power to define them, and who, conversely, has no means to oppose these frameworks. In accordance with the analysis of Judith Butler (2009), those who dictate the rules within institutions both produce and presuppose 'certain operations of power that work primarily through establishing a set of "ontological givens". Among those givens are precisely notions of subject, culture, identity, and religion whose versions remain uncontested and incontestable within particular normative frameworks' (Butler 2009, p. 149). Within my research context, this means that, even though there is a hypothetical way to oppose this power—for instance, by trying to change the 'particular normative frameworks' that shape the givens—the amount of power and acknowledgement required to do so is huge and difficult to attain, especially for people from minorities facing discrimination, poor social networks and difficulties in raising their voice and gathering social support.

Refugees can act only within a series of conceptual frameworks created by others (institutions and organizations), which are culturally and socially shaped, are currently almost exclusively focused on securitization arguments (cf. Crépeau et al. 2007; Atak and Crépeau 2014), and define the characteristics that matter in describing refugees' behaviours and identities, and against which refugees have no power or voice. In accordance with the symbolic-interactionist approach, and specifically Mead's work (1934) on the complex interaction among the 'I', 'me' and 'self', it is arguable that the creators of these labels and frameworks determine, or significantly affect, the experiences of the subjects labelled.[3]

Social and institutional operators often use these labels without perceiving their consequences, such as the reproduction and perpetration of stigma and stereotypes (Sigona 2003; Manocchi 2011; Nawyn 2011). Therefore, the characteristics of the many resettlement support projects, rather than producing the positive effects that they claim, reduce refugees' self-efficacy (defined by Bandura [1997] as one's belief in one's ability to succeed in specific situations or to accomplish a task) by forcing them to rely on welfare assistance, hindering their achievement of autonomy, and pushing them into situations of deep social vulnerability. And these risks are equally present in projects that consciously aim not to produce such negative impacts.

My work focuses on the combined effect of the practical difficulties that refugees face due to the legal and administrative management of the reception system, and the labelling processes that take place in the interactions between refugees and institutions and organizations, both in the formal reception system and in the more spontaneous one, as illustrated below. My conclusion is that although some of the labels used by government authorities seem to be necessary and legitimate in order to safeguard the right of a nation-state to control its domestic threshold and to decide who can enter and who cannot, still their effects on refugees' experiences, alongside the labelling processes framed by the reception system's organizations, result in situations of deep vulnerability. Refugees are marginalized, and deprived of their voices and of the possibility to express their opinions, perspectives or expectations, thereby trapped in a vicious circle that starts with the label of 'victim' and ends with that of 'crook' (cf. Malkki 1996; Van Aken 2008).

The decisions made by refugees in response to this system are often ineffective because of the poor information they receive, the inaccurate beliefs they have about the reception system, and the high expectations they have regarding resettlement. Indeed, as emerged from my fieldwork, in addition to the stereotypes and prejudices that inhabit representations of refugees that institutions, organizations and social workers use in their daily activities, stereotypes can also be found among refugees' interpretations of what the reception system should provide, what system workers should do, and what rights refugees can claim. From this myriad of voices, the actions of refugees emerge, which we could in part define as practices of resistance (Foucault 1976), but which are often ineffectual and lead only to suffering, disorientation and vulnerability. In fact, the burden of labels and the consequences of predetermined paths provide refugees with only restricted possibilities for action (Bakewell 2010). Under these circumstances, the agency (Bandura 1999) of refugees is limited, and their ability to achieve a stable autonomy is weakened—as evidenced by the periodic falling back onto assistance among many refugees.

Sewell's (1992) definition of 'agency' highlights that this is a quality embodied in all the members of a specific society. By engaging their agency, citizens can reflect on their own positions and conditions in society, providing a basis from which to plan and implement strategies to fulfil their desires and objectives. Additionally, an inherent characteristic of agency is that it supports the individual in transforming the social relationships in which that individual is involved. In this regard, in order to imagine it possible to modify one's own social condition, it is first necessary to fully recognize one's membership in society. Through this recognition, the individual is authorized to engage in dialogue with other members, express his/her points of view and criticize others' opinions in a dialectical relationship.

However, for asylum seekers and refugees, this level of recognition and legitimization is rarely achievable (cf. Marchetti and Manocchi 2016). First, we need to consider the difficulties facing refugees—and immigrants—in dealing with the socio-cultural distance between refugees and the mainstream dominant culture of the host country, which, when present, constitutes a huge challenge for both creating fruitful relationships and finding a path to integration. In this context, the meaning of 'recognition' can change and be affected by cultural biases from both sides, leading to unforeseeable results (cf. Kirmayer et al. 2007, 2014). Second, the current reception system, instead of fostering that social legitimization—for instance, by helping migrants to achieve some kind of membership of the host society that, even if not fully recognized, is at least acceptable—puts into action practices of unilateral acculturation and indoctrination of the host country values. This will be particularly clear in the examples described later in the chapter—of projects being more focused on the sustainability of the system than on supporting refugees. But first, the nature of the Italian asylum system will be considered.

The Aleatory Italian Reception System

The administrative procedure governing asylum applications is under the exclusive direction of the Ministry of Interior. Asylum claimants must manifest their request immediately upon landing on Italian soil. Once a request is submitted, the claimants are provided with a temporary residency permit and, after some days or weeks, depending on the congestion in the system, they will be given a date on which the hearing with the Territorial Commission (see note 1) in charge of the evaluation of their application will be held.

During this period, and up to a maximum of six months, asylum claimants cannot work, and may ask to be included in the Protection System for Asylum Seekers and Refugees.[4] The system should provide full support to claimants in terms of both their basic needs and preparation for social integration, through a series of services such as Italian language courses, recognition of prior qualifications and vocational training. However, the system is chronically undersized and thousands of asylum claimants are unable to be serviced. Therefore, many only have the options of receiving assistance from private organizations (such as non-profit organizations, churches and volunteer associations), acquiring help from ethnic communities or other refugees who arrived years ago, or using squatting as a means of finding shelter.[5]

The Italian reception system must be read within the context of the broader trends that have developed across Europe in the past few decades regarding the right of asylum. These trends continue to be focused almost exclusively on 'closure' and 'securitization' (Huysmans 2000), ignoring the need for uniformity among the different reception conditions in European countries and for the improvement of the quality standards of these services. However, these systems have failed to guarantee the 'protection from invasion',[6] as is claimed by conservative parties, and they have produced a rapid decline in the safety of asylum seekers and refugees

(Zetter 2009)—as has been evidenced by numerous European agencies (cf. ECRE March 11 2016; FRA 2016, Chapter 3; AIDA 2013, Chapter Reception Conditions; Swiss Refugee Council, SFH-OSAR 2013; UNHCR 2013), as well as the EU institutions (European Commission 2016; EASO 2013, esp. para 3.2.1.4. Italy[7]).

At the Italian national level, multiple programmes coexist within the limited asylum reception system, managed by mixed sets of public and private actors and funded mostly through local, national and European temporary grants (see AIDA document 'Short overview of the Italian reception system').

The first national reception system was tested in Italy in 2001 under the acronym of PNA (*Piano Nazionale Asilo*—'National Asylum Plan') and then formalized in 2002 as SPRAR (*Servizio di Protezione Richiedenti Asilo e Rifugiati*—'System for the Protection of Asylum Seekers and Refugees'). Thereafter, the system was reshaped and reorganized several times, until the last modifications were included in the Legislative Decree 18 August 2015, n. 142. One element that has remained present, as it is crucial for the implementation of the system, is the involvement of local authorities or municipalities. Indeed, because of the administrative and bureaucratic nature of the system, refugees have to comply with the obligations at the local level in order to receive formal documents and public services and to prove their right to be considered legal residents of a specific municipality (Bolzoni et al. 2015).[8] Therefore, only with the full involvement of municipalities as crucial actors in the reception system can the country adequately welcome asylum claimants, provide them with support and enhance their integration into society after the recognition of their refugee status.

However, at the time of my fieldwork, the participation of municipalities in the SPRAR was not mandatory, but voluntary. Usually municipalities, together with a consortium of local non-profit organizations, have to submit a proposal for a temporary project—of up to three years' duration—that is evaluated by the SPRAR's Central Office appointed to manage the national system (Servizio Centrale), to be supported by the national fund. If the local consortium wants to continue providing reception services to asylum claimants and refugees after a project ends, it must reapply for other funds, on a project-by-project basis, via a three-year cycle. But in those cases in which municipalities are not interested in entering the SPRAR, there are no formal mechanisms to force their participation.[9] In this regard, the majority of municipalities involved in the SPRAR entered the system due to their circumstances, such as an already huge presence of refugees or the establishment of a Territorial Commission for International Protection that catalyses the influx of asylum claimants and refugees.

Thus, even if on paper it appears that the services provided are helpful in supporting asylum claimants and refugees through the provision of accommodation, counselling, and language and professional training for a period of 6–12 months, and even if there are many successful local projects around the country, overall the national system is chronically undersized and unable to offer prompt support. For instance, among the several reorganizations of the system that I mention above, in 2013, the Italian Ministry of Interior allocated three years of funding (2014–16) to support a capacity of 16,000 spots (Ministerial Decree, 17 September 2013[10]). However, in previous years, the total capacity was around 3000 spots, to receive support for six months each. The latter was the situation at the time of my fieldwork.[11]

Alongside the national reception system (SPRAR), which, as discussed above, involves the central and local authorities, together with consortia of local non-profit organizations, many other local reception and integration projects also exist. Usually, these additional projects are coordinated by small non-profit organizations, religious organizations or volunteer organizations, working on specific geographic areas. Often, these projects are implemented with only partial collaboration with the municipal authorities, and without formal support from the national system. The main consequence of this is that the collaboration and communication between the formal national system and these local small projects are poor or absent. I had the occasion to observe this dynamic in Piedmont, the region in which I conducted my study, and through discussions with colleagues who work in other Italian regions—and it appears that this lack of communication and collaboration is a problem throughout Italy.

It is necessary to consider that, in addition to asylum claimants who arrive on Italian soil, there are several other categories of refugee that, by law, are entitled to be supported by the formal system. Among these are refugees who have spent a period of time in the Asylum Claimants Reception Centres ('CARA', in the Italian acronym); refugees who are not yet self-sufficient by the time of completing their involvement in a SPRAR programme, and are still eligible to apply for further support; and refugees who have left Italy to seek their fortune elsewhere but face deportation orders from certain European countries back to Italy, according to the Dublin Regulation.[12]

The final overall result of this situation, at the national level, consists of a fragmented patchwork of services, with huge disparities from city to city, and a failure to provide adequate reception and support services to all of the asylum claimants and refugees legally entitled to such services—and consequently a systematic contraction of rights guaranteed (Sassen 1999; Algostino 2005; Marchetti 2006, 2009; Ambrosini and Marchetti 2008; Schiavone 2009; Schuster 2009; Rastello 2010). Indeed, in Italy, at the time of my study, thousands of refugees—though the number was difficult to quantify precisely—were neglected and left to stay in the country without any kind of formal support (Manocchi 2012). The absence of systematic support affects refugees' experiences for a long time, putting at serious risk the possibility of full integration into the new society. The vicious circle produced by this lack of adequate support creates situations of deep vulnerability and precariousness, whereby refugees are pushed into finding temporary survival solutions. Squatting and other informal housing solutions often emerge as the only options available (Sanyal 2009; Bolzoni et al. 2015).

The Role of Institutions

Anthropologist Liisa Malkki (1996) pointed out that, in order to be identified as an asylum seeker, a refugee must demonstrate a series of physical characteristics and social behaviours that are consistent with the idea of 'good', 'real' asylum seekers, and that, in Malkki's experience, are strongly linked to the concept of 'victim': 'As the visible signs of one's social refugeeness faded, one's worthiness as a recipient of material assistance was likely to decrease' (1996, p. 385).[13] Consequently, what is relevant for the system are not the refugees' 'stories' (their subjective narratives about what happened and the causes of their fleeing), but the 'immediately ascertainable facts' (Feldman 1994, p. 406). Moreover, these 'facts' should be sufficiently malleable in order to be turned into 'cases', or bureaucratic, standardized stories (cf. Ticktin 2005, especially the 'logic of exceptionalism', p. 350) that can be understood within the system's rules and frameworks (cf. Zetter 1991; Butler 2009). Through this rite of passage, the subject enters the anonymous corporeality described by Feldman (1994), whereby every personal connotation dissolves into an anonymous and indistinguishable mass. Refugees are perceived as rootless because of their escape from their origin country, according to a prejudice that perceives culture as naturally rooted in places and not people (cf. Malkki 1992). Therefore, a rootless subject has no culture, history, arguments or perspectives, and these elements must be instilled again in a 'bare life' (Agamben 1995), without the possibility of expressing one's own ideas of family, gender, assistance or values (cf. Van Aken 2008). According to Rajaram, this process consists of 'a de-historicizing generality that makes it difficult to understand that there are individual politics and histories behind the pictures of teeming masses of bodies' (2002, p. 252).

Exemplary of this process is the narrative outlined below, reflecting the experience of Nadir, one of the refugees I met during my fieldwork.

Nadir (a Sudanese refugee—not his real name), after receiving several months' worth of institutional aid, is now in a situation where he can no longer ask for support. A request, in any case, would be denied by the institutions due to the behaviours he exhibited while he was being assisted. Operators described him as violent, irascible, rude, not willing to respect his commitments and an individual who lives life in his own way, not according to the rules set in the apartment where he was living:

> He was demanding to cook what he wanted, when he wanted. He was used to get up late in the morning and insist to have breakfast when the kitchen was already closed. Once he entered the kitchen anyway, he prepared his breakfast and then he nearly threw at a worker a pan of hot oil, just because the worker told him he could not do these things! (City of Turin's case manager)

However, to the volunteers for the associations that support refugee squatters, with whom Nadir worked, he was a reliable point of reference, able to mediate with other refugees as an interpreter and provide his knowledge of the Italian reception system. To these people, he embodied the role of wise mentor, who helped other refugees make good decisions. From my field notes:

> Last night I went with a volunteer to talk to the Sudanese boys who tomorrow must leave for Ivrea (a town north to Turin), to see how they were and if everything was ready. Talking to them, I noticed that Samir was very nervous: he could not sit still, he was sweating a bit, in sitting he was continuously dancing the leg. I asked him what was wrong and he did not speak, he was hiding. Then Nadir intervened and the two have spoken a few seconds thickly in Arabic. Then Nadir told me that Samir was scared for the next day, he was worried because he was afraid that things would go wrong. He was no sure anymore to leave. After he told me this, Nadir started talking in Italian to all those present, explaining that this was an opportunity not to be missed, that tomorrow everything would be fine and that Samir and others who were leaving should not to be afraid, because he understood that things were well organized. After this, Samir calmed down a little bit. (Field notes, 15 May 2009, squat located in a former medical clinic)

The huge difference between the two representations of Nadir is clear. Here my goal is not to identify the most accurate one; indeed, both illustrations are coloured by labelling processes. Instead, it is interesting to highlight that the judgement of the local authorities prevents Nadir from accessing certain services and obstructs his pathway to integration, pushing him out of the national system and out of several non-institutional projects. As a consequence of his alleged behaviour, Nadir lost all support from the authorities and it was difficult for him to find any additional help. To cope with this difficult situation, he travelled across Europe—just as he had when he was an asylum claimant—but was still unable to find any viable alternative, so he decided to return to Turin and settle in one of the squats that was active at the time. Before being washed out of the system, Nadir asked for family reunification for his wife and son, and obtained permission to bring them to Italy. But at the time of our interview, he was living in a squat, without a job or home, and without any concrete plans to improve his situation, awaiting the arrival of his family. The pressure, in his words, was 'really devastating'. Nonetheless, he continued to assist volunteers and support organizations with their interactions with squatting refugees, contributing towards keeping alive a social network that provides alternative forms of support. When his family arrived, his final (albeit temporary) solution was to ask for hospitality from one of his friends in Turin, worried about the expectations of his wife and the future of his son.

The Role of Non-profit Organizations

As mentioned above, non-profit organizations also take part in labelling processes, due to their close involvement with each stage of asylum seeker and refugee pathways (cf. Rivetti 2013). Here, Roger Zetter's (2007) concept of 'bureaucratic fractioning' is at work.[14]

For the purposes of this chapter, it is fruitful to highlight two findings that emerged during my fieldwork, which reveal the complexity of labelling processes engaged in by non-profit organizations, and some of their consequences.[15] The first is related to the idea that refugees need to adapt to the system instead of holding on to their own expectations, habits and preferences when these are in conflict with the predefined and standardized beliefs and routines inherent to that system. The second finding relates to the bias that refugees are victims who need to be taken care of.

The example that I present regarding the first finding relates to refugee inclusion in vocational training courses and internships. Often, the training courses that are offered to refugees within the Italian reception system—by both SPRAR programmes and non-profit organizations' projects—only cover a small number of professional fields. The choice of course is based on what training agencies are able to offer at the time and on the decisions made by organization workers—with very little involvement on the part of refugees in such decisions. Some of the social organizations that are involved (such as voluntary groups, civil society organizations and human rights organizations that advocate for refugees' rights) are critical of this process, because it rarely aligns with refugees' expectations and desires, and is ineffective at helping refugees find a job once they have completed their training.

However, it is clear that, even where more innovative options are available (such as courses for specialized positions like wine-grower), the courses that are most popular among refugees, whether provided through the SPRAR or other projects, are those that are usually offered to refugees—introductory courses for jobs related to the construction industry, cleaning and sanitizing sector, healthcare services and tourism.[16] A sort of vicious circle emerges, where organization and operator biases are reinforced by refugees' decisions, which support those organizations that propose the same courses year after year and discourage more innovative projects.

Even if workers and refugees alike are aware of the inefficacy of these training courses in helping refugees find jobs, all of the actors involved find ways to justify this situation. In relation to this, some case managers—within the SPRAR and non-profit organizations—criticize refugees for their poor attitude. Refugees become profiled as persons who are low achievers and lack enthusiasm to improve their prospects, due to their choice of a relatively easy path that does not require much time or effort. In contrast, other case managers try to perceive agency in refugees' choices, albeit not without a certain degree of frustration, noting that participation in these courses is seen by refugees as the only chance to find a job, even if this means not taking into consideration their own experiences, expertise and expectations: 'You do this and that, organize, propose, but at the end of the day they choose the same old things, because with those ones they believe to find a job, even if only under the table [regarding the course of cleaning and sanitizing]' (Case manager). Finally, some refugees keep their plans and expectations secret from their case managers. For many, the most important goal is to be flexible and ready to leave Italy for another European country as soon as conditions allow it. Therefore, the best training course is perceived as the easiest one—a course that is not too demanding and leaves refugees with adequate time to plan their departure from Italy. Such hopes and plans are often not shared with case managers since refugees do not want to lose their 'spot' in the Italian system.

Additionally, it is relevant to consider those cases in which organization workers insist on representing refugees as vulnerable and weak, arguing that they could hardly manage more challenging situations—such as vocational training—because of the amount of suffering they have endured. The following extract from an interview with a case manager is a good example of these representations:

> If you have to run away, you have to do that today, not tomorrow. The goal that they have is something more imaginary than real. What I have observed in the last four years is that people are able to stay only till they are able to resist, face their suffering. Otherwise they leave.
>
> *Interviewer: So, they move because of the suffering?*
>
> Yes, because moving they feel they are doing something: 'I'll go, so I am not forced to sit still and think about my problems that the others throw in my face every time I make a plan, because they [workers in support organizations] say to me, "You cannot do that, you cannot go on, you need specific support"'. And then, inevitably, the subject cannot make it, is not able to move on, the only option that feels is to go away. We have had cases like that, one in particular I will never forget it. Such was the weight, because the more they are intelligent and have problems, the more they are able to have an introspective phase that they cannot cope. And this girl had to confess, in front of me: 'I'm going away'. And when I asked: 'But why? There is some problem here?'. 'No, there is no problem, but I cannot stay here'. (Case manager)

Case managers draw on these kinds of representations in order to interpret and label the daily situations that they encounter, showing clear emotional involvement with the experience of refugees, even if reflecting opposing nuances: sometimes sympathizing with refugees and standing up for them against the system, at other times criticizing refugees' decisions and behaviours. Such representations are welded to the structural characteristics of the reception system. Additionally, they are reproduced in the Italian and European grants available to organizations. Within these grants, the victim label is reinforced: refugees are weak people who have to fit into the system's theoretical framework. Of course, there is a general economic crisis to take into account in explaining the difficulties in finding internships for refugees that turn into employment contracts. However, here it is more crucial to highlight the requirements imposed by funders and the bureaucratic institutional apparatus on organizations seeking to implement support projects. Many grants require applicants to propose projects designed for specific categories of people, such as vulnerable groups, single mothers with children, unaccompanied minors or refugees who have already received support from the national system but still need help. This proliferation of sub-labels demonstrates that it is no longer sufficient to be merely a 'victim' in order to receive support. Instead, refugees need to display additional characteristics of vulnerability. In the words of a project manager, 'Last year we had funds to work with refugees, just refugees, but this year we can only accept refugees with health issues, so they [the refugees] started telling us that they were tortured, they have this and that, and so on. But we need to prove these stories with documents, to justify the enrolment in the project. So we are asking them for medical reports, but this doesn't work, and actually is not the idea of the project that we had at the beginning'. The fragmentation of labels results in more rigidity and obstacles, which reduce the flexibility that organizations would like to have to better support refugees. And the refugees are pushed through processes of continual dehumanization and re-humanization according to the characteristics that, grant by grant, have to be highlighted, rather than hidden. They thus become that *homo sacer* ('sacred man'—see Agamben 1995) who can be sacrificed on the altar in order to preserve and perpetuate the system itself. The result is a situation in which organizations are forced to seek out specific characteristics in refugees in order to obtain funds, instead of tailoring interventions based on refugees' needs and expectations. At the same time, as refugees are passed from one project to another, they increasingly seek to be served by several projects in parallel.

Furthermore, refugees who participate in these projects fail to understand this underlying logic, because it is completely different from their expectations and that 'common sense' that they often invoke: 'I have no particular needs, I have no particular problems. I am only a young man. For me there are no projects. But if you do not help me I will become a homeless, needy person that will ask for welfare assistance' (young refugee residing in a squat). A common consequence is the attempt to leave Italy for another European country, where refugees will eventually start a life in the shadows, without the possibility of being formally recognized and therefore able to access services,[17] forced to take under-the-table jobs, live with other refugees in precarious situations and periodically return to Italy to renew their visa (see the interesting work of Borri and Fontanari 2015; Borri 2016; Fontanari 2016). And for those who cannot afford this solution, the only alternative is to stay in Italy and deal with the daily difficulties that arise—and this frequently leads to refugees finding themselves in a worse situation than they were in when they first landed in the country (cf. Nadir trajectory illustrated above).

The overall result is an extremely inefficient and ineffective system of support, where the poor outcomes achieved by refugees—in terms of socioeconomic integration—are not due to a lack in case managers' abilities or errors made by organizations, but to the profound distance between what funders decide to support and refugees' expectations.

On the one side, refugees are consumed by certain beliefs and pressures that they perceive as absolutely urgent, such as their responsibility for the situations of family members left in the origin country or in temporary situations (for instance, in refugee camps or squats in a transit country), or the necessity of immediately obtaining a job in order to be able to send money home or save it for another trip to reach other European countries (where they will be on their own, without the possibility of accessing formal supports or services). On the other side, the institutional system and the non-profit and social organizations respond to these urgencies with slow and overly complex actions. Exemplary here is the complex and difficult process of recognition of prior educational qualifications, which slows refugees' integration into Italian society—a problem that affects not only refugees but also economic immigrants (Reyneri 2004). For instance, enrolment in university courses is difficult for refugee students, who need recognition of their completion of high school to enter the Italian university system.

Additionally, non-institutional programmes have to deal with a level of bureaucratic complexity that is not present for SPRAR projects. For instance, in terms of funds management, non-profit organizations that use European funds often do not have the same liberties in managing money as are available to SPRAR programmes. An example here is the rigidity with which expenses are managed and reported. Within non-profit organizations' projects that are supported by the European Refugee Fund (ERF)—with which I have more experience—economic support for food expenses is provided via vouchers that are useable only for specific supermarket brands. Usually, supermarkets in Italy are very expensive and they supply almost exclusively Italian and Western products. Open-air markets are much more affordable and, especially in specific neighbourhoods, they provide a larger variety of food from a broader range of sources. But the majority of open-air market vendors do not accept vouchers. Therefore, refugees who are supported by ERF projects have very limited options. They can use the vouchers at appointed supermarkets, which means spending more when buying a similar product that could be less expensive in an open-air market, and losing the opportunity to eat their preferred foods. Refugees may also try to find vendors who are willing to accept vouchers; and based on the refugees' stories that I collected, this means finding someone who accepts vouchers but will attribute less value to them in order to make a profit. Finally, refugees may ask case managers or settlement workers to exchange vouchers for cash. But case managers have confirmed that this solution is not practicable for everyone due to the large amount of money that they have to pay in advance and because case managers are obliged to use the vouchers as prescribed by law.

At this point, it is necessary to clarify a number of points. At the time of my fieldwork, non-profit organizations were applying for those European funds focused on the so-called second integration[18]—that is, the phase, after the first reception system assistance, during which refugees should achieve their full autonomy. Accordingly, the most suitable recipient is deemed to be a refugee who has already received national assistance for a period (e.g., a year), has already taken part in several activities like language classes or vocational training, and has achieved a certain level of autonomy. Given that such recipients are already following a positive pathway, any additional support they could ask for in theory would be related to less urgent needs, such as establishing a small business, enrolling into a university course or covering medical expenses. However, non-profit organizations know that the refugees they will serve using the European resources focused on the second phase, of integration, are people still at the emergency stage, needing support for their basic needs even if they had arrived in Italy years ago and had already been processed by the first reception system. The lacks in the reception system and the inadequate supports provided to refugees when they arrive in Italy are the main causes of this situation—a situation in which non-profit organizations try several ways to reach funds and so be able to support refugees, even if this means adjusting, as much as possible, the profile of people whom the organizations want to serve, in order to fit the formal characteristics requested by the European funds. The implications of this are numerous and significant (cf. Busso et al. 2013). In sum, the final outcomes achieved by refugees, which could actually be very positive in terms of being really out of the emergency phase and being ready to attain full autonomy, are often quite poor if measured against the indicators stipulated by the European funders and in relation to the second integration. At the completion of a project, organizations face numerous difficulties in reporting the project experience, for example, because the activities the project supported—likely aimed at meeting refugees' basic needs—are quite distant from European expectations around project activities and outcomes, which jeopardizes the organization's chances of obtaining the required funds. They therefore have trouble covering all of their expenditure, as well as obtaining economic support for future projects.

These negative consequences further impact organizations and their case managers in terms of capability in achieving project outputs and outcomes, and fatigue. The nature of refugees' stories and the characteristics of cases are complex and emotionally challenging. Violence, loss, suffering, long periods of deprivation and precariousness are often present in the narratives of refugees. Among workers, frustration, helplessness and anger often emerge, which may result in severe forms of abandonment and burnout. Additionally, a large number of case managers are on temporary contracts, which are renewed year by year, only when organizations receive funds. As mentioned earlier in the chapter, non-profit organizations receive funds and economic support discontinuously, based on applications for grants that only cover temporary projects (usually up to three years in the case of the ERF—the most used source of support in Italy). This results in a high turnover among workers, who often move from one organization to another, chasing the available funds. An important consequence of this situation is the potential waste of experience and expertise that workers have developed while working on projects.

Psychological supervision for these workers is allowed by the ERF budget rules, but the amount of money available for that is sufficient only for sporadic meetings with experts, and the impact of such supervision on workers' mental well-being is consequently negligible. If the organization does not assure continuity in funds, such loss can also have negative repercussions for refugees—for instance, in terms of the quality of the services received, the discontinuity and interruptions in relationships with case managers, the fatigue generated by constantly rebuilding social relationships with new case managers, and the loss of trust in organizations and the system.

The final result negatively impacts refugees, organizations and the European reception system as a whole. Indeed, besides the deficiencies prevalent in the Italian national system, it is also important to consider the absence of a common asylum reception system at the European level, generously outlined in several regulations and treaties (the 1997 Amsterdam treaty,[19] the 1999 Schengen acquis[20] and the 2007 Treaty of Lisbon[21]) but never fully implemented, with almost all the attention focused on immigration rules.

Conclusion

As mentioned above, introducing the concept of the labelling process, one of the most affecting characteristics of the refugees' conditions in Italy and Europe is the difficulty, if not impossibility, of achieving a level of social recognition that would make them, and their arguments and expectations, hearable and acceptable by the host country citizens and by the reception and supporting system more broadly. This lack renders refugee agency weak and ineffective. There are several causes of this situation. First, the absence of a unified European system, and the fact that the current system seems to be incapable of moving beyond the rhetorical debates around quotas and access modalities, perpetuates an unwillingness to recognize the negative consequences of current regulations for both refugees and the system itself. Second is the national political decision to maintain the right of asylum as a matter of national security rather than a question of social integration. And third is a system of economic supports and grants that, in the face of ever-increasing complexity, responds with greater rigidity instead of flexibility. This situation also results in organizations being compelled to shut down since projects are not able to provide the required services when they are needed, so that refugees are forced to find solutions outside the formal system in order to survive.

Within this scenario, the 'helping' relationship—which can be understood as the indoctrination of and the taking care of vulnerable victims—becomes characterized by identity dynamics that shape refugee experiences and reify the labels that are used to manage them. This dysfunctional and ineffective relationship is supported and reinforced by the decisions and actions of the administrative apparatus that determine resource distribution and define needs (cf. Van Aken 2008). One of the most evident consequences is the unilateral attribution of stifling characteristics (Sciolla 2000) that are intelligible by the reception system but not necessarily understood by refugees themselves. Throughout their participation in reception projects, refugees are compelled to redefine themselves, accepting, or dealing with, the definitions and labels imposed upon them by institutional employees, social workers and case managers. Under the influence of these processes, they somehow have to connect their past selves with their new ones, reorganizing their preferences, expectations, behaviours, habitus and way of understanding the world (Goffman 1961; Pizzorno 2007).

The result is a system that does not provide adequate tools and strategies that enable refugees to achieve autonomy. Instead, it produces disparities in treatments and opportunities, and an over-reliance on welfare assistance, and, ultimately, is more focused on its own reproduction than on the improvement of refugee conditions. Through my observations, I was able to demonstrate that, even in cases where project workers are committed to finding effective pathways for refugees, it is very hard to break the vicious circle that is determined by the system's structural characteristics. Consequently, the system is mostly reduced to a government apparatus (Foucault 1991) that, on the one hand, often reproduces forms of marginalization and social suffering (Kleinman and Kleinman 1997) and, on the other, keeps many refugees at the border of the law, trapped in legislative, bureaucratic and organizational structures that fail to effectively support their integration.

In this context, the practices of resistance undertaken by refugees turn into dramatic situations in which refugees' physical and mental integrity is jeopardized, due to the actions that they have to carry out in order to overcome the increasing number of obstacles that are generated by national and international systems. As Zetter highlighted, '[t]he resulting discontinuities, between expectation and outcomes – an accentuated sense of alienation and deprivation, overcrowding, loss of privacy – are a clear and sharp reflection of an institutionalized definition embodied in the label refugee. Needs and aspirations became structured into technocratically manageable programmes with unwanted effects on the lives of the refugees' (1991, p. 52).

Notes

1. The Territorial Commissions for Refugee Status Recognition (*Commissioni territoriali per il riconoscimento della protezione internazionale*) are the only authorities competent for the substantive asylum interview (LD 119/2014, which modifies Article 4 LD 25/2008). They are nationally coordinated by the Department of Civil Liberties and Immigration, Ministry of Interior. In Turin, the Commission was established in the summer of 2008. Before that, asylum claimants residing in Turin were referred to other Commissions in other Italian cities.
2. See the section on 'The Aleatory Italian Reception System'.
3. See also the works of Cooley (1902, 1998), and Thomas and Znaniecki (1927).
4. By law, after six months the claimant can ask for a special work permit as an asylum claimant, but the time needed to obtain it is long—at the time of my fieldwork, more than two months—with the consequence that the claimant is still unable to work, forced to keep receiving social assistance while awaiting their interview, and not in possession of a long-term residency permit.
5. There are four possible results that can arise out of a Commission's decision (cf. Manocchi 2012): (1) the recognition of refugee status stipulated under the 1951 Refugee Convention (adopted by Italian legislation in 1954, law 722); (2) the concession of a three-year temporary residency permit, as a subsidiary form of protection; (3) a one-year residency permit for humanitarian reasons; and (4) the applicant may receive a denial, against which they may appeal at ordinary court.

6. The formal committees set up by the Italian national authorities to investigate the results of the Dublin Regulation emphasize the inefficiency and ineffectiveness of this system, as well as the negative impact on asylum seekers and refugees (Central Service SPRAR, Servizio di Protezione Richiedenti Asilo e Rifugiati—System for the Protection of Asylum Seekers and Refugees).
7. As it is possible to read in the latest EASO annual reports (2016 related to the situation in 2015, and 2015 related to the situation in 2014), Italy implemented a series of improvements in all aspects of the asylum claimant process and the reception system, especially increasing the number of available spots in the national System for the Protection of Asylum Seekers and Refugees. However, although it is important in this chapter to refer to the situation at the time of the fieldwork in order to support the conclusions and arguments I propose, it is worthwhile to note here that, even after the changes were introduced, non-profit and practitioner organizations (such as the Association for Juridical Studies on Immigration—ASGI) still highlight several issues that remain present in terms of accommodation and social integration support.
8. Bolzoni et al. (2015) highlight that, 'Within the Italian legal order, the notion of *residency* corresponds to the place in which a person is settled (Art. 43 of the Civil Code), and develops into a well-defined formal status when the registration at the municipal registry office takes place (Law n. 1228 of 1954 and the Decree of the President of the Republic n. 223 of 1989). Through local registration, therefore, the effective recognition of residency materialises' (pp. 405–6).
9. At the moment of the final editing of this chapter (end of 2016), the Italian reception system was going through a huge reorganization aimed at changing municipalities' voluntary involvement to encompass a more systematic engagement of them. Shortly thereafter, instead of needing to propose a temporary project, municipalities had to go through an accreditation process in order to become formally entitled to receive systematic and continued national support. The positive impacts of this change are not clear, because the participation of municipalities is still not mandatory, and if they do not want to go through the accreditation process, the Italian system will continue to be undersized. However, the negative consequences remain very clear. Through the process of accreditation, a series of formal requirements will be requested, and several of the current non-profit organizations that are running reception projects

will not be able to adequately meet those requirements, creating a serious risk that they will have to exit the system, meaning that all of their experience and expertise will be lost.

10. Decreto del capo dipartimento Libertà civili e Immigrazione 17 settembre 2013, available at (Italian text): http://www1.interno.gov.it/mininterno/export/sites/default/it/assets/files/27/2013_09_18_capacitx_ricettiva_SPRAR_2014_2016.pdf.
11. As source, consult the annual reports on the SPRAR website prepared by the Central Service, Ministry of the Interior (www.serviziocentrale.it). See also the previous note no. 12, about the current changes in the Italian system.
12. Now in its third edition, issued in 2013 through the Regulation (EU) No 604/2013 of the European Parliament and of the Council of 26 June 2013, the Dublin Regulation establishes the criteria and mechanisms for determining the Member State responsible for examining an application for international protection lodged in one of the Member States by a third-country national or stateless person.
13. This labelling process is also present in the current European Refugee Fund (ERF) grants, which specifically target people who are able to demonstrate vulnerabilities, such as chronic disease, mental health issues and disabilities, or who are single parents and elderly people (see below).
14. As Zetter points out 'Labels do not exist in a vacuum. They are the tangible representation of policies and programmes, in which labels are not only formed but are then also transformed by bureaucratic processes which institutionalize and differentiate categories of eligibility and entitlements. In this way, labels develop their own rationale and legitimacy and become a convenient and accepted shorthand' (2007, p. 180).
15. During this period, I worked on four annual projects with the involvement of more than 20 organizations, consisting of leading non-profit organizations (which were the recipients of the European funds), supportive organizations and voluntary associations.
16. These courses were the most popular at the time of my fieldwork.
17. As mentioned above, the Dublin Regulation impedes the free circulation of asylum seekers and refugees within European borders, instead, forcing refugees to stay in the first country that took their fingerprints because that is the only country entitled to manage their case.
18. That phase of social and economic integration that follows the first period of the reception during which the focus is on the formal reception of the refugee and the provision of services for basic needs.

19. Available here: http://www.europarl.europa.eu/topics/treaty/pdf/amst-en.pdf.
20. Available here: https://www.consilium.europa.eu/uedocs/cmsUpload/SCH.ACQUIS-EN.pdf.
21. Available here: http://eur-lex.europa.eu/legal-content/EN/TXT/?uri=OJ:C:2012:326:TOC.

References

Adler, P. (1990). Ethnographic research on hidden populations: Penetrating the drug world. In E.Y. Lambert (Ed.), *The collection and interpretation of data from hidden populations* (NIDA Research Monograph 98, pp. 96–112). Rockville: National Institute on Drug Abuse.

Agamben, G. (1995). *Homo Sacer: Il potere sovrano e la nuda vita*, Torino: Einaudi. Trans. Daniel Heller-Roazen as *Homo Sacer: Sovereign Power and Bare Life*. (1998). Redwood City: Stanford University Press.

Algostino, A. (2005). *L'ambigua universalità dei diritti. Diritti occidentali o diritti della persona umana?* Napoli: Jovene.

Ambrosini, M., & Marchetti, C. (Eds.). (2008). *Cittadini possibili: Un nuovo approccio all'accoglienza e all'integrazione dei rifugiati*. Milano: Franco Angeli.

Asylum Information Database [AIDA]. (2013). *National country report – Italy*. Available at: http://www.asylumineurope.org/reports/country/italy

Asylum Information Database [AIDA]. *Short overview of the Italian reception system*. Available at http://www.asylumineurope.org/reports/country/italy/reception-conditions/short-overview-italian-reception-system

Atak, I., & Crépeau, F. (2014). National security, terrorism and the securitization of migration. In V. Chetail (Ed.), *Research handbook on migration and international law* (pp. 93–112). Cheltenham/Northampton: Edward Elgar Publishing.

Atkinson, R., & Flint, J. (2001). Accessing hidden and hard-to-reach populations: Snowball research strategies. *Social Research Update, 33*, 1–4.

Atkinson, P., Coffey, A., Delamont, S., Lofland, J., & Lofland, L. (2001). *Handbook of ethnography*. London/Thousand Oaks: Sage Publications.

Bakewell, O. (2010, August). Some reflections on structure and agency in migration theory. *Journal of Ethnic and Migration Studies, 36*(10). doi:10.1080/1369183X.2010.489382.

Bandura, A. (1997). *Self-efficacy: The exercise of control*. New York: W.H. Freeman.

Bandura, A. (1999). Social cognitive theory: An agentic perspective. *Asian Journal of Social Psychology, 2*, 21–41.

Bolzoni, M., Gargiulo, E., & Manocchi, M. (2015). The social consequences of denied access to housing for refugees in urban settings: The case of Turin, Italy. In *International Journal of Housing Policy*. Abingdon/Oxfordshire: Taylor & Francis.

Borri, G. (2016). Mobilità' intra-europea: il caso dei movimenti di ritorno a Torino di migranti titolari di protezione umanitaria. *Mondi Migranti*, Franco Angeli, 1/2016.

Borri, G., & Fontanari, E. (2015). Lampedusa in Berlin: (Im)Mobilität innerhalb des europäischen Grenzregimes. In *PERIPHERIE, Zeitschrift für Politik und Ökonomie in der Dritten Welt*, 138/139, 35.

Busso, S., Gargiulo, E., & Manocchi, M. (2013). *Multiwelfare: Le trasformazioni dei welfare territoriali nella società dell'immigrazione*, FIERI research report commissionato da Fondazione Compagnia di San Paolo e Fondazione Cassa di Risparmio di Cuneo. www.fieri.it.

Butler, J. (2009). *Frames of war: When is life grievable?* London: Verso.

Cardano, M. (2011). *La ricerca qualitativa*. Bologna: il Mulino.

Cardano, M., Manocchi, M., & Venturini, G. L. (2011). *Ricerche sociali: Un'introduzione alla metodologia delle scienze sociali*. Roma: Carocci.

Cooley, C. H. (1902). *Human nature and the social order*. New York: Scribner's.

Cooley, C. H. (1998). *On self and social organization* (S. Hans-Joachim, Ed.). Chicago: University of Chicago Press.

Crépeau, F., Nakache, D., & Atak, I. (2007). International migration: Security concerns and human rights standards. *Transcultural Psychiatry, 44*(3), 311–337.

European Asylum Support Office [EASO]. (2013). *Annual report on the situation of asylum in the European Union 2012*. Available at: http://www.statewatch.org/news/2013/jul/eu-easo-annual-report.pdf

European Commission. (2016). *FACTSHEET: Managing the refugee crisis – Italy: State of play report*. Brussels, 10 February 2016. Available at: http://ec.europa.eu/dgs/home-affairs/what-we-do/policies/european-agenda-migration/background-information/docs/managing_the_refugee_crisis_-_italy_state_of_play_report_20160210_en.pdf

European Council on Refugees and Exiles [ECRE]. (2016). Memorandum to the European Council Meeting 17–18 March 2016, *Time to save the right to asylum*. Brussels March 11, 2016. Available at: http://www.ecre.org/wp-content/uploads/2016/03/ecre-memorandum-time-to-save-the-right-to-asylum-11-march-2016.pdf

European Union Agency for Fundamental Rights [FRA]. (2016). *Asylum and migration into the EU in 2015*. Available at: http://fra.europa.eu/sites/default/files/fra_uploads/fra-2016-fundamental-rights-report-2016-focus-0_en.pdf

Feldman, A. (1994). On cultural anesthesia: From Desert Storm to Rodney King. *American Ethnologist, 21*(2), 404–418.

Fontanari, E. (2016). Soggettività en transit: (im)mobilità dei rifugiati in Europa tra sistemi di controllo e pratiche quotidiane di attraversamento dei confini. *Mondi Migranti*, Franco Angeli.

Foucault, M. (1976). *Histoire de la sexualité I : La volonté de savoir*. Paris: Gallimard.

Foucault, M. (1991). Governmentality, trans. R. Braidotti and revised by C. Gordon. In G. Burchell, C. Gordon & P. Miller (Eds.), *The Foucault effect: Studies in governmentality* (pp. 87–104). Chicago: University of Chicago Press.

Goffman, E. (1961). *Asylums: Essays on the social situation of mental patients and other inmates*. New York: Anchor Books.

Gold, R. (1958). Roles in sociological field observation. *Social Forces, 36*, 217–213.

Huysmans, J. (2000). The European Union and the securitization of migration. *JCMS: Journal of Common Market Studies, 38*(5), 751–777.

Kirmayer, L. J., Lemelson, R., & Barad, M. (2007). *Understanding trauma: Integrating biological, clinical, and cultural perspectives*. Cambridge: Cambridge University Press.

Kirmayer, L. J., Guzder, J., & Rousseau, C. (2014). *Cultural consultation: Encountering the other in mental health care*. New York: Springer.

Kleinman, A., & Kleinman, J. (1997). The appeal of experience: The dismay of images – cultural appropriations of suffering, in our times. In A. Kleinman, V. Das, & M. Lock (Eds.), *Social suffering* (pp. 1–23). Berkeley: University of California Press.

Malkki, L. H. (1992). National geographic: The rooting of peoples and the territorialization of national identity among scholars and refugees. *Cultural Anthropology, 7*(1), 24–44.

Malkki, L. H. (1996). Speechless emissaries: Refugees, humanitarianism, and dehistoricization. *Cultural Anthropology, 11*(3), 377–404.

Manocchi, M. (2011). "Questo sì che è un rifugiato": La valutazione della domanda d'asilo e i processi di etichettamento. *Interdipendenze, 4*, 3–23.

Manocchi, M. (2012). *Richiedenti asilo e rifugiati politici: percorsi di ricostruzione identitaria – Il caso torinese*. Milano: Franco Angeli.

Marchetti, C. (2006). *Un mondo di rifugiati: migrazioni forzate e campi profughi*. Bologna: EMI.

Marchetti, M. (Ed.). (2009). Rifugiati e richiedenti asilo. *Mondi Migranti, 3*. Milano: Franco Angeli.

Marchetti, C., & Manocchi, M. (2016). Introduzione: Rifugiati in transito attraverso l'Europa. *Mondi Migranti*, Franco Angeli, 1/2016.

Mead, G. H. (1934). *Mind, self, and society: From the standpoint of a social behaviorist*. Chicago: University of Chicago Press.

Nawyn, S. J. (2011). "I have so many successful stories": Framing social citizenship for refugees. *Citizenship Studies, 15*(6–7), 679–693.

Pizzorno, A. (2007). *Il velo della diversità: Studi su razionalità e riconoscimento*. Milano: Feltrinelli.

Rajaram, P. K. (2002). Humanitarianism and representations of the refugee. *Journal of Refugee Studies, 15*(3), 247–264.

Rastello, L. (2010). *La frontiera addosso: Così si deportano i diritti umani*. Laterza: Roma-Bari.

Reyneri, E. (2004). Education and the occupational pathways of migrants in Italy. *Journal of Ethnic and Migration Studies, 30*(6), 1145–1162.

Rivetti, P. (2013). Empowerment without emancipation: Performativity and political activism among Iranian refugees in Italy and Turkey. *Alternatives: Global, Local, Political, 38*(4), 305–320.

Rodgers, G. (2004). Hanging out with forced migrants: Methodological and ethical challenges. *Forced Migration Review, 21*, 48–49.

Sanyal, R. (2009). Contesting refugeehood: Squatting as survival in postpartition Calcutta. *Social Identities: Journal for the Study of Race, Nation and Culture, 15*(1), 67–84.

Sassen, S. (1999). *Migranti, coloni, rifugiati: Dall'emigrazione di massa alla fortezza Europa*. Milano: Feltrinelli.

Schiavone, G. (2009). Il diritto d'asilo in Italia dopo il recepimento nell'ordinamento delle normative comunitarie: uno sguardo d'insieme tra il de iure e il de facto. *Mondi Migranti, 3*, 57–78.

Schuster, L. (2009). Dublino II ed Eurodac: esame delle conseguenze (in)attese. *Mondi Migranti, 3*, 37–56.

Sciolla, L. (2000). Riconoscimento e teoria dell'identità. In D. Della Porta, M. Greco, & A. Szakolczai (Eds.), *Identità, riconoscimento, scambio*. Laterza: Roma-Bari.

Sewell, W. H. (1992). A theory of structure: Duality, agency and transformation. *American Journal of Sociology, 98*(1), 129.

Sigona, N. (2003). How can a "nomad" be a "refugee"? Kosovo Roma and labelling policy in Italy. *Sociology, 37*(1), 69–79.

Spradley, J. (1979). *The ethnographic interview*. Belmont: Wadsworth.

Swiss Refugee Council, SFH-OSAR. (2013). *Reception conditions in Italy: Report on the current situation of asylum seekers and beneficiaries of protection, in particular Dublin returnees.* Berne, October 2013. Available at: https://www.refugeecouncil.ch/assets/news/english-website/reception-conditions-in-italy.pdf

Thomas, W. I., & Znaniecki, F. (1927). *The Polish peasant in Europe and America.* New York: Alfred A. Knopf.

Ticktin, M. (2005). Policing and humanitarianism in France: Immigration and the turn to law as state of exception. *Interventions: International Journal of Postcolonial Studies, 7*(3), 347–368.

United Nations High Commissioner for Refugees [UNHCR]. (2013). *Raccomandazioni dell'UNHCR sugli aspetti rilevanti della protezione dei rifugiati in Italia, Luglio 2013.* Available in the Italian language at: http://www.unhcr.it/wp-content/uploads/2016/01/raccomandazioni.pdf

Van Aken, M. (2008). *Rifugio Milano: vie di fuga e vita quotidiana dei richiedenti asilo.* Torino: Carta Editore.

Zetter, R. (1991). Labelling refugees: Forming and transforming a bureaucratic identity. *Journal of Refugee Studies, 4*(1), 39–62.

Zetter, R. (2007). More labels, fewer refugees: Remaking the refugee label in an era of globalization. *Journal of Refugee Studies, 20*(2), 172–192.

Zetter, R. (2009). La securitizzazione e le politiche europee in materia di asilo e rifugiati. *Mondi Migranti, 3*, 7–28.

10

Asylum Seeker Materiality and Identity-Building: Shapers of Socio-legal Incarceration

Francesco Vecchio

This chapter is intended to explain why many asylum seekers in Hong Kong want to live in spaces that can be defined as 'slums', namely 'informal settlements with makeshift dwellings, deficient basic services and insecure tenure' (Turok and Borel-Saladin 2016, p. 1). These are spaces at the margin of urban areas, where structures are mostly erected unlawfully. Slums in Hong Kong consist of purpose-built or remodelled compounds, the function of which was originally to house animals or gardening tools but where asylum seekers now live. In my research, I found that these asylum seekers were mostly South Asians, and their livelihoods were most reliant on their community of fellow asylum seekers with whom they shared such slum dwellings, often made of a dangerous mixture of brick, wood, cardboard and iron sheets, and lacking sewers and sometimes toilets or running water.

I draw on my participatory observation conducted as an outsider with two groups of about ten male asylum seekers each. One group comprised

F. Vecchio (✉)
Department of Anthropology, The Chinese University of Hong Kong, Shatin, Hong Kong

F. Vecchio, A. Gerard (eds.), *Entrapping Asylum Seekers*, Transnational Crime, Crime Control and Security, DOI 10.1057/978-1-137-58739-8_10

Bangladeshi and the other Pakistani asylum seekers, both living in the northern territories of Hong Kong, where clusters of asylum seeker slums are located. The trust I built with these asylum seekers produced testimonies collected through semi-structured and unstructured interview techniques, which I digitally recorded or reported in notes during or after conversations. Access to these asylum seekers was facilitated by my previous experience as an aid worker for a local non-governmental organization (NGO) and by research I conducted with a group of 75 asylum seekers in 2010–11 (Vecchio 2015). Many of these 75 asylum seekers were interviewed again in 2013–14. They helped me gain access to the two slum communities in which some of them lived, to observe their lives over several months in 2015.

My motivation for engaging with slum dwellers was to produce ethical research based in the understanding that social researchers must advance knowledge of the world while being committed to ensuring that the research they generate is used to protect the people who are the objects of analysis (Jacobsen and Landau 2003). My aim was to challenge contemporary assumptions about asylum seekers by exploring their particular liminal materiality and to identify one assemblage of factors that contributes to a visible process of entrapment for asylum seekers in Hong Kong.

In what follows, I explain how asylum seekers' choice of dwelling is a consequence of their socio-legal incarceration or confinement within a condition akin to detention, which limits and structures their identity—an identity that was also the enabler of a context that shaped their struggle to survive and gain a measure of control over their lives, albeit within a slum.

Asylum Seeker 'Incarceration' in Hong Kong

This chapter includes three interrelated and overlapping levels of analysis. On one level, I account for the factors that produce a socio-legal condition wherein asylum seekers' residential spaces take form as the result of policy and power relations that construct a painful 'truth', one that speaks of asylum abuse and asylum seekers as a burden and threat to Hong Kong—a depiction that in turn supports the rationale underpinning stringent immigration controls and minimal welfare assistance as a deterrence measure (LegCo 2015). That asylum seekers in Hong Kong must negotiate inadequate welfare provisions by working illegally in most cases has been discussed at length in the previous literature (Vecchio 2015). However, stiff penalties apply to those caught working or committing crimes.[1] In fact, media images of asylum seekers being taken away from alleged crime scenes have become recurrent in the Hong Kong newspapers (see, e.g., On.CC 2015). These news reports can be said to instil anxiety, if not contempt and rage, among the general populace at the increasing risks to which Hong Kong is purportedly exposed as asylum seeker crime rates appear to rise (Fung 2015). Calls for more stringent policies to deter their arrival are consequently met by a receptive public (Cheung 2016), with the result that asylum seekers continue to be denied economic and legal rights, while their welfare provisions have not increased since early 2014. Indeed, access to such welfare has been curtailed, despite Hong Kong becoming one of the most expensive cities in the world, with soaring rents affecting anyone sitting at the lower end of a very polarized social ladder (Sun 2016). As a consequence, asylum seekers speak of an enduring condition of deprivation and 'mental torture' that restricts their agency without the need for concrete walls.

The concept of wall-less confinement is not new. Media and political accounts that present an alarmingly negative discourse about asylum seekers born of outrage at certain aspects of asylum seekers' agency have become the norm in many countries (see several chapters in this volume). Media reports uncritically associate asylum seekers with increasing challenges experienced by citizens in relation to welfare and crime, ingraining perceptions of asylum seekers as a threat to be deterred, against which society must be guarded (Moore 2013). A number of legal barriers have therefore been erected to curtail the asylum seeker space of manoeuvre (Dauvergne 2008). And a cohort of people has been enlisted at various levels and in different capacities to police a tight mesh of rules and regulations that construe what Bruzzone (2016) recently called a continuum of 'spatial unfreedom'—namely, a space where internal and external regimes of detention similarly limit the agency of asylum seekers. On the one hand, Martinez and Slack (2013) speak of prison and detention as spaces where detainees are exposed to values, norms and survival strategies to which they might not otherwise have been exposed. On the other, Coutin (2010) speaks of irregular migrants acquiring a 'territorial personhood', or an illegal persona resulting from their immigration status, which negatively impacts their mental state while limiting their movements within the host country, as well as the spaces where they may view their attempts to live a 'normal' life as more likely to succeed. Within this context, the spatial limitations and the ensuing risks that irregular migrants may need to take to survive most often produce social isolation, which often accentuates public perceptions of the socioeconomic and cultural difference of and the threat posed by the inhabitants of such spaces (Sciurba 2009). Marginal groups in certain urban areas may be perceived to be, or may actually be, more inclined to engage in criminal and illegal activities as a result of both their frustration at the lack of opportunities available to them (Agnew 1992) and the fact that illegal forms of work become their main source of income (Pellegrino 2012). In Hong Kong, asylum seekers are 'tortured' (in their own words), and their identity challenged, in that they feel compelled to enter and remain within spaces where their agency is limited by their depiction as welfare abusers and threats, which shapes and reinforces their socio-legal marginalization.

On a second level, I rely on my experience as an NGO worker in Hong Kong in 2005–07, and research conducted within and outside the premises of this and other NGOs, to identify additional factors that determine the space within which asylum seekers exist and act, and thus the condition upon which their classification as a threat is based. In this regard, the label 'refugee' is here explained in light of how it is viewed or understood by NGOs and asylum seekers themselves (cf. Harrell-Bond 2002).[2] The narratives of this latter group are particularly revealing of the objectification this population endures at the hands of institutions and people who are either receptive and involuntarily supportive of hegemonic discourses surrounding alleged asylum abuse, or consciously reject such discourses but use the refugee label to claim rights the asylum seekers are denied in Hong Kong.

Finally, I focus on my participants' construction of a political and cultural identity that impacts their spatial and socio-legal banishment. Lamont and Mizrachi (2012) argue that people labelled as inferior (or a threat) seek to either negotiate or avoid the associated stigma by developing identity-based strategies that resist or distance them from such labelling. It has been argued that in detention, as well as in slum areas, morale and self-esteem are sapped as detainees and slum dwellers feel saddled by rejection, forced boredom and inactivity, increasing their mental stress (Bosworth 2012; Turok and Borel-Saladin 2016). Consequently, these spaces can transform into sites of resistance wherein asylum seekers oppose broader structural settings to regain a measure of control over the boundaries of their self. Bosworth (2012) speaks of detainees developing pride and belonging to their origin country in response to their classification as dangerous foreigners. Similarly, the slums in which my participants lived can be seen as spaces of prideful resistance, and renew agency.

The asylum seeker slums in Hong Kong were brought to the public's attention in 2013, when the NGO Vision First lamented the inadequacy of government welfare for asylum seekers, with rental assistance being insufficient to secure safe and legal housing (Vision First 2013). Rather than increasing the assistance, the government gradually halted rental payments in the slums, apparently persuaded that such housing posed a risk to life, as revealed by the media after the death of asylum seeker 'Lucky' in a fire in January 2015 (Bandara 2015). Yet, my participants, as well as other asylum seekers, continued to live in these spaces. On the one hand, they were offered no valid alternative, as they were unable to find legal and affordable housing. On the other, even when offered an alternative, many asylum seekers refused to leave the slums. It is with this peculiar stance—of asylum seekers preferring to live in dreadful conditions in slums—that this chapter is concerned, to understand the motivations behind this choice.

I argue that these slums are a means of protection from below. As such, however, these slums are also the outcome of, and are functional to, the institutionalization of a prison without visible walls. In a way similar to the 'ghetto' theorized by Wacquant (2004), the Hong Kong refugee slums resemble a Janus-faced device—namely, a highly peculiar form of urban organization warped by asymmetrical relations of power between two *legally* different groups. On the one side, discriminatory and violent policies, politics and practices by the majority 'control and corral' asylum seekers in a space akin to detention (Melossi 2015, p. 3). On the other, the slum dwellers' socio-legal and spatial banishment provides them with reason to resist such a condition by forming protective in-group relations. In seeking internal affinity, however, slum dwellers give form to a support mechanism that augments their social marginalization and illegalization. In fact, borrowing from Sigona (2015), asylum seekers in slums create opportunities for themselves to engage with broader society by asserting a degree of political and cultural subjectivity through the creation of an internal support mechanism. Yet, as this mechanism is based on a process of identity-building that is shaped in relation to and against mainstream society, asylum seekers' opportunities for legal integration are diminished inasmuch as their agency confirms their socioeconomic difference—representing the process of entrapment that forms the focus of this research.

Soaring Pain Behind Invisible Walls

All my participants experienced incarceration in Hong Kong. They had been confined in prison or immigration detention for crimes committed in Hong Kong, or for unlawfully entering or overstaying in the territory. They had been released after being provided with a 'recognizance' paper that attested to their illegal status, and pending assessment of their asylum claim.[3] Incarceration, however, was lived in multiple ways, experienced at its worst as a combination of anxiety, anomie, alienation and anger in the face of the relentless uncertainty felt while their (better) future was placed on hold. 'I'm always in stress. I'm thinking if I don't have a job, I live where', protested a young Pakistani asylum seeker. This participant painted different shades of incarceration, whereby 'prison is better than being outside'. Work is available and can be legally performed in prison, while immigration detainees cannot work but need not worry about paying their rent, food and utility bills. The power of the state machinery to corral and subjugate was unexpectedly felt more intensely on the outside.

In fact, outside concrete walls, my participants' morale was affected by factors that intersected with and constituted relationships of power that effected a condition wherein asylum seekers were reminded daily of their transience and inferiority, which enmeshed with shame and uneasiness at being frowned upon by people who they felt did not understand the boundaries compelling their agency. In effect, asylum seekers are controlled by state and non-state institutions that operate separately and differently, and yet feature a host of interrelated policies and practices that most often inflate the exclusionary boundaries defining asylum seeker behaviour. My participants' lived experience was hence impacted by structures that resulted in a condition of isolation, vulnerability and shame which in turn shaped their identity and agency.

First, asylum seekers are given A4-size recognizance papers that attest to their illegality and thus extraneousness to Hong Kong. While these papers provide them with an 'identity' that prevents them from receiving services to which legal residents are entitled, they also raise or contribute to their prejudicial and discriminatory treatment. Hospital staff can refuse non-emergency visits, property agents and landlords can either turn asylum seekers away or exploit them for extra money, and the authorities may act rudely when recognizance papers are produced, especially in certain areas (Refugee Union 2016). Butler (2004) argues that in settings where certain groups are legally or discursively made inferior, both state and non-state institutions may either be delegated or simply seize powers that control and regulate such groups. Other than authorities exercising legitimate power, in Hong Kong other institutions appear to administer power that diminishes the spaces of manoeuvre of asylum seekers while affecting their dignity. One Bangladeshi participant revealed that when he visited several real estate agencies to find accommodation in urban areas he was turned away upon showing his recognizance papers, apparently because the agents did not want 'troubles', as if possession of this paper defined one's persona. 'They don't see me as a person, but as a refugee', he said.

With recognizance papers, asylum seekers are afforded government rental assistance. However, such assistance was equivalent to HKD1500 per month in 2015, which is insufficient to rent a single room in the poorest urban areas of Hong Kong. Further, some agents may not want to rent rooms to asylum seekers as their rental assistance may take too long a process. Because asylum seekers receive only limited food assistance and toiletries, and about HKD300–500 for utilities and transportation, they may also be seen as destitute (Ramsden and Marsh 2013)[4] and thus incapable of paying the balance of their rent. While some participants recognized that the existence of asylum seeker welfare pulled an ostensibly compassionate mask over a stringent policy designed to marginalize them, such assistance and its mode of disbursement reduced their chances of obtaining their preferred housing. The nature of this assistance had two additional consequences.

On the one hand, delays in the disbursement of assistance, and the requirement that asylum seekers produce a tenancy agreement before rental payments can be arranged, mean that asylum seekers usually have to find a home on their own and produce the money required upon the signing of their tenancy agreement, before they can obtain their rental allowance. The obvious implication of this is that accommodation can be sought only in the cheapest areas, where housing is often precariously built and unlawful. On the other hand, the provision of such assistance is dependent on discourses of ethnicity and security that are imbued with fears that exacerbate asylum seekers' frustration and sense of isolation in Hong Kong. One Bangladeshi participant lamented that 'They give us one razor per month but no shaving cream. What's the meaning of this?! Then people must think this guy must be a terrorist'. The Hong Kong government's policies and procedures related to asylum seekers' survival led my participants to feel the brutal objectifying power of exclusionary politics.

Second, it was the asylum seekers' understanding that they lived in a punitive reality of service framed by stringent rules arguably coupled with the desensitization of many caseworkers to the plight of asylum seekers. Provision of the assistance to asylum seekers has been contracted by the government to the local branch of the International Social Service (ISS) since 2006. One Pakistani interviewee who had been paying for his room in a slum by himself, because his rental assistance had been terminated, emotionally recalled what he described as the uncaring attitude of his ISS caseworker, in turn revealing the public attitude towards asylum seekers:

> You are my case officer, just to sit in your office and each month I come here [to renew the monthly assistance contract], I say, 'Hi', and you say, 'Hi' and 'Sign here', and then go? Then why you have that name, caseworker, what do you work in my case? Even you don't look for a room for

> me, what do you work in my case? I'm telling you, I cannot find a room because I don't know the language and Hong Kong people hate talking to us. (Pakistani asylum seeker)

A housing crisis, involving many asylum seekers being forced to either pay for all the rent on their own or face homelessness, followed the government's decision to suspend rental payments for unlawful slum structures. While my participants revealed that they could not find cheap accommodation in urban areas, this crisis was exacerbated by the ISS staff apparently inviting asylum seekers to share rooms with each other to make up for higher rents in the city. However, this solution was deemed unviable by the asylum seekers in this research. They believed that living in the city amplified their vulnerability. As the above Pakistani participant articulated:

> [W]e don't have any family, relationships or friends to share room. And even if I share … I find one roommate … and I move … and then after one month or so my roommate is caught by the police in some criminal activity, or fighting, and he is sent to jail, for two, three or eight months. At that time, that building agency, or owner, will not understand my problem. They must ask me to move, right? – And in the room, there must be many other problems. You see, maybe I have a drug business and I share room with you, and one day police find some drugs in our room; so they catch me or they catch you? We are living together! (Pakistani asylum seeker)[5]

Over long conversations with my participants I often recorded their frustration at the seemingly disconnected and yet enfolding and apparently unscalable barriers they encountered, their imprisonment being enforced across status and service.

Third, the time asylum seekers spent in Hong Kong, due to the lengthy and ostensibly dysfunctional screening mechanism (Daly 2009), was said to weigh heavily on their mental health. While some were distressed from sleep deprivation, because 'I can't control my life', others maintained that 'when you work you feel tired and you can sleep nicely'. It was this sense of fulfilment that was missed in Hong Kong. Remarkably, many participants argued that they would have happily endured emotional, social and economic deprivation and isolation if this was a temporary situation, and a solution to their problems would eventually materialize.

On this point, Bosworth's (2014) ethnography of immigration detention in the United Kingdom relays the narratives of people whose foreignness is shaped by walls that remind detainees of their immigration status. If Bosworth deals with life behind bars that recasts detainees' subjectivity to produce estrangement, in Hong Kong, life outside actual walls produces similar narratives. Bosworth's participants complained of confinement that negates their humanity by enforcing boredom, uncertainty and pain that are akin to 'mental torture'. In Hong Kong, my participants often lamented that they would have resorted to extreme measures to end their circumstances had other asylum seekers not been listening to their frustration. I did not observe self-harm during my research. And yet their narratives spoke of violence and borders that define power, identity and uncertainty. 'I feel everyone hates me, because you have that kind of feeling that you are a refugee, and people need to help you … you wonder and you see no future', argued one interviewee. It comes as no surprise that asylum seekers and their supporters have used placards at public protests that read 'Hong Kong is a prison' and 'Hong Kong tortures us' (see, e.g., Vision First 2015).

Understanding and Affecting Asylum Seeker Identity

As Jenkins (2014) explains, identity is a label constructed and negotiated by individuals based on social roles defined by structural settings that are shaped by power relations and the unequal distribution of resources. Multiple factors thereby impact the processes by which people identify with, individualize and interiorize the borders that differentiate them socially and legally (Jenkins 2014; Fassin 2013). In this section, I complement my research with my personal NGO experience to delineate the contours of the kind of refugee, or 'genuine' asylum seeker, that most NGOs wish to serve or believe they are serving. This label is understood to have consequences for my participants' materiality and identity-building.

Only a very small number of NGOs in Hong Kong assist asylum seekers. As has been argued elsewhere (Vecchio and Beatson 2014), the majority of these NGOs emphasize services for asylum seekers' immediate survival, while a limited others argue that merely filling the gaps in government assistance risks perpetuating policies and practices that engender prejudice and the asylum seekers' feeling of being mistreated and unwanted. Regardless, both approaches appear to be largely based on a label that may not always represent or serve the asylum seekers' best interests.

Lawshan (2012) convincingly argues that the term 'NGO' has come to encompass a moral and political signifier of collective action that improves human lives. The work of NGOs is thereby often imagined to be inherently selfless, free of worldly desires and thus 'good' for the underprivileged, who would otherwise have no-one to attend to their needs. Yet, an increasing volume of literature argues that such an understanding risks shaping social understandings of need and privilege, and hence who is deserving of 'our' help (Harrell-Bond 2002; Kapoor 2013). Motivated by a desire to identify the outcomes of NGO work, in my research I spent time with the asylum seekers with whom I had only limited access in 2005–07, and towards whom I had been told not to provide aid. I then discovered the divide, to which my NGO work had contributed, between refugees 'deserving' of assistance—most often seen as grateful, obedient and pitiful individuals whose agency, or lack thereof, testified to their indigence (Vecchio 2015)—and other refugees, who fail to visit NGOs on a regular basis. Most often this latter group lived far from the urban centre where NGO offices are located. Thus, these asylum seekers were forced to 'manage on their own', by engaging in working activities that, it was believed, 'genuine' asylum seekers would not take up for fear of arrest and repatriation (Bernal 2010). Their agency fuelled the suspicion that they had travelled to Hong Kong for reasons other than to flee persecution (cf. Moore 2013), and since they did not seek help from NGOs, it was assumed that they were not deserving of sympathy. As an aid worker, I was often told not to help such asylum seekers in order to focus on more vulnerable cases.

Obviously, this classification had implications in terms of who was awarded assistance. Considering that many NGOs are resource-limited, and currently there are about 11,000 asylum seekers in Hong Kong (ImmD 2016), many asylum seekers live without NGO aid. As I witnessed, this lack of assistance led asylum seekers to seek out situations, environments and networks that provided them with (albeit limited) resources, such as the slums. When I asked my participants whether they had heard of NGOs helping asylum seekers, only a few had some vague knowledge. Many had tried to approach an NGO, while others had not because friends who had tried had been quickly dismissed, giving them an impression of 'how things go'.

The following section demonstrates that a sense of 'groupness' developed in both the slum communities under my scrutiny. They each adopted values and expectations based on a sense of their mutual exclusion and isolation, which in turn produced a sense of shared belonging. It is understood that identity-based claims are often made as a form of adaptation or resistance to some kind of imposition (Jenkins 2014). In this vein, Wacquant (2004, p. 3) maintains that 'external hostility' generates corresponding 'internal affinity', which can be asserted through surging pride (Bosworth 2012), as well as 'learned isolation' (Leung 2014, p. 7), whereby a segregated segment of the population retreats within their in-group's protective walls. In Hong Kong, the two groups of slum dwellers I met led a secluded life, far from the judgmental gaze of mainstream society. 'We are refugees. If something happens [on the outside], they blame us. So better we stay here', explained one Bangladeshi participant.

Importantly, the feeling expressed in the above quote was strengthened by the activity of one NGO that argued that asylum seeker suffering cannot be relieved by resource-limited NGOs alone, but should be tackled at the policy level (Vision First 2014a). I am a non-executive director of this NGO, Vision First, which allows me to both gain knowledge and critically reflect on what I observe. Banking on the internal affinity among asylum seekers in Hong Kong, Vision First tried in 2014–15 to mobilize this population and help them take ownership of the 'refugee' label in order to construe a political identity that opposed normalized representations of victims and system abusers (Vision First 2014b). This mobilization began with a few asylum seekers in the slums. It was founded on the understanding that they had come to perceive themselves in line with the socio-legal status they were assigned in Hong Kong, which, however, was contested by their assertion of their own superior morality (see following section). The first refugee-led NGO in Hong Kong was consequently formed. And its member base grew via word of mouth to reach a few hundred asylum seekers, including many of my participants. These asylum seekers acted on their sense of marginalization to shift their stance from one of learned isolation and proud retrenchment to being 'refugees' visibly exercising their rightful agency (Vecchio and Ham 2017).

Their mobilization was, however, met with resistance. On the one side, it appears that it did not raise the sympathy and support of other NGOs (cf. Sigona 2015), who were worried that this line of reasoning would antagonize the authorities and blur the boundaries between genuine and bogus asylum seekers, on which the demands of funding agencies and donors in Hong Kong have long rested (Vecchio 2015). On the other, after the ISS terminated their rental assistance, slum dwellers were vexed by the sudden need to pay for all of their rent. As a result, all of my participants silently withdrew from political engagement.

In hindsight, this mobilization did not alter the general perception that asylum seekers are foreigners. As Bosworth (2012, 2014) argues, the socio-legal otherness of immigration detainees is confirmed by their claiming an identity that elevates their status to the realm of a living and rightful agent, in opposition to what O'Malley (2010) calls the 'simulated anonymity' of risk categories. The visibility of Hong Kong's refugees was grounded on a sense of communality established around their illegal immigration status and different ethnicity. In addition, most slum dwellers who participated in this surge of activism came to share the opinion of other asylum seekers who had not taken part in the mobilization: that protesting and becoming too visible in the eyes of the authorities would only reinforce their stigmatization (Vecchio and Beatson 2014). Whether this view stands up to empirical analysis is debatable. Nonetheless, it is clear that the slum dwellers believed that the little they had, such as rental assistance, was swept away by the state restoring the order disturbed by these protests. For people without secure legal status, who had previously learnt to master resources that allowed them to get by and sometimes even to prosper in isolation, flying under the radar became a preferable option when their livelihood became more dependent on raising an income illegally.

For my participants, a visible process of entrapment emerged wherein the spatial limitations of their geographical banishment structured their agency: initially, by informing public discourses of deservedness, which exacerbated their isolation, and later, by generating an identity-shaping exercise that returned them to even harsher conditions, which were then negotiated through illegal work—the resource that fuelled the public image of asylum seekers as deviant economic migrants.

Building Support in the Face of Marginalization

As Turok and Borel-Saladin (2016) argue, there are generally two contrasting views on the impact of slums on the mental health and socioeconomic status of their inhabitants. On one side, it is argued that slums function as sites where migrant populations form or access new social networks (Turner 1968). According to this view, slums are areas where shelter is affordable and resources can be shared. Internal affinity among people who share similar living settings and conditions can be developed in ways similar to that seen in the ghetto, as theorized by Wacquant (2004), although the integrative and protective nature of this space is conceptualized most notably as a means to enable inhabitants to save enough money to leave the slum and socially and economically integrate into the city. The intensification of social relations and cultural sharing inside slums, fuelled by the inhabitants' isolation, is also featuring in the literature that views slums as 'cul-de-sacs'—namely, sites where slum dwellers suffer from a lack of employable skills, environmental hardship and mental stress (Turok and Borel-Saladin 2016). Here, however, hopes and expectations are sapped by the slums and the lack of opportunities they entail. In Hong Kong, in the two communities I studied, my participants shared a condition akin to this 'cul-de-sac' scenario (cf. Davis 2006). However, these slums were also spaces where asylum seekers organized their community around a collective identity and resourceful pride. In fact, the structural barriers they faced on the outside were negotiated through companionship and peer assistance.

In this regard, it is noticeable that asylum seekers generally have only limited knowledge about Hong Kong before arriving there, which can be eased by contact with co-nationals in Hong Kong after arrival (Vecchio

2015). For example, one Bangladeshi participant described how he arrived in Hong Kong with only a phone number he was given by a friend of someone in Hong Kong that could be contacted in an emergency. Finding himself without means of survival he called this person and was taken to a slum where other asylum seekers from Bangladesh lived. It is here that, as he said, 'slowly, slowly we learn everything', adapting to and normalizing their life on the margins. Migration indeed implies that former support ties are often replaced with new connections in the destination country (Koser 1997). Further, such ties are formed over a shared background, whether it be ethnic, cultural or even grief at the loss of their home (Butler 2004). On the one hand, my participants explained that, despite their having been involved in many confrontations in their home countries, in Hong Kong conflict among asylum seekers was manageable, and indeed rarely affected life in the slums, because these complex networks had become key to their survival. 'We have so many problems that people can even commit suicide', said a Pakistani participant. These 'problems' meant that refugees in Hong Kong were motivated to foster and maintain their connections with each other, as they could be useful at any time. Speaking about an asylum seeker who the night before had been evicted by his landlord, and was now housed by him, the above participant said: 'That's why it's important to stay here [in the slums]. People have friends. Like me and him. I help him today, other people will help tomorrow'. Saunders (2010) similarly recalls a conversation in a slum in Kenya during which he was told that 'Neighbours are important. … When you have a good understanding and relationship with them, they can keep you alive. … Friends here are very important'.

On the other hand, such friendship was born of their collective indifference of, if not aversion to, both the local Chinese community and the legal residents that shared the asylum seekers' ethnic background. First, from my interviews emerged the view that not only did the local population not understand asylum seekers, but also that this occurred because asylum seekers believed the local Chinese population to be morally and culturally deficient—a circumstance that arguably softened asylum seeker in-group divisions in the face of adversity. Referring to the meagre social services provided for the local elderly (cf. Lam 2016), the above Pakistani participant stated that 'These people can't help their own kind, how can they help us? We need to help ourselves'. Further, one eloquent Pakistani participant complained about the overtly 'materialistic' approach to life adopted by the local population, who placed excessive importance on money and success as a way to define and classify individuals, and in so doing dehumanized asylum seekers. In response, this participant advanced his group as the depository of a rightful behaviour, values and thinking, by arguing that 'Our mentality is different'. Very often I was involved in discussions in which participants praised their own country's laws, religion and cultural traditions above that of Hong Kong (cf. Bosworth 2012), despite these often having caused their migration.

In relation to diet, my participants stressed that cooking and eating were valued as important social events focused on sharing food, which was a practice they believed distanced their culture from that of Chinese people. It is noteworthy that slum residents rarely ventured out to densely populated urban areas, for public transportation is expensive. Instead, their time was spent at home where compounds usually comprised ten or more rooms and large common areas often furnished with chairs and sofas. These areas facilitated the exchange of views, knowledge and experiences among the tenants. I was told by my participants that in these shared spaces they would regularly talk about their future and unfulfilled dreams, as well as their past, family and homeland. Such conversations would occur most often at night, as asylum seekers often have disturbed sleep (Mellah 2001). Through such conversations, they revived a sense of belonging to their homeland and distant traditions, which was often expressed in their insistence on cooking and sharing traditional food. When I visited their homes, I was frequently invited for lunch. However, the grocery items needed to cook their food were not available through the limited government assistance provided. In this regard, some commented that shopping for grocery items was an activity that, on the one hand, was frustrating as these items should have been provided given that they were not allowed to work, and, on the other, gave them a sense of dignity, control and self-worth. 'We don't want to get assistance. We want to get things by ourselves', said one Pakistani asylum seeker. However, generating an income risked arrest.

Second, local residents who shared the asylum seekers' ethnicity were rarely respected by my participants. When asked about whether asylum seekers could obtain help from these residents, one Bangladeshi slum dweller argued that their untenured legal status affected co-ethnic relationships with these residents: 'They don't like us. They are residents and we are refugees. They are rich and we are poor. The majority is like that. Maybe one or two want to help, but they want to find their own benefit for the help'. As in Wacquant's (2004) argument about the ghetto, even Hong Kong's refugee slums appear to be marred by stigmatization based on ethnicity, which is further demonstrated by the local ethnic minorities' resenting asylum seekers, for their illegal stay is seen as tarnishing the local residents' precarious reputation in the eyes of the majority group (Lahtoo 2016; Law and Lee 2013). And yet it is the asylum seekers' illegal status that enforces their marginalization, enshrining their ethnic inferiority. Older migrant generations may in fact feel they are in competition with newly arrived co-ethnic migrants (Schierup et al. 2006), or they may bank on the asylum seekers' precarious status and reputation to exploit their vulnerability in housing, health and labour (Grzymala-Kazlowska 2005). Consequently, many of my participants commented that they felt 'at home' in the slums, away from both Chinese and ethnic residents (cf. Wacquant 2004). Not only the slums protected them from the threats faced on the outside, but this environment also resembled the settings in which they had lived in their own country, in turn revealing the collective pride of participants who opposed the perceived lifestyle of the majority of the Hong Kong population. 'We don't like the city. We need our peace. This place [the slum] is similar to our home and we can help each other', I was told by a group of Bangladeshi participants.

The help available to asylum seekers in slums was to be found via their daily associations with each other, through which they shared food, experiences and coping strategies. Such strategies often involved local opportunities to 'integrate' into Hong Kong (cf. Turner 1968), by working illegally, although this largely increased their extraneousness from the law-abiding society. The risks they incurred while working in the informal economy also caused friendships in the slums to be often tenuous and formed out of convenience, in turn explaining asylum seekers' need to forge a large base of neighbours who cluster in these areas. On the day we met, one Bangladeshi participant had told another asylum seeker about a job that he had refused to take in order to honour our meeting, on the promise that he would be called by this friend were other opportunities to arise in future. However, his friend was arrested when the workplace was unexpectedly busted by immigration authorities. Saddened and angry that asylum seekers were subjected to this kind of policing, this participant feigned a smile at the realization that, 'If I had taken that job, I would be in jail now'.

Conclusion

The purpose of this chapter was to analyse why certain asylum seekers in Hong Kong preferred to live in slums than in other settings, even after their rental assistance was terminated. In so doing, the aim was to document and explain a process of entrapment to which the asylum seeker population is subjected, their agency funnelled by their securing a 'home' in spaces where a supportive mechanism exists that becomes the mast around which their identities and collective pride take shape. On this note, particular mention is made of the context of these asylum seekers' 'incarceration', and specifically the mental torture caused by their illegal status which structures the life chances that foster this state of mind. In this context, in which they feel poorly tolerated by the majority population, asylum seekers seek companionship and assistance from each other. Through communal living in the slums, they raise a collective and cultural identity that entrenches their stigmatization, which, coupled with their financial needs, ensures their entry into the informal economy, out of necessity and as an instrument to retain or reclaim a measure of agency.

It follows from the above that the slums form part of a self-supporting machinery whereby asylum seeker identity and agency effectively contribute to their incarceration and mental torture. Their confinement creates state power that marks and violently regulates them to enforce their integration into specific segments of society, regardless of their individual aspirations (cf. Mezzadra 2011). It can be argued that the slums render their inhabitants, as per Wacquant (2004), both objectively and subjectively dissimilar from the local population, while their coping strategies are limited to spaces in which their difference is permitted although constantly policed.

An important question to raise then regards the real purpose of the asylum and welfare system for asylum seekers. Based on official statistics, the number of asylum seekers in Hong Kong has increased from a few hundred when assistance for them was provided for the first time by the ISS in 2006, to about 11,000 today, de facto demonstrating the inadequacy of deterrent policies. Further, it is noteworthy that my participants, who endorsed a more engaged identity through political action, retraced their steps to return to their previous livelihoods, disengaging from politics which they felt had failed them twice. On the one side, asylum seekers are still foreign to Hong Kong. On the other, political engagement did not ensure any positive change. The state exerted its power to subdue and appease asylum seekers, who unwillingly returned to the spaces of their confinement and the same activities that previously shaped their prideful existence.

To answer the above question, it is then valuable to recall that the economic exploitation of its inhabitants is central to the function of the ghetto (Wacquant 2004). In Hong Kong, it might be that the socio-legal incarceration of asylum seekers is both the reason for their marginalization and the enabler of exploitative labour conditions in the marker (Vecchio 2015). While incarceration institutes transience, uncertainty and vulnerability (Bosworth 2014), it also pleases overarching economic forces in terms of employment (Martinez and Slack 2013). There might be here the case for the preference for legal restrictions that impose conditions akin to incarceration over the use of physical walls in relation to extant economic conditions and the task that those labelled superfluous and damaging to society are required to perform in Hong Kong.

Notes

1. Sentencing guidelines impose 15–22 months' imprisonment on illegal immigrants and others pending removal who are caught working illegally (*HKSAR v Usman Butt and others*, HCMA70/2010).
2. 'Asylum seeker' and 'refugee' are terms used here interchangeably with preference to the former for asylum is extremely hard to obtain in Hong

Kong. Further, the label refugee is traditionally associated with migration from China and Vietnam in the 1950s through to the 1990s that was believed to be largely economically motivated. In the contemporary discourse, the international usage of the label refugee can be said to be equivalent to the use of 'genuine asylum seeker' in Hong Kong.

3. In 2004, the Hong Kong Government introduced a screening mechanism to assess *non-refoulement* claims of people demanding protection from torture, cruel or other inhuman treatment, following a decision to that effect of the Court of Final Appeal, Hong Kong's highest court (Loper 2010). This mechanism has since been enhanced and expanded in scope. However, the government maintains that asylum seekers are to be considered illegal immigrants and overstayers (LegCo 2015). In fact, immigration policies can require people seeking protection to pursue their claim only after they have either entered Hong Kong illegally or their permitted period of stay has expired (*CH v Director of Immigration*, CACV59/2010). Consequently, asylum seekers are illegal migrants or overstayers against whom is generally handed down a removal order, which can warrant the asylum seeker detention if his or her removal is foreseeable in the short term. Most asylum seekers are detained only for the purpose of verification of their identity, after which they are released into society pending determination of their asylum claim.
4. For the government assistance they receive is to be distributed in a form that should avoid creating a 'magnet effect which may have serious implications on the sustainability of the assistance programme and … immigration control' (LegCo 2015, p. 8).
5. Asylum seekers in slums generally retain some privacy as rooms are cheaper than in urban settings, and thus they can live alone while sharing the compound common areas only.

References

Agnew, R. (1992). Foundation for a general strain theory of crime and delinquency. *Criminology, 30*(1), 47–87.

Bandara, K. (2015). Sri Lankan fatally burned in Hong Kong refugee slum. *The Sunday Times*, 4 February, viewed 5 February 2015. http://www.sundaytimes.lk/150201/news/sri-lankan-fatally-burned-in-hong-kong-refugee-slum-133282.html

Bernal, J. K. (2010). Begging for basic rights. *South China Morning Post*, 13 November.

Bosworth, M. (2012). Subjectivity and identity in detention: Punishment and society in a global age. *Theoretical Criminology, 16*(2), 123–140.

Bosworth, M. (2014). *Inside immigration detention*. Oxford: Oxford University Press.

Bruzzone, M. (2016). On exterior and interior detention regimes: Governing, bordering, and economy in transit migration across Mexico. In D. Conlon & N. Hiemstra (Eds.), *Intimate economies of immigration detention: Critical perspectives* (pp. 105–119). Abingdon: Routledge.

Butler, J. (2004). *Precarious life: The power of mourning and violence*. London: Verso.

Cheung, K. (2016). HKFP lens: "gas them" – Activists satirise anti-refugee campaigners at competing rallies. *Hong Kong Free Press*, 9 May, viewed 9 May 2016. https://www.hongkongfp.com/2016/05/09/hkfp-lens-gas-them-activists-satirise-anti-refugee-campaigners-at-competing-rallies/

Coutin, B. (2010). Confined within: National territories as zones of confinement. *Political Geography, 29*, 200–208.

Daly, M. (2009). Refugee law in Hong Kong: Building the legal infrastructure. *Hong Kong Lawyer, 9*, 14–30.

Dauvergne, C. (2008). *Making people illegal: What globalization means for migration and law*. Cambridge: Cambridge University Press.

Davis, M. (2006). *Planet of slums*. London: Verso.

Fassin, D. (2013). *Enforcing order: An ethnography of urban policing*. London: Polity Press.

Fung, K. (2015). Crime wave shows folly of open-door policy to refugees. *China Daily*, 7 October, viewed 7 October 2015. http://www.chinadailyasia.com/opinion/2015-10/07/content_15325622.html

Grzymala-Kazlowska, A. (2005). From ethnic cooperation to in-group competition: Undocumented Polish workers in Brussels. *Journal of Ethnic and Migration Studies, 31*(4), 675–697.

Harrell-Bond, B. (2002). Can humanitarian work with refugees be humane? *Human Rights Quarterly, 24*(1), 51–85.

Immigration Department [ImmD]. (2016). *Statistics on non-refoulement claims*, as at end of June 2016, viewed 22 September 2016. http://www.immd.gov.hk/eng/facts/enforcement.html

Jacobsen, K., & Landau, L. B. (2003). *The dual imperative in refugee research: Some methodological and ethical considerations in social science research on forced migration* (Rosemarie Rogers Working Paper No. 19). The Inter-University

Committee on International Migration, viewed 1 June 2009. web.mit.edu/cis/www/migration/pubs/rrwp/19_jacobsen.htm

Jenkins, R. (2014). *Social identity*. Abingdon: Routledge.

Kapoor, I. (2013). *Celebrity humanitarianism: The ideology of global charity*. Abingdon: Routledge.

Koser, K. (1997). Social networks and the asylum cycle: The case of Iranians in the Netherlands. *International Migration Review, 31*(3), 591–611.

Lahtoo, Y. (2016). Grim prospects for Hong Kong's South Asian asylum seekers when their own governments want them in a gulag. *South China Morning Post*, 14 April, viewed 15 April 2016. http://www.scmp.com/comment/insight-opinion/article/1935979/grim-prospects-hong-kongs-south-asian-asylum-seekers-when

Lam, J. (2016). Hong Kong government slammed as poverty figure hits six-year high. *South China Morning Post*, 15 October, viewed 16 October 2016. http://www.scmp.com/news/hong-kong/politics/article/2028422/hong-kong-government-slammed-poverty-figure-hits-six-year

Lamont, M., & Mizrachi, N. (2012). Introduction: Ordinary people doing extraordinary things: Responses to stigmatization in comparative perspective. *Ethnic and Racial Studies, 35*(3), 365–381.

Law, K. Y., & Lee, K. M. (2013). Socio-political embeddings of South Asian ethnic minorities' economic situations in Hong Kong. *Journal of Contemporary China, 22*(84), 984–1005.

Lawshan, A. (2012). How progressive culture resists critique: The impasse of NGO studies. *Ethnography, 14*(4), 501–522.

Legislative Council [LegCo]. (2015). *Legislative Council Panel on Security: Unified Screening Mechanism for Non-refoulement Claims*, LC Paper No. CB(2)1832/14-15(03), 7 July, viewed 7 September 2016. http://www.legco.gov.hk/yr14-15/english/panels/se/papers/se20150707cb2-1832-3-e.pdf

Leung, W. S. (2014). The fragmentation, shift and adaptation of the "asylum seeker" identity in Hong Kong. *VF Research Insight Series*, 2.

Loper, K. (2010). Human rights, non-refoulement and the protection of refugees in Hong Kong. *International Journal of Refugee Law, 22*(3), 404–439.

Martinez, D., & Slack, J. (2013). What part of "illegal" don't you understand? The social consequences of criminalizing unauthorized Mexican migrants in the United States. *Social & Legal Studies, 22*(4), 535–551.

Mellah, F. (2001). *Clandestino nel Mediterraneo*. Trieste: Asterios Editore.

Melossi, D. (2015). *Crime, punishment and migration*. London: Sage.

Mezzadra, S. (2011). The gaze of autonomy: Capitalism, migration and social struggles. In V. Squire (Ed.), *The Contested politics of mobility: Borderzones and irregularity* (pp. 121–142). Abingdon: Routledge.

Moore, K. (2013). "Asylum shopping" in the neoliberal social imaginary. *Media, Culture & Society, 35*(3), 348–365.

O'Malley, P. (2010). Simulated justice: Risk, money and telemetric policing. *British Journal of Criminology, 50*, 795–807.

On.CC. (2015, November 30). 外國快速評核免遣返聲請 港平均滯留2.7年 (Average of 2.7 years required to assess non-refoulement claims), viewed 30 November 2015. http://hk.on.cc/hk/bkn/cnt/news/20151130/bkn-20151130161257180-1130_00822_001.html

Pellegrino, V. (2012). La clandestinità come progetto trans-nazionale: Un caso di studio sulle migrazioni marocchine in Emilia (Nord Italia). *Mondi Migranti, 3*, 205–226.

Ramsden, M., & Marsh, L. (2013). The "right to work" of refugees in Hong Kong: Ma v Director of Immigration. *International Journal of Refugee Law, 25*(3), 574–596.

Refugee Union. (2016). Does race count in police profiling?. Refugee Union, 4 February, viewed 7 November 2016. http://www.refugeeunion.org/7648/race-count-police-profiling/

Saunders, D. (2010). *Arrival city: How the largest migration in history is reshaping our world*. London: William Heinemann.

Schierup, C. U., Hansen, P., & Castles, S. (2006). *Migration: A European dilemma*. Oxford: Oxford University Press.

Sciurba, A. (2009). *Campi di forza: Percorsi confinati di migranti in Europa*. Verona: Ombre Corte.

Sigona, N. (2015). Campzenship: Reimagining the camp as a social and political space. *Citizenship Studies, 19*(1), 1–15.

Sun, N. (2016). To stay or not to stay? Hong Kong low-income households say rents rising faster than government subsidies. *South China Morning Post*, 11 September, viewed 11 September 2016, http://www.scmp.com/news/hong-kong/economy/article/2018436/stay-or-not-stay-low-income-households-say-rents-rising

Turner, J. C. (1968). Housing priorities, settlement patterns, and urban development in modernizing countries. *Journal of the American Institute of Planners, 33*, 167–181.

Turok, I., & Borel-Saladin, J. (2016). The theory and reality of urban slums: Pathways-out-of-poverty or cul-de-sacs? *Urban Studies*. doi:10.1177/0042098016671109.

Vecchio, F. (2015). *Asylum seeking and the global city*. Abingdon: Routledge.

Vecchio, F., & Beatson, C. (2014). Asylum seekers' Occupy movement in Hong Kong. *Race & Class, 56*(2), 96–104.

Vecchio, F., & Ham, J. (2017). From subsistence to resistance: Asylum seekers and the other "Occupy" in Hong Kong. *Critical Social Policy, 37*(3), 1–21.

Vision First. (2013). The compound under the tree, 9 May, viewed 7 November 2016. http://www.vfnow.org/3780/the-compound-under-a-tree/

Vision First. (2014a). SWD incapable of thinking outside the box with new tender. Vision First, 8 December, viewed 9 December 2014. http://www.vfnow.org/page/3/?filterYear=2014&filterCategory=-1&filterKeyword

Vision First. (2014b). VF commend refugees for sharing stories with world. Vision First, 20 December, viewed 23 December 2014. http://www.vfnow.org/6225/vf-commend-refugees-sharing-stories-world/

Vision First. (2015). Refugees are turning to crime because of Hong Kong's botched asylum system. *Hong Kong Free Press*, 25 August, viewed 25 August 2015. https://www.hongkongfp.com/2015/08/25/refugees-are-turning-to-crime-because-of-hong-kongs-botched-asylum-system/

Wacquant, L. (2004). Ghetto. In *International encyclopedia of the social & behavioral sciences*. London: Pergamon press.

Index[1]

[1] Note: Page numbers followed by 'n' refers to note.

F. Vecchio, A. Gerard (eds.), *Entrapping Asylum Seekers*, Transnational Crime, Crime Control and Security, DOI 10.1057/978-1-137-58739-8

G

H

I

J

K

L

Printed by Printforce, the Netherlands